D. H. LAWRENCE AND THE AUTHORITARIAN PERSONALITY

D. H. Lawrence and the Authoritarian Personality

Barabara Mensch

Department of English
Concordia College, Edmonton, Alberta

MACMILLAN

First published 1991

Published by
MACMILLAN ACADEMIC AND PROFESSIONAL LTD
Houndmills, Basingstoke, Hampshire RG21 2XS
and London
Companies and representatives
throughout the world

Printed in Hong Kong

British Library Cataloguing in Publication Data
Mensch, Barbara
D. H. Lawrence and the authoritarian personality.
1. Fiction in English. Lawrence, D. H. (David Herbert)
1885–1930
I. Title
823.912

ISBN 0–333–55543–0

For my husband and my son

Fred and Julian

Acknowledgments

Thanks and acknowledgement are due to Henry Holt and Company, Inc. for permission to quote, in the United States edition of this book, from *The Three Faces of Fascism: Action Française, Italian Fascism, National Socialism* by Ernst Noltë. Copyright © 1963 by R. Piper and Co. Verlag. Translated by Leila Vennewitz. Translation © 1965 by R. Piper and Co. Verlag. Reprinted by permission of Henry Holt and Company, Inc.; for the U.K. rights to quote from this publication I thank George Weidenfeld and Nicolson Ltd. Thanks are also due to the University of California Press for permission to quote from Fritz Stern, *Politics of Cultural Despair: A Study in the Rise of the Germanic Ideology.* Copyright © 1961, The Regents of the University of California. Finally, I gratefully acknowledge permission from Harper & Row to quote from the definitive study by T.W. Adorno, et al., *The Authoritarian Personality,* Harper & Row, 1950.

A warm thanks to the following individuals, all of whom had considerable input with regard to the direction and form that this book, which was originally my doctoral dissertation, has taken: Fred Radford, Chris Bullock, Nora Stovel, Gary Watson, George Zytaruk and Jerald Zaslove.

Thanks also to Kermit Hummel for taking on the project, and to Simon Winder for his enthusiastic and encouraging support.

Finally, a very warm note of love and thanks to my husband Fred, for all the typing, grammar checks, editorial and production work which he has put into the project.

Contents

He ran out, blindly, as if from the dark, probably thinking that now he was free. Then he stopped short, seeing he was not free, but surrounded in an unknown way.

The Plumed Serpent

Preface

Almost sixty years after Lawrence's death, some of the major themes dominating his work still seem unreconcilable. How could this poet of consumate spontaneity, tenderness and sexual freedom also endorse charismatic leaders and obedient followers, as well as authoritarian personality elements that have led to accusations of "fascism" in his work? Bertrand Russell is one of Lawrence's strongest detractors in this area, claiming that Lawrence's theory of blood consciousness "led straight to Auschwitz" (115). The rigid authoritarian attitude that emerges in some of Lawrence's work seems totally at odds with the spontaneity of perception, and the complexity of character that dominates most of his writing. The incongruity of these elements in Lawrence's work has never been satisfactorily analyzed.

There is also considerable ambiguity surrounding the term "fascism" and how it relates to authoritarianism. Fascism might be defined as the political externalization of authoritarian personality elements; there are, of course, different kinds of fascism, though the tendency is to identify the term strictly with German National Socialism. Hannah Arendt distinguishes between fascism and totalitarianism; whatever the distinctions, and these will be examined later, at bottom of any fascist or totalitarian platform are the psychological forces of the authoritarian.

Lawrence's work shows very clearly that he recognized the authoritarian personality and incorporated it into his writing; this recognition, however, does not constitute an endorsement of the rigid personality that would be receptive to the negative, life-denying political structures of fascism and totalitarianism. Wherever Lawrence draws an authoritarian personality type, he counters it with another personality that is honest, feeling, and what might even be defined, in the fullest sense of the word, as "liberal."

Fascism is a difficult concept to deal with, even in the 1980s; it is doubly difficult to ascertain correctly what was understood as fascism within Lawrence's time. Those early years of fascist development, and of political affiliations in general, were a time of extreme confusion. As evidence of the political instability of the period, Winston Churchill, elected to Parliament as a Conservative, crossed the floor in 1900 to join the Liberals instead (he was accused of "socialist" leanings for this move). England, like other European countries, had coteries of socialist movements since the late nineteenth century, and the real fear in the English "establishment" of this time was not of authoritarianism, but of socialism. King George V "thought of any individual or movement tinged with 'socialism' as inimicable to the throne," and thought that Churchill's views were "very socialistic" (Jenkins 235).

This concern with socialism, rather than with right-wing authoritarian politics, was reinforced by conservatives throughout Europe after the 1917 Russian revolution, with its attack on the aristocracy and established order. Mussolini's "fascism," on the other hand, attracted amused, but rarely fearful notice, as Lawrence himself notes as late as 1928:

> Why, having come out from England to find mountains, lakes, scythe-mowers and cherry trees, does the little blue-eyed lady resolutely close her blue eyes to them all, now she's got them, and gaze away to Signor Mussolini, whom she hasn't got, and to Fascism, which is invisible anyhow? (*Phoenix II* 533)

There was very little negative reaction to fascism during Lawrence's lifetime because few people viewed it as the regressive tyranny it turned out to be; there is little evidence of any active protest against the dangers of an authoritarian order until the time of the Spanish Civil War. By then, the protesters were a curious blend of ardent socialists, people like Nancy Cunard, the model for Lucy Tantamount in Aldous Huxley's *Point Counter Point,* who worked as a war correspondent in the Spanish civil war (Fielding 121). Many writers of the twenties were apathetic – or contemptuous – toward existing political systems. Virginia Woolf is a good case in point; her view of politicians is expressed in the comment: "…what humbugs they all are! – or rather hypnotised by the incantation of some siren quite invisible to the outside world…" (*Letters* 283). Lawrence's battles with political criticism centered primarily around the censoring of erotica in his works; no critic found fascist themes in *The Plumed Serpent* at that time. It was not until three years after Lawrence's death that T.S. Eliot wrote:

> A man like Lawrence … with his acute sensibility, violent prejudices and passions, and lack of intellectual and social training, is admirably fitted to be an instrument for forces of good or for forces of evil;

> or as we might expect, partly for one and partly for the other. A trained mind like that of Mr. Joyce is always aware what master it is serving; an untrained mind, and a soul destitute of humility and filled with self-righteousness, is a blind servant and a fatal leader. (*After Strange Gods* 58-59)

Eliot accuses Lawrence of promoting the forces of evil through his art, but Eliot would not necessarily have argued that authoritarian systems are evil. In the same lectures he emphasizes that "the struggle of our time [is] to concentrate, not to dissipate; to renew our association with traditional wisdom; to re-establish a vital connexion between the individual and the race; the struggle in a word, against Liberalism" (48-49). Eliot's belief in a renewed classicism is really another approach to an authoritarian order. As Peter Ackroyd notes, Eliot, by his twenties, had identified himself with an intellectual movement, "the main tenets of which were an attack upon humanitarianism and liberal democracy, the espousal of a hard classicism after the flatulence of Rousseauist 'self-expression,' the affirmation of absolute and objective values, and the recognition of the need for order and authority to discipline man's fallen state" (76). If Eliot disapproves of Lawrencian art, it is because he feels that Lawrence lacks any "moral or social sense" (Ackroyd 36-37), not because of a specific political philosophy that Lawrence endorses.

There exists, then, a need to distinguish clearly between authoritarianism, totalitarianism and fascism. With these definitions established, they may be applied to the actions and behavior of specific characters in Lawrence's novels, to determine whether or not these characters display authoritarian attributes. In *Women in Love*, Gerald Crich is an authoritarian personality; the novel ends, however, with Birkin's unfulfilled desire for an intimate community of people that extends beyond the marriage bond.[1] After *Women in Love*, Lawrence moves toward a further examination of communal relationships and the need for a leader. *Aaron's Rod* may be seen as Lawrence's attempt to be a leader, *Kangaroo* as his trial at being a follower, and finally, *The Plumed Serpent* as a futuristic attempt on his part to imagine the perfect relationship between leader and follower.

[1] Lawrence also expresses this desire outside the fictional world in his ideal of Rananim, as expressed most clearly in a letter of January 1915 to Koteliansky, in *The Quest for Rananim*. (Zytaruk 22)

Chapter 1

Lawrence, Authoritarianism and Fascism: The Critical Response

One of the first critics to address the fascist issue in Lawrence's writing was Christopher Caudwell, who, in *Studies in a Dying Culture* (1938), accused Lawrence of producing "fascist" art. Caudwell defines fascist art as a return to "old primitive values, to mythology, racialism, nationalism, hero-worship and *participation mystique*.... Fascist art is like the regression of the neurotic to a previous level of adaptation" (56). Caudwell understands Lawrence's conception of blood intimacy to be an atavistic urge, a regression from rationalism and complexity to an instinctual, primitive level of behavior, in fact, to a grossly insensitive, hence regressive, state:

> If ... we are to cast off intellectualism and consciousness we must abandon all symbolism and rationalism *tout court*, we must *be* and no longer think, even in images. Yet on the contrary Lawrence again and again *consciously* formulates his creed in intellectual terms or terms of imagery. But this is self-contradiction for how can we be led intellectually and consciously *back* from consciousness? It is our consciousness that Lawrence attempts to extend and heighten even at

> the moment he urges us to abandon it. (Caudwell 59)

Caudwell concludes his argument by stating that Lawrence has romanticized "the old bourgeois pastoral heaven" (70). This is a serious misreading of Lawrence, whose writing shows the need to expand and extend the range of human sensitivity, not decrease it. Caudwell views thinking and feeling in a linear or evolutionary sense, hence rationalism is a development from primitivism; Lawrence, however, explores the areas of being that are outside of rational thought. Hence, it makes more sense to use the terms conscious and unconscious, rather than rational and primitive; the human unconscious exists alongside the conscious sphere, not prior to it.

In 1939, William York Tindall also finds that Lawrence's anti- intellectualism and primitivism resemble that of the Nazis, but Tindall feels that Lawrence is "more sentimental than any except the earliest of the Nazis; he wanted to destroy machines and money, not control them" (178). Tindall finally categorizes Lawrence as a theocratic fascist. In a similar vein, Bertrand Russell's comment that Lawrence's theory of blood consciousness "led straight to Auschwitz" appeared in Russell's autobiography in 1968. Russell is also naive here in his estimation of Frieda's influence and interaction with Lawrence:

> Lawrence, though most people did not realize it, was his wife's mouthpiece. He had the eloquence, but she had the ideas. She used to spend part of every summer in a colony of Austrian Freudians at a time when psychoanalysis was little known in England. Somehow, he imbibed prematurely the ideas afterwards developed by Mussolini and Hitler, and

> these ideas she transmitted to Lawrence, shall we say, by blood consciousness. (115)

In 1950, Lionel Trilling, in *The Liberal Imagination*, articulates his theory that Lawrence, along with Proust, Joyce, Eliot, Yeats, Mann, Kafka, Rilke and Gide, cannot be defined or judged within a political spectrum at all. Trilling is concerned with liberal ideology, which he defines as "a love of the ideas and emotions which liberal democracy, as known by our educated class, has declared respectable," and concludes that "there is no connexion between the political ideas of our educated class and the deep places of the imagination" (98-99). This is an important statement, inasmuch as Lawrence had, as becomes evident through a study of his later novels, some very strong social and class feelings, and possessed attributes that could certainly be considered "liberal."

In 1955, Mary Freeman attempts to refute the charge of fascism in Lawrence's art in her study, *D.H. Lawrence: A Basic Study of His Ideas*. She is right to note the complexity and multi-faceted nature of this concept, finding that fascism is "a massive loose-jointed composite" (191). She qualifies the charge of fascism in Lawrence's work from this perspective:

> No one element abstracted from the fascist composite makes fascism or a fascist. Even a cluster of similar elements organized differently, or in a different context, may have a different meaning. (192)

The problem with Freeman's attempt to vindicate Lawrence is that she deals solely with the actual historical practice of fascism, and not at all with fascist ideology. Her point that "fascism was the complete subjugation of men to the productive machine" (200) is true with regard to the actual enactment of fascism in Germany in 1941, but how was this ideology originally presented to the German people in a form palatable enough to find the wholesale acceptance that it did? Nazi propaganda took great care to romanticize and disguise the harsh facts. The myths and religiosity that were used in the presentation of fascist ideology must be evaluated, and their appeal must be better understood in order to decide whether a writer is finally fascist or not. It is too narrow to focus only on the actual events (although these must be considered as part of the examination of fascism), without recourse to the elemental reactionism of the movement itself.

The 1960s offer a brilliant plethora of stimulating and insightful critics who attempt to understand the relationship of fascism and art. In 1963, Julian Moynahan is highly critical of the political solutions that Lawrence offers in *Aaron's Rod* , *Kangaroo,* and *The Plumed Serpent*:

> The leadership novels reflect a temporary breakdown in Lawrence's morale.... The chief characters of these novels are, overwhelmingly, self-exiles from the European bourgeoisie who fall into positions of political and social extremism from despair at finding anything tenable to cling to. The same formula may cover Lawrence himself during some of those years. (113-14)

In 1967, Laurence Lerner calls *The Plumed Serpent* "the worst of all: ... it is the most ambitious (and the most fascist)" (173). Lerner pinpoints the cruelty of the ritual sacrifices as the most undigestible element in the novel:

> ... the long ritualistic slaying ... would be frightening if it were not ludicrous. What is frightening is Kate's subsequent reaction:... There is no such thing, we see, as rising above morality. The ecstasy which drives Kate to feel "what do I care," drives her to condone very specific acts that exist on a down-to-earth

> level. It is never safe to say of any man "he is of the gods." (176)

John Harrison parallels these sentiments, which are perhaps intrinsically part of the sixties' ethos of moral-political consciousness. In *The Reactionaries* (1966), published a year before Lerner's *The Truthtellers,* Harrison agrees with Lawrence that modern civilization is in need of change: two world wars only twenty years apart are not indicative of health, but Harrison chides Lawrence for childish irrationality in his vehement response to the first world war: "... to rage and stamp one's foot at being medically examined does not do much good" (166). Like Lerner, Harrison focuses on the sacrificial murders in *The Plumed Serpent,* which he finds an example of how Lawrence is fascinated "by the idea of blood-sacrifice, even human sacrifice" (184). Harrison states that:

> Lawrence's views on social leadership are inherently close to the fascist conception of society.... Lawrence anticipated the fascist emphasis on ritual and symbols. In *The Plumed Serpent* the semi-religious, semi-political movement seems to consist of ritual and symbols, and very little else. In politics, the casting off of mental consciousness leads straight to the mass hysteria of the regimes of Hitler and Mussolini. Belief in the power of a natural leader, in "dark gods," in irrationalism and racialism, had disastrous results in the 1930s, when Nazism gave them perverted political forms.

In 1970, Kate Millett's *Sexual Politics* designates Lawrence's art as fascist, but more as a sideline than as the central issue: her primary purpose is to uncover male dominance and female exploitation. Nevertheless, she finds in Lawrencian art "the political structure of patriarchy itself, and Lawrence's fine new talk of dark gods, his jargon about spontaneous subordination, is simply a very old form of bullying, which in other contexts we are accustomed to call fascistic" (269). Millett finds that fascism and male supremacy go hand-in-hand in Lawrence's works, much as they did in actual practise in Nazi Germany:

> *Aaron's Rod*, *Kangaroo*, and *The Plumed Serpent* ... are unquestionably strident, and unpleasant for a number of reasons, principally a rasping protofascist tone, an increasing fondness of force, a personal arrogance, and innumerable racial, class, and religious bigotries....

In 1971, Norman Mailer wrote *The Prisoner of Sex* as a rebuttal to Millett's work. Mailer presents a strong case for Lawrence's art as being an endorsement of sexual love between man and woman – difficult as that love may be to achieve. But his endorsement of Lawrence's political stance is more evasive, especially with regard to some of Lawrence's later novels like *Aaron's Rod* and *Kangaroo*. Mailer even notes, with some relief, that "perhaps it was just as well Lawrence died when he did, for he could have been the literary advisor to Oswald Mosley about the time Hitler came in" (136-37). Mailer concludes, finally, that "Lawrence was not only trying to sell dictatorial theorems, he was also trying to rid himself of them" (139), much as he attempted to overcome the Oedipal complex in *Sons and Lovers*. Mailer feels that the ideas presented in Lawrence's art are presented to be tested, lived through vicariously, and then discarded:

> ...his ideas cannot simply triumph, they have to be tried and heated and forged, and finally be beaten into shapelessness against the anvil of his profound British skepticism which would not buy his ideas,

> not outright, for even his own characters seem to wear out in them. (138-39)

Lawrence criticism after the 1960s seems to label his work fascist under varying degrees of censure, dependent upon whether or not the critic is finally pro Lawrence or anti Lawrence. The 1970s critics are more given to a qualification of the term; K.K. Ruthven argues that the term "fascism" meant something different to Eliot, Yeats, Lawrence, Pound and Lewis than it means to us – that, in fact, the political programme of fascism should be strictly distinguished from the actual political activities pursued. Earlier, in 1956, Graham Hough had argued that, although Lawrence's leadership phase embodied many fascist ideas, "Lawrence died too early to be put to the only really diagnostic test" (239). Similarly, Ruthven feels that Lawrence and other artists of the twenties have been labelled "fascist" or "proto-fascist" not because they endorsed Mussolini, but because of certain attributes they applauded, such as strong-arm government, racism, and an élitism based on social standing or circumstances of birth: these attributes *are* proto-fascist, independent of a particular political creed. Ruthven feels that:

> Lawrence's fascination with vigorous alternatives to wimbly-wombly young men brought him to the attention of more sinister believers in *Blutgefühl*, but he would have laughed at the idea of *The Plumed Serpent* being recommended as reading suitable for British Fascists, as it was by Rolf Gardiner in *World Without End* [1932]. (225-30)

But how can we be sure that Lawrence would have laughed; Ruthven's assertion here is hypothetical. Ruthven does, however, recognize that art may influence actual events. He cites W.B. Yeats as an example, suggesting that some of Yeats's plays and poetry actually helped instigate the Easter uprising of 1916 (227).

In 1970, Baruch Hochman's study, *Another Ego*, presents the main thesis that "Lawrence moves from a radical individualism to … a radical (if qualified) communalism – not out of waywardness, but out of a sustained engagement with the issues and observations that underlie his initial individualism" (xi). Hochman finds that Lawrence anticipates both Norman O. Brown and Herbert Marcuse in finding "no necessary conflict between nature and civilization or between culture and the instincts. Hence, [Lawrence] can argue so vehemently for enactment of man's spontaneous desires without threat to the civilized community" (19). Hochman's examination of Lawrence's critique of democracy is helpful, pointing out Lawrence's recognition that "the 'world' of modern group-life is, paradoxically, an amorphous realm that, for all its chaos, is absolute (totalitarian) in its demands" (187). Despite this, Hochman finds that the charge of fascism in Lawrence's work is basically unjustified, because "'the personal-passional' relationship to a leader [is] so different from the mechanism of fascist self-subordination, yet formally so like the formulation of the leadership principle in fascist ideology" (221). Hochman does admit that Lawrence's "need for socially sanctioned outlets for repressed blood lust comes close to fascism" (220); Hochman's conclusion, however, is that Lawrence's "later reversion to what I have termed communalism represents a capitulation, an acknowledgement that the pains of individuation are too keen, that the candle is not worth burning" (258). Hochman's conclusion is refuted by Jerald Zaslove, who, in reviewing the book, states:

> what is not seen is that [Lawrence] is, however idealized, an anarchist, an asocial being more like the Cezanne who could paint an apple, a man who had learned the "reciprocity of tenderness." (62)

In 1973, Scott Sanders asserts that *The Plumed Serpent* embodies a "totalitarian social order" (167). Citing Wilhelm Reich's analysis of the authoritarian patriarchal family as the basis of authoritarian political receptivity, Sanders notes that Lawrence, "proceeding along the same psychological path but in the reverse direction, … embraced an authoritarian model for the state because it assured male dominance in marriage" (227). Sanders falls on one side of a division amongst various critics in his conclusion that Lawrence was, finally, a political thinker, or rather that Lawrence's works embrace political stands:

> Defenders of Lawrence … often argue that we must distinguish the mythic visions of a writer from the political shapes they take.… Thus in *The Plumed Serpent*, one might argue, Lawrence is imagining a reintegration of the self, or a rediscovery of the religious faculty, not a revival of some neo-fascist pre-Columbian state. But men's imaginings about nature, personality and society *do* take political shapes, which often mirror personal anxieties and desires. (170)

Paul Delaney's vivid account of the war years in Lawrence's life, published in 1978, presents the view that Lawrence was "too naive and wilful" (135) to understand or construct a viable political program. Recently, Keith Sagar's study, *D.H. Lawrence: Life Into Art*, argues with Raymond Williams' earlier charge that Lawrence ends *Women in Love* with an evasive flight from society, from social reality. Sagar finds the "star-polarity" balance proposed by Birkin to be the start of the social impulse in Lawrence's art. Daniel J. Schneider's *D.H. Lawrence: The Artist as Psychologist* takes this view further through his analysis of Lawrence as a self-psychoanalyst – one who:

> in his thinking about the social causes of neurosis, never persuaded himself that personal therapy, or "mind-cure," is enough, or that freedom is within the reach of most men. A healthy humanity, he knew, cannot exist in a sick society. Social and political rebellion are a precondition of psychic health. (4)

Two recent studies, Judith Ruderman's *D.H. Lawrence and the Devouring Mother* and Sheila MacLeod's *Lawrence's Men and Women*, parallel each other in determining that Lawrence was primarily motivated throughout his career and his life by the dominance of females in his life; the political side of the novels is scarcely mentioned and certainly not emphasized by either critic. Ruderman does examine the formation of the totalitarian personality in chapter ten of her study. But her opinion that "... political programs in and of themselves never interested Lawrence..." (7) coincides with Delany's viewpoint. These opposing viewpoints bring into focus a problem that is significant within the context of this study: how consciously – or self-consciously – must a political stance be assumed by an artist before he is said to be "political" (whether liberal, conservative, socialist or fascist)?

Sheila MacLeod, a year after Ruderman's study, argues that "...Somers is not much of a political animal..." (62).[1]

[1] Brian Moore has commented that an artist need not *be* overtly political for his political and social prejudices to show: "*Ginger Coffey* was highly successful ... as a film, in Russia, of all places, because the Russians saw it as an attack on migration to capitalist countries.... I think deep down, buried in every writer, his prejudices show, even if they're not directly visible" (74).

Anthony Burgess, in *Flame into Being,* is evasive about Lawrence's political proclivities: he concludes that "...the political theme had best be ignored: this philosopher writer can rarely be swallowed whole" (124). Furthermore, Burgess asserts that Lawrence "...was not as anti-democratic as he liked to think; he was merely honest enough to state openly that we all need living models of superior energy and genius, that there is a *canaille* around, and that politicians are, for the most part, inferior animals" (204). Burgess, himself a highly socialized, urbane novelist, assumes here that Lawrence will define "politics" and political issues from a similarly "socialized" perspective. Lawrence, however, examines a more profound, or "primal" psychological reality through his novels; this reality nevertheless embodies strong social/political repercussions. Like Burgess, Ross Parmenter, in his study of *Lawrence in Oaxaca,* admits that "Huitzilopochtli's Night" is "a stumbling block" (304). His apologia for Lawrence as a possible fascist is bewildering:

> Lawrence ... did not preach ... fascism personally, and he saw his religion as anti-fascist in spirit. His Ramón, too, tries to insure that his religion will not become fascist. Yet such is the honesty of the novel that its religion takes the step of public murders as a fascist means to frighten the villagers from further attempts on their lives. (304)

This seems to be an attempt to exonerate the ideology, but it finally exonerates nothing; to adopt fascist or totalitarian methods is to err, finally, where fascism did.

Peter Scheckner's book *Class, Politics, and the Individual* analyzes Lawrence's awareness of class differences, and by extension, illuminates the milieu of Lawrence's time. His conclusion is that the "ghost that most haunted

Lawrence was neither sexual nor psychological but social" (19). It is interesting to note that both Paul Delany and Scheckner point out that Lawrence began as a socialist; both critics cite Lawrence's letter to Bertrand Russell in which he states: "It is no use saying a man's soul should be free, if his boots hurt him so much he can't walk." Still, socialism in England in 1915 had a hazy, undefined, all-encompassing aura, evolving as it had from a pastoralized guild system. On the other hand, the term "fascism" had not even been coined at the time, but extreme conservatism is virtually indistinguishable from authoritarianism, and these political platforms were the precursors to the fascism of the 1930s.[2]

When an awareness of fascism did emerge, the radical connotations attached to both socialist and fascist ideologies made them almost indistinguishable political alternatives to many people. Lawrence, in one of his letters to Koteliansky (Feb. 1, 1929), refers to Sir Oswald Mosley as "the Socialist" (Zytaruk 47). Two years later, Mosley headed the British Fascist movement. Mercurial transformations of political stands such as this are evidence that the terms "fascist," "socialist," etc. were neither clearly understood nor agreed upon. Another example of the unstable political affiliations - or distinctions - that characterized the period is found in Germany in the early 1920s, when Moeller van den Bruck, the writer of the reactionary right, drew fatefully close to negotiating with German Communists:

> For a brief moment, in the streets, in meeting halls and in the columns of party newspapers, German

[2] It is interesting to note that Mussolini too began his political career as a socialist. George Watson maintains there was little awareness of fascist ideology in England until the 1930s, even by the intelligentsia. In fact, he states that "[b]efore 1933 intellectual fascism is scarcely to be seen or heard in Britain" (72).

nationalists and fascists collaborated with the Communists. (Stern 308)

Clearly, neither side understood the other, nor even, perhaps, itself; the possibility of such a merger now seems ludicrous, but we have a retrospective vision to aid us. It was difficult for artists in the 1920s to understand these terms, especially since the politicians themselves could not adequately define them. If most English intellectuals became aware of fascism as late as the 1930s, however, Lawrence's recognition of this ideology came ten years earlier, since he was in Italy at the time of Mussolini's ascendance to power. But Lawrence's estimation of fascism at this early date was that "[i]t was an anti-socialist movement" that was reduced only to "another kind of bullying" (*Movements* 316).

If the terms "fascism" and "socialism" were confusing during the '30s, they are no less confusing now, with socialists defining fascism as a reactionary or right-wing program that is inherently anti-socialist, while conservative critics like George Watson claim that fascism is essentially socialism and that "the myth of fascism as a conservative force … [is] fundamentally a Marxist myth" (94).

Perhaps one of the strongest approaches to Lawrencian political ideology is by John Carey in his essay "D.H. Lawrence's Doctrine." Carey pleads for honesty in looking at Lawrence's art; apologetics from narrow points of view, whether from politics, psychology, sociology or Christianity, are not, he feels, facing the dilemma squarely. Neither is "the pretence that really he was a decent, moderate sort of fellow, almost a Christian" (133), much of an insight. Carey states, however, that "it is in the final paradox of Lawrence's thought that, separated from his warm, intense, wonderfully articulate being, it becomes the philosophy of any thug or moron" (134). What is very important about Carey's essay is that he recognizes the shallowness and superficiality of some of the charges of fascism against Lawrence. This, he says, is not the first artist who appears at times authoritarian, naming others such as Carlyle, Nietzsche and Yeats, who "thought much as Lawrence did" (133). Carey distinguishes Lawrence's authoritarian qualities from that of the Nazis in accordance with the final outcome of each:

> Even granted that the beliefs of Lawrence and the Nazi killers coincided to some degree (and it would be futile to deny this) ... Lawrence's beliefs did not issue in mass murder but in writing novels. Unless life is to be deprived altogether (and how could it be deprived?) of violent and destructive and irrational ways of feeling, it is ludicrous not to distinguish between people who can bring these feelings to a life-enhancing end in great literature, and people who can produce only a pile of corpses.... As well blame stabbing on cutlers.... If the responsibility for Auschwitz is to be transferred to men of letters, it will need to be thinly spread. (133)

The review of Lawrence criticism relating to the issue of authoritarianism and fascism reveals two major flaws in many of the critical works. One flaw is that the critics' definitions of the terms are often fuzzy and inadequate. This inadequacy is further exacerbated by the problem of perspective. Contemporary critics tend to view Lawrence's works from the contemporary perspective; this includes a recitation of the atrocities committed in the name of fascism, even though none of these atrocities were actually committed during Lawrence's lifetime; Nazism never became a reality until three years after Lawrence's death. The retrospective vision has tended to cloud Lawrence criticism with emotional connotations that are confusing and often detract from the integrity of the critical analysis.

The second flaw in criticism to date is that critics are too anxious to praise or damn Lawrence unconditionally. This is due, in part, especially with respect to the early critics, to Lawrence's own personality, which, like his writings, seemed to invite either outrage or idolatry. Clearly, a need still exists for an objective analysis of fascist, and accompanying authoritarian and totalitarian, elements in Lawrence's works. This analysis must also be based on an adequate definition of these political stands, and a comparison of how they relate to each other.

Chapter 2
The Problems of Definition

A major problem regarding Lawrence criticism relating to the authoritarian personality and to fascism, is a lack of authoritative definition of the terminology. What constitutes an authoritarian? What does the word "fascism" really mean? Does fascism consist of the historical factors leading to the development of the movement, the methodology or actual practice of fascism, the ideology of fascism as a political program, or the psychological make-up of the fascist mass – or of the fascist individual? Some critics have adopted a very narrow definition, often resulting in political condemnation of much of Lawrence's art. Others have defined fascism so nebulously that it becomes a simple matter to distinguish "art" from "politics" and thus exonerate Lawrence of virtually any charge. It is especially difficult to define aesthetics in relation to a fascist perspective, unless we clearly understand what the term itself means.

The subject becomes all the more complex when other terms that are almost analogous, but not equal to the word "fascist," are used. The concepts of "totalitarian" and "authoritarian" are often incorrectly used as synonyms for "fascism." Nor can these concepts be ignored, since they *are* all interrelated, and more importantly may, within the context of this study, all define various aspects or nuances of Lawrence's work that need to be differentiated from the term fascist.

The complexity of the terminology may be clarified to an extent through reference to the works of established authorities on the subjects of fascism, totalitarianism and authoritarianism. Some of the scholars who have examined at length and from various perspectives the issues that this study attempts to define include T.W. Adorno, Ernst Noltë, Hannah Arendt, Fritz Stern and Wilhelm Reich. Even with this intimidating body of scholarship devoted to an understanding of authoritarian politics, fascism and totalitarianism, it remains difficult to formulate a clear and simple theoretical definition. A summation might be that fascism consists of a reactionary force which, growing slowly in cultural and intellectual milieus, and abetted by certain historical conditions in both politics and economics, finally emerges with a simplistically idealistic program. This program is emotionally and pseudo-religiously served to the masses, until the power of the reactionary force is complete and, in certain cases, enforced through totalitarian means.

At this point the problem of perspective becomes significant as well. The fascist issue has been defined from sociological, moral-philosophical, historical and psychological perspectives. Each perspective has its own level of significance, and the differing viewpoints may, in fact, be of critical importance in analyzing Lawrence's progress as a writer. Terry Eagleton has pointed to the fact that Lawrence started writing from a "social" or proletarian viewpoint (157). A possible hypothesis regarding the leadership novels would be that they chronicle a change in Lawrence's art from a social to a continuously more individual/psychological perspective. Defining the terms from varying, but interrelated disciplines may therefore uncover a richness in these novels that would otherwise not be noted.

Lawrence's art does not reveal human nature in terms of simplistic categories, such as political disposition, psychological makeup or erotic appetite. The power and success of his writing at its best is based on a portrayal of the interrelated aspects of these different areas of human experience. A composite or multi-layered interpretation of his work is therefore essential to fully understand Lawrence's relationship to authoritarianism and to fascism. Superficially, his outward, conscious and rather flippant response to Italian fascism, at least, was a guffaw. Mussolini, he claimed, should wear a ring through his nose (Barr 23), but, in the leadership novels, we find a closer entanglement with "fascist" concepts: this is the area that requires examination.

T.W. Adorno and his associates provide an exhaustive examination of authoritarian attributes in *The Authoritarian Personality* (1950), a study that relates the reactionary personality to a psychological profile of a specific type of political personality. This profile is extremely significant in determining authoritarian and fascist elements in Lawrence's fictional characters, because it presents a complete, interrelated approach to fascism. Adorno's study is a lengthy, complex analysis of reactionary attitudes found within a wide variety of topics. The analysis is based on extensive testing of various groups of people in an objective and scientific manner. Topics examined include attitudes towards stereotyping, superstition, aggression, sexuality, power and "toughness," destructiveness and cynicism.

The results of these studies are predictable at times; in other instances they are surprising.

Leading up to a definition of authoritarianism or "pseudo-conservatism," the authors outline the major trends in liberalism and conservatism. Conservative trends include (1) support of the American *status quo*, (2) resistance to social change, and (3) support of such conservative values as practicality, ambition, and upward class mobility:

> The values for practicality and rugged competitiveness stand in rather marked contrast to other, psychologically related, values for charity and community service.... [In contrast], [f]rom the "liberal" point of view charity is mainly a soothing of conscience and a means of maintaining an unjust state of affairs. (155)

Liberals, states Adorno, "tend to view social problems as symptoms of the underlying social structure, while conservatives view them as results of individual incompetence or immorality" (155). Conservatives view political problems "in moral rather than sociological terms" (155). Adorno's study, significantly enough, indicates that the authoritarian does not evolve naturally out of the conservative personality. The authors define the "genuine conservative" as a personality that supports the democratic tradition in specific elements of competitiveness and economic mobility.

The authoritarian personality, on the other hand, evolves from a political-psychological makeup that masquerades as conservative, but is in fact opposed to the tenets of democracy. This stance is defined as "pseudo-conservative" and, in its *reaction* to democracy, it incorporates fascism:

> It is, rather, a totally new direction: away from individualism and equality of opportunity, and toward a rigidly stratified society in which there is a minimum of economic mobility and in which the "right" groups are in power, the outgroups subordinate. Perhaps the term "reactionary" fits this ideology best. Ultimately it is fascism. (182)

The Authoritarian Personality does not contain a definition of "reactionary" or "fascism" as such. The term reactionary, however, is assigned to "the relation between ethnocentrism and 'conservatism'" (183). It is distinguished from conservative in the sense that it is a "distortion of conservatism – a distortion which retains certain surface similarities but which changes the basic structure into the antithesis of the original" (182). Without actually defining fascism, the authors suggest that the use of "anti-democratic propaganda" is indicative of "the *potentially fascistic* individual" (1). The key discovery of this study parallels the psychological-political type of personality which emerges out of Fritz Stern's examination of Lagarde, Langbehn and Moeller van den Bruck in Germany. Jean-Paul Sartre's *Anti-Semite and Jew* (1948) parallels the findings of the Adorno team as well, albeit from a less scientific, more individual perspective. Reich's description of authoritarian familial structures is also echoed in Adorno's study of the authoritarian personality. Finally, some of the basic themes of Noltë's definition of fascism and Arendt's definition of totalitarianism are found in the reactionary personality:

> ... it is one of the major findings of the present study that individuals who show extreme susceptibility to fascist propaganda have a great deal in common. (They exhibit numerous characteristics that go together to form a "syndrome": although typical variations within this major pattern can be distin-

> guished.) Individuals who are extreme in the opposite direction are much more diverse. … Nevertheless, it was possible to distinguish several types of personality structure that seemed particularly resistant to anti-democratic ideas. (Adorno 1-2)

Adorno and his collaborators carefully and extensively elucidate the characteristics that apply to the authoritarian personality. Briefly, these attributes can be summarized in the portrait of an individual who identifies with the form of organized, conventional, socially-accepted religion (209). This personality does not recognize or exhibit the self-questioning, evaluative attitude that is often indicative of true religious conviction; rather, he is likely to adhere blindly to the "familial or maternal choice of religion" (215). The elements of the religious ideology which most serve to reinforce reactionary attitudes, which the authoritarian personality will hold to most strongly and unquestioningly, are firstly, a "complete faith in some supernatural force," and secondly, the conviction that man can never understand everything (321). This is a belief that rests on superstition and the sense of man's ultimate frailty and insecurity, rather than in a hope for the progress of reason. Such assumptions imply the individual's submissiveness and willingness to surrender the control and autonomy of his individual choice. The authoritarian is characterized by strongly conventional values, specifically those of the middle classes. People who fit this description possess a "[s]ubmissive, uncritical attitude toward idealized moral authorities of the ingroup" (228), and strongly condemn and reject those who flout convention. Authoritarians exhibit an "[o]pposition to the subjective, the imaginative, the tenderminded" (228). They believe in fatalistic determinism and are inclined to think in terms of stereotypes, for example, anti-Semitism. They are preoccupied with:

> the dominance-submission, strong-weak, leader-follower dimension; identification with power figures; overemphasis upon the conventionalized attributes of the ego; exaggerated assertion of strength and toughness. (228)

The authoritarian personality, characterized by this emulation of power, is finally both cynical and destructive; it is anti-utopian, with a consequent "vilification of the human" (228). There exists a proclivity within such a make-up to believe in the lurid perversity of man's true nature or, as Adorno says, a "projectivity" of "wild and dangerous things go[ing] on in the world" (228). Such projectivity extends to an "exaggerated concern" with sexual depravity and perversity. (Adorno defines this projectivity psychologically as "…the projection outwards of unconscious emotional impulses" [228].) It is significant that all these psychological characteristics are evident in many of Lawrence's character portrayals, especially in *Women in Love* and the "Leadership" novels.

Predictably, the authoritarian personality is likely to be less intelligent and less educated than his opposite, the liberal thinker (287). Further, he espouses overly idealized parental stereotypes and is either unable or unwilling to analyze "conflicts in inner experiences" (342-43). Because this personality type is intimidated by self-questioning, he is "[f]earful of any reproach or hostility felt towards authority-parent figures" (343). The domination of parental authority, especially a harsh and unbending authority, is often evident in the background of the authoritarian personality, and the reverse is true of the non-authoritarian:

> For the establishment of the psychology of the unprejudiced man a non-threatening father figure may indeed be of great importance. It makes it possible for the son to include in his conception of masculinity some measure of passivity. (364)

Adorno, like Reich, notes that homes of authoritarian personalities tended to be father-dominated, "or just dominated" (370). This last phrase suggests inclusion of a form of maternal domination that also results in authoritarian conditioning. In contrast, the liberal personality very often comes from a background that is "mother oriented." It is essential to establish the difference between domination and maternal orientation in the conditioning of personality; as Judith Ruderman has shown, the female may be defined as simultaneously succouring and devouring.

The childhood of the non-authoritarian personality is often oriented "*toward the adult and the espousal of internalized standards* as manifested in reading a lot, an interest in school and teachers, and in achievement striving" (439). Non-authoritarians also reported a tendency toward "relative *isolation* in childhood, while the authoritarian types refer to what may be defined as gang-sociability, including such aspects as popularity and the holding of offices in clubs and high school fraternities and sororities" (439). Lawrence admitted his own lack of popularity, describing himself as "a delicate brat with a sniffy nose" (Spender 15).

The study stresses that the unprejudiced or non-authoritarian individual will readily examine psychological hostilities and conflicts, with regard to "... where they originate: with their parents and with themselves" (485). Lawrence, as a young artist, certainly grappled with the possessive hold his mother had on him, and reached a clearer understanding of this relationship through his art in *Sons and Lovers*.

Adorno describes the political attitudes of the high scorers, the authoritarians: "ignorance and confusion" characterize the content of their thought on the whole, although this is covered up by an "official optimism." They assume a "'practical' bias" (658) to hide their emotional detachment from everything that is beyond their well defined range of action.

In general, pseudo-conservatism is defined as "conventionality and authoritarian submissiveness on the ego level, with violence, anarchic impulses, and chaotic destructiveness in the unconscious sphere" (675). Fear of politicians and bureaucrats occurs in both the authoritarian and non-authoritarian personality types (693), but the strong anti-utopian element is a form of "realistic" thinking that exists only in the authoritarian (695). Similarly, authoritarian personalities do not sympathize with the under-privileged or poor: to do so would imply an identification with weakness on their part.

Adorno's study was published in 1950, and evoked varied critical responses. Cox and Dyson, in *The Twentieth Century Mind*, note that it does not clearly distinguish whether the authoritarian personality can be defined within a specific class system or if it is a "phenomenon of individual psychology" (173).[1] Adorno's later work embodies a vision of a "non-autonomous self" that is in contrast to his more optimistic contemporaries, such as Herbert Marcuse, and the resulting association of pessimism

---

[1] Seymour Martin Lipset's *Political Man: The Social Bases of Politics*, suggests that authoritarian tendencies are more pronounced in lower class segments of society (104-5).

with his work – for example, he worked with Thomas Mann to produce the character of Adrian Leverkuhn in *Doktor Faustus* – is attributed to his belief in the inescapability of conditioning, of the historical process itself. Finally, William P. Kreml's *The Anti-Authoritarian Personality* (1977) shows how a left-wing extremist stance satisfies "many of the same authoritarian personality characteristics" (2) as the reactionary personality defined in Adorno's study. Kreml's thesis offers an interesting insight into the analysis of Gerald Crich's personality later in this study. The moot point here, however, is that Lawrence has never been accused of *left-wing* extremism, but rather of a reactionary stand, so Kreml's study is, to a large extent, irrelevant.

Adorno, then, has provided a very rich, research-oriented definition of authoritarianism. Another approach to the central political-historical- ideological and psychological concept of fascism is presented by Ernst Noltë in *The Three Faces of Fascism* (1963), which considers the political theory of fascism in the 1920s and '30s. Hannah Arendt's *The Origins of Totalitarianism* (1951) examines a political structure that is often confused with fascism, and which emerges alongside of fascism in Germany. Wilhelm Reich's *The Mass Psychology of Fascism* (1933) is an historical-psychological study of the specific characteristics that contribute to the rise of fascism, while Fritz Stern's *The Politics of Cultural Despair* (1961) offers insight into the historical-ideological trends that, beginning in the early nineteenth century with three ideologists (Paul de Lagarde, Julius Langbehn, and Moeller van den Bruck), led to the ideology of fascism in Germany.

A thorough examination of fascism requires more than a study of the psychological make-up of the kind of personality attracted to fascism. We also need to look at the historical perspective, the specific political practice of fascism from the 1920s to '40s, as well as its historical base and its ideological approach. Obviously, several approaches toward learning are present here; equally obvious is that one single approach (for example, a specific political theory, without recourse to an understanding of the historical milieu, the economics, the psychological climate of the time, and the time immediately preceding it) is inadequate because it is too narrow.

Because fascism, once established, so brutally controls individual freedoms, especially when it is also a totalitarian system, it becomes necessary to understand how such a power evolves and succeeds. Fascism effectively blocks every area of human thought, so the political theory alone cannot define the term adequately, cannot explain such complete control. An individual supporting fascism may rationalize his position on grounds that the fascist ideology is a form of anti-socialism, considering that an authoritarian system will politically block the advance of socialism, and that this is why it is desirable. Implicit in the appeal of fascism, however, is also a psychological impulse to turn away from the burden of responsibility toward submission and suspension of responsibility. This shifting of responsibility from the individual to an authoritarian ideology appears as a relief, especially in an environment already dominated by confusion and widespread dissatisfaction. Politically, the support for fascism may appear to the voter to be a strong response to a desperate situation, yet psychologically it is regressive, even childish.

At the same time, we must consider the "Zeitgeist" or climate of thought – that reaches backwards and thus becomes a historical view – which begins the receptivity towards fascism. The ideological motifs may have been present a hundred years before, although not immediately recognizable as such. Many critics who lay the charge of "fascism" in the field of aesthetics offer no comprehensive definition of the term. At most, they pinpoint coincidental attributes between fascist regimes and the artist's work. Ernst Noltë cites the example of President Roosevelt being charged with fascism and compared to "Mussolini as long ago as 1934" (8-9). Yet it becomes obvious, when examining Roosevelt's career, that the charge is undeserved:

> ...it is precisely from this example of Roosevelt that we see how careful we must be not to infer fascism from isolated "fascist" traits. There is no doubt whatever that in his ideas and personality Roosevelt was fundamentally opposed to fascism (and not only to Hitler and the fascism of Germany). Apparently there must be a "fascist minimum" without which the noun would be meaningless and even the adjective "fascist" doubtful (9).

It is necessary, therefore, to approach the political phenomenon of fascism from various points of view. The harmony between ideological viewpoints may vary, yet each is truthful in its own distinct sense. Fascism is a reality that existed in parts of Europe from the 1920s to '40s: the definitions of this phenomenon are varied, often contradictory, because the approach to fascism "does not merely 'double' ... [its] self-understanding, but constructs an interpretation of that self-understanding, an ideology of that ideology" (Noltë 68). The ideological approach here connotes a complex structure, "an inherently complex formation which, by inserting individuals into history in a variety of ways, allows of multiple kinds and degrees of access to that history" (Noltë 69).

At one point in this multi-levelled approach to fascism, it becomes necessary to deal with Noltë's definition, that fascism is a direct response to the rise of socialism. This is an apparent contradiction to Hannah Arendt's assertion that totalitarianism is characterized above all by genocide. The two writers almost seem to discuss different methodologies, and yet we know that in the case of Nazi Germany they are certainly speaking of the same model. Each theorist, because of the inherent value of the ideological approach, articulates a particular reality that is not accessible through other perspectives. On this basis, then, the most complete and honest approach toward a definition of fascism is of necessity multi-layered, with each layer bringing to light its own truths.

The term fascism was coined by Mussolini (about 1920), and defined loosely, evasively, and attractively as an all-encompassing ideology: "organized, concentrated, authoritarian democracy on a national basis" (Noltë 7). Noltë pinpoints a more concise definition of the term:

> Fascism is anti-Marxism which seeks to destroy the enemy by the evolvement of a radically opposed and yet related ideology and by the use of almost identical and yet typically modified methods, always, however, within the unyielding framework of national self-assertion and autonomy. (20-21)

Noltë is primarily interested in establishing fascism as a specific political revolutionary *reaction* to certain conditions of the times during and between the two world wars:

> The war, the revolution, imperialism, the emergence of the Soviet Union and the United States, were not locally confined phenomena. Neither could a movement which came into being as an outcome of the

> war, a movement which fought revolution with revolutionary methods, which radicalized imperialism, and which saw in the Soviet Union ... the greatest of all threats, be called a locally confined phenomenon, no matter how many differences might be attributable to it due to local conditions. *This movement would have found its place in the Europe of the postwar period even if Mussolini and Hitler had never lived.* No term other than "fascism" has ever been seriously proposed for it. [italics mine] (6)

Noltë defines the term "fascism" within the parameters of political *theories*, the "ideas and values" that it embodies. The leaders, he says, might have been different people, but the essential political movement would have occurred regardless, because of the special set of circumstances of that time.

Noltë isolates many characteristics of fascism, which he alternately (and erroneously, if we accept Arendt's distinction) calls totalitarianism. First and foremost, he cites the establishment "of an ideologically oriented single party" which enforces strict uniformity, "if necessary by terroristic methods" (12). Under such rule, the individual's "religious and moral obligations toward God" (12) are dissolved, and the state has total claim over the individual. Three further characteristics that Noltë cites as attributes of totalitarianism are:

> terrorism, which proceeds with extreme harshness against the familiar and the traditional; ... universalism, which aims at world domination; ... [and] perversion, which demands those very things which are contrary to the laws of God and humanity. (18)

Finally, Noltë finds that fascism is characterized by: "The unshackling of primitive instincts, the denial of reason, the spellbinding of the senses by pageantry and parades"

(20). He acknowledges that, in practice, "ideology [is] of a secondary and instrumental nature in fascism" (70). Noltë also diagnoses the fear expressed by Maurras and Hitler, the feeling that "culture" would be lost, drowned in the mediocrity of the rise of the masses. This was a prevalent theory, one that was also reiterated by Ortega y Gasset, in his *The Revolt of the Masses* in 1932:

> There is no culture where there are no standards to which our fellow men can have recourse. There is no culture where there are no principles of legality to which to appeal. There is no culture where there is no acceptance of certain final intellectual positions to which a dispute may be referred. There is no culture where economic relations are not subject to a regulating principle to protect interests involved. There is no culture where aesthetic controversy does not recognise the necessity of justifying the work of art.
>
> When all these things are lacking there is no culture; there is in the strictest sense of the word, barbarism – properly speaking, there are no barbarian standards. Barbarism is the absence of standards to which appeal can be made. (79)

But Ortega has no sympathy with fascism, and holds liberal democracy to be the only possible political salvation from socialism. At any rate, one finds people as different in their political sympathies as Maurras and Ortega y Gasset expressing the same concern over the stultifying power of the conformist masses. In the western world, the 1920s and '30s represent a time when men from all backgrounds and callings rebelled against such mass-produced mediocrity in a mood of bitter post-war disillusionment. Certainly, British literature alone gives ample evidence of such a mood.

Noltë traces the fascist concept of "liberty" to the early Rousseauian idea; by restricting *all* levels of choice and experience in an individual's life, and by substituting complete obedience to, and the total domination of one ideal, Rousseau – and later, the fascists – could offer man the illusion of "complete" liberty:

> Since human and social conditions must mean restriction and dependence, a form of dependence would have to be found, the nature of which would no longer be particular but total, and which in its very totality would coincide once again with the nature of original liberty. If each person surrenders himself completely, that is, uniformly, to the law of the *volonté générale*, total obedience is equivalent to total liberty, since each human being no longer faces another human being, or a chance institution, but only the universality of his own self. (32-33)

This concept of liberty through complete submission and/or domination is in line with Mussolini's definition of fascism:

> Fascist man does not lead a life apart from all others, independent, self-indulgently following the whim of the moment: instead he personifies 'nation and *patria*,' moral law which links individuals and generations together in tradition and vocation. (Noltë 245)

This theory of "unfreedom" is idealized most at times when the individual has little power to change existing conditions, for example, during the labour unrest in Britain at the time, or during the period of weak hypocrisy of the Weimar Republic in Germany in the 1920s. The democracy of the western world is equally blemished, as John Harrison points out: "the men who possess the real power are not the elected delegates, but the men who control the purse strings, the financiers and the controllers of big business" (207).

Noltë analyzes the three models of fascism that were dominant in Europe for a time: Action Française, Italian Fascism and National Socialism. His approach is to analyze the phenomenon from a political-theoretical perspective. Hannah Arendt, in her three-volume study, *The Origins of Totalitarianism*, offers an historical-sociological approach to a definition, not of fascism, but rather of the more specific term "totalitarianism." Unlike Noltë, who does not differentiate fully between the terms fascism and totalitarianism – indeed, at one point he defines totalitarianism as simply "a secularized theocracy" (36)[2] – Arendt is very clear in her distinction between the two terms. Fascism exists as a political movement in Germany, Italy and France, yet Italy and France do not evolve into *totalitarian* regimes, while Germany does. Arendt agrees with Noltë's view that ideology is of secondary importance in fascism, although she identifies the ideology within the context of the totalitarian movement. She finds that "adherence to a totalitarian movement ... did not depend upon an ideological consensus, upon rigid devotion to racial or class credos" (Whitfield 26). She also agrees with Noltë's notion that the individual under a fascist regime is totally dependent on the state. Human spontaneity and diversity are restricted so completely that the void left in the individual "soul" is easily converted, trained or terrorized into belief in a rigid ideology:

---

[2] Noltë's definition of "totalitarian" is extremely loose and all-inclusive; at another time he states that "[t]he word 'totalitarian,' in the sense of laying full claim to, and obligation on, a human being, is applicable to every religion, every outlook on the world and on life, even the liberal. But only in the eyes of liberalism is this form really purely formal – that is, not ultimately concretizable..." (219).

> Total domination, which strives to organize the infinite plurality and differentiation of human beings as if all of humanity were just one individual, is possible only if each and every person can be reduced to a never-changing identity of reactions, so that each of these bundles of reactions can be exchanged at random for any other. The problem is to fabricate something that does not exist, namely, a kind of human species resembling other animal species whose only "freedom" would consist in "preserving the species." (Arendt, III 136)

Arendt underscores the substitution of total bondage for total freedom by quoting Hitler's assertion that the fascist strives "for a condition in which each individual knows that he lives and dies for the preservation of his species" (III, 136). The fact that Arendt is talking about concentration camp prisoners and Noltë about the general populace in a fascist state does not deny their agreement here: the two kinds of victims differ only in the degree of the intensity of the control that is exercised over their lives, although that control at its most intense often resulted in the death of the victim.[3]

Noltë points to the *kind* of violence used in the fascist state, which "is organized, not elemental; brutal not wildly passionate" (70). Arendt parallels this definition through her description of the tactics used by Hitler's SA troops and later the SS troops in their administration of the concentration camps. She relates how the early SA administration used perverse, impassioned, spontaneous brutality, which was later changed, under the SS troops, to efficient indifference:

---

[3] Reich's theory that fascism is not a surrender to an authentic, spontaneous emotion, but a surrender to a super-imposed abstract myth, an artificial "liberty" from self, is also a parallel that might be noted here.

> The real horror began ... when the SS took over the administration of the camps. The old spontaneous bestiality gave way to an absolutely cold and systematic destruction of human bodies, calculated to destroy human dignity.... (III 151-52)[4]

In exploring his theory of fascism, Noltë cites many characteristics that parallel much of what Arendt is saying. Noltë, however, has established a link between three primary models of fascism, and has tried to show how they exemplify the theory. While much of Arendt's work coincides with Noltë's, she does not define fascism as such. In fact, she has little interest in the Action Française or Italian Fascism as embodying the heart of the fascist problem. Arendt's concern is not with the theory, the "ideas and values" that are specific to fascism, but rather with the *method*, the means and ways of enactment, and she defines these as "totalitarian," rather than as fascistic. She finds only two models of authoritarian rule, Stalinist Russia and Nazi Germany, to be strictly totalitarian, since the one overriding characteristic of totalitarianism is the mass extermination of human beings.

Again, Noltë's central thesis that "Fascism is anti-Marxism which seeks to destroy the enemy by the evolvement of a radically opposed and yet related ideology" (20) represents a *theoretical* assessment and definition of the growth of fascism as the simple polarization of authoritarianism versus socialism, but utilizing basically the same methods as socialism. Arendt, however, makes a

---

4 Arendt's later study of Eichmann on trial in Jerusalem supplements this aspect of totalitarian violence: what she found in Eichmann was a man who was "coldly efficient, indifferent, and 'banal' in his evil" (Whitfield 210). What would have bothered Eichmann's conscience most was the feeling that he had failed or disappointed his superiors as a bureaucrat (Whitfield 226).

critical distinction in the methods used: "the difference between Fascism and totalitarianism might be summed up in one word: genocide" (Whitfield 39). While Noltë defines fascism as an authoritarian reaction *to* Bolshevism, Arendt isolates Stalinist Russia (*not* Bolshevism as such) and Nazism as parallel examples of totalitarian rule.

When we examine literary works for possible "fascist" theories and motifs, how do we distinguish between a "fascist" theory and a "totalitarian" method? Does Céline, for example, illustrate traits that are characteristic of fascism or totalitarianism? More specifically, when Birkin entertains the possibility of the annihilation of man in *Women in Love*, is this a fascist trait, or a possible example of totalitarian method, or an artistically objective vision of man's decline? Charles Maurras, theoretician of the Action Française, shows a fear of annihilation of the species that may be somewhat parallel to Lawrence's articulation:

> For Maurras, the swamp, the power which destroys life and beauty, and liberalism, the dominating thought pattern of the modern age, are identical. And at this point it becomes clear that in his fear – a fear which may seem purely political – Maurras is in the last resort concerned with himself and mankind: "Should the liberal lie spread over the earth, should anarchism and universal democratism spread the 'panbeotie' announced by Revan, should the barbarians from the depths, as predicted by Macaulay, appear at the appropriate time, then man will disappear as a human being, just as he will have disappeared in the form of Frenchman, Greek, or Latin" (Noltë 103).

Noltë talks about the "totalitarian" character of Mussolini's Italian Fascism, and even of the "partial totalitarian" nature of the Roman Catholic Church. Arendt would say the twentieth-century Catholic Church could not possibly be called totalitarian, because no mass extermination of sectors of the populace was committed. Furthermore, the authoritarian hold that Italian Fascism had on its people, although repellent to a liberal, was never as complete and total as the totalitarian power of Nazism and Stalinism over its people. The power of Nazi Germany was due partly to the *terror* inculcated through mass exterminations, "known but not known" by the populace. The presence of the Vatican in Italy may have had a mitigating effect on the Italian movement. At any rate, Italian Fascism may be characterized as "authoritarian," while German fascism and Stalinism is characterized as "totalitarian." Towards the end of his book, Noltë states:

> The poles of authoritarianism and totalitarianism bracket a span ranging from Pilsudski's regime, via the political totalitarianism of Falangist Spain, to the all-encompassing totalitarianism of Mussolini and Hitler. (460)

In the light of Arendt's more specific definition of totalitarianism as always accompanied by genocide, Noltë's above statement makes little sense; the terminology is too abstract and undefined. Noltë does, however, establish fascist theory as a direct reaction to Marxism. This is significant, as Hitler, in calling his ideology "National *Socialism*," insidiously incorporated the illusion of significant socialistic content into his program. Where Marxism uses slogans like the "brotherhood of man," National Socialism refers to the "Volk," a nationalistic form of brotherhood. But socialism was never truly a part of the fascist doctrine, as David Schoenbaum has stated:

> "Socialism" in its conventional senses was difficult, if not impossible, to locate in Nazi practice. But as

> an effective concept it had a very real meaning in Nazi attitudes. It was hortatory and defined a state of mind. (56)

Marxist-related ideology was "typically modified," to suit fascistic purposes. This again reinforces the most vital distinction between the varying forms of fascism, the distinction of the *methods* adopted to enforce the ideology. The fascist methods practiced in Italy, France, and Franco's Spain were clearly different from those practiced by National Socialism and Stalinism. Because only one of the totalitarian models is coincidentally fascist as well, it must be stated that totalitarian regimes are not necessarily fascist regimes, and conversely, fascist regimes are not *necessarily* totalitarian. By extension, then, the charge of fascism should not instantaneously conjure up the image of genocide, which is solely the attribute of totalitarian systems.

Reconsidering Bertrand Russell's remark that Lawrence's theories of blood-consciousness "led straight to Auschwitz" reveals some over-generalization of thought. Is Russell accusing Lawrence of fascism or totalitarianism? Probably Russell himself would be unaware of the difference.

While Noltë and Arendt examine fascism from a historical-political-sociological base, Wilhelm Reich analyzes the psychological elements of the German fascist regime in an attempt to understand the masses' unquestioning acceptance of this reactionary political program. In *The Mass Psychology of Fascism* (1946), he defines the concept as:

> characterized by metaphysical thinking, unorthodox faith, obsession with abstract ethical ideals, and belief in the divine predestination of the fuhrer. These basic

> features are linked with a deeper layer, which is characterized by a strong authoritarian tie to the fuhrer-ideal or the nation. The belief in a "master race" became the principal mainspring of the tie to the "fuhrer" on the part of the National Socialist masses, as well as the foundation of their voluntary acceptance of slavish submission. (80)

Reich sees the authoritarian family structure as the mainspring of fascism. This emphasis on an authoritarian patriarchal family structure as a primary source of fascism is vital to the study of Lawrence's leadership novels. For Reich, authoritarian families were dominated by "compulsive" marriage and family ties, as well as by a heavy reliance on mysticism:

> The greater part of this mysticism and what is most important about it is a biological energy process, an extreme expression of reactionary sexual ideology, irrationally and mystically conceived. *The creed of the "soul" and its "purity" is the creed of asexuality*, of "sexual purity." Basically, it is a symptom of the sexual repression and sexual shyness brought about by a patriarchal authoritarian society. (84)

Reich perceives fascism as a universal psychological quality, potentially active in all people. In an attempt to assess it objectively, he finds that:

> wherever we encounter authoritarian and moralistic suppression of childhood and adolescent sexuality, a suppression backed up by the law, we can infer with certainty that there are strong authoritarian-dictatorial tendencies in the social development, regardless of which slogans the ruling politicians use. (215)

Reich is more concerned about the personality of the fascist and the mass appeal of the ideology than he is about actual ideological or political platforms. He attributes the rise of fascism in Nazi Germany to the Germans' unshakeable belief in the *state.* Fascism became a dominating force because the form of the state was invested with more importance, security and hope than was the *essence,* the people. Reich cites the multitude of weak political parties in Germany between the wars as an essential cause of the German populace turning to fascism (280). His final analysis is that the mass of people themselves act *irresponsibly* when they turn power over to the state, rather than retaining it as their own right:

> If we take *"freedom"* to mean first and foremost the *responsibility of each individual to shape personal, occupational, and social existence in a rational way,* then it can be said that *there is no greater fear than the fear of the creation of general freedom.* (320)[5]

Such an analysis is innately revolutionary;[6] this view of freedom as social responsibility would require a complete transformation of self and society in order to work. Reich's theory also ignores, or makes meaningless, the specific rise of reactionary politics in the 1930s. Fascism and totalitarianism may be the outcome of a long trend toward authoritarian self-definition, but why, at that particular time in history (1930s), did it gain such prominence, not in an isolated instance, but in many countries and parties?

As an actual governing power, fascism was successful in only three countries. In this sense, it would appear to be an isolated phenomenon of the 1920s to '40s. In a less rigid sense, authoritarian trends, or elements of psychological readiness for authoritarianism, have been found

---

[5] Erich Fromm, in *Escape From Freedom,* also deals with the ambiguous, often frightening elements of freedom and the appeal of an authoritarian structure that represents an "escape" from the responsibilities inherent in "freedom."

[6] Reich cautions, however, that "We have to be on our guard against allowing our wishful revolutionary thinking to get the best of us and regarding as a realistic possibility that which is only right 'as such'" (200), the "as such" meaning that the desire for change is evident, but the necessary social conditions have not yet been met.

in the western world long before this period. It is notable that the 1960s were also a time of heightened political and moral awareness. But only the intellectual strata, a fairly small fraction, of the "hippie" movement were politically sophisticated. The majority of the young represented a dangerous wish to be free of middle-class North American conventionality, without any real awareness of their ideological vulnerability. Joan Didion describes their innocence in her essay "Slouching Towards Bethlehem" (1967):

> Anybody who thinks this is all about drugs has his head in a bag. It's a social movement, quintessentially romantic, the kind that recurs in time of real social crisis. The themes are always the same. A return to innocence. The invocation of an earlier authority and control. The mysteries of the blood. An itch for the transcendental, for purification. Right there you've got the ways that romanticism historically ends up in trouble, lends itself to authoritarianism. (125)

Didion's description of the migration of the masses of flower children to Haight-Ashbury parallels the young German drifters whom Stern analyzes in Moeller van den Bruck's milieu and time. Thus, the possibility of authoritarian control over such rootless, valueless and hopeless groups is underlined by their break with reality and by their naiveté.

Reich's theory must be examined in comparison with the more precise political, historical theories of fascism offered by Noltë and Arendt, defining the fascism of the period from 1920 to 1945.

A comparison of Reich's theories to Lawrence's belief in the rejuvenation of man through sexual fulfillment affirms the fact that both point to the tie between sexuality or unconscious life and political/social life. The similarity between Reich's theories and Lawrence's art is striking, in that both emphasize the need for sexual fulfillment as indicative of self-integration, as well as the integration of the self with others and within society. For Reich this integration would define the individual as a free, *responsible* political entity, totally opposite to the fragmented, unwholesome, *irresponsible* authoritarian personality that chooses to serve blindly, rather than to exercise the option of freedom. Some critics have noted the tendency in Lawrence to associate authoritarian characteristics in males with sexual fulfillment. While Lawrence does appear to identify a healthy sexuality with authoritarian characteristics in his leadership novels, the intent of the present study is to examine the validity of this identification, which has caused a great deal of critical controversy.

Two critics who deal very specifically with the questions of integration and authoritarianism in Lawrence's works are David Boadella and Scott Sanders; they are consequently dealt with here, rather than in the preceding chapter.

Boadella finds a close similarity between Reich's theory of orgonotic energy (Sharaf 280) – the spontaneous flow of energy, within and without the body – and Lawrence's recognition of the need "of the right kind of contact between men and women, the restoration of the capacity for merging" (134). Lawrence, in exposing the counterfeit nature of modern love, "is aware of the extent to which, since genuine feelings so often do not exist, they have to be faked and are faked on a mass scale, as well as in individual lives" (40). Boadella compares Lawrence's recognition of "sentimentality and counterfeit feeling" (Boadella 40) to Reich's theory of "substitute contact," which may be characterized by "'loud obtrusive laughter; forced rigid handshake; ... lukewarm friendliness; ... rigid sticking to certain views, plans or goals; ... exaggerated hail-fellow-well-met behavior [and a] rigid conversational way of talking'" (Boadella 40). In contrast to this empty, artificial form of contact, Lawrence and Reich both emphasize their reverence for individual life and freedom. Boadella quotes Lawrence's advice on educating a child: "First rule, leave him alone. Second rule, leave him alone. Third rule, leave him alone. That is the whole beginning" (63). Reich's dictum is synonymous: "remove every obstacle in the way of this naturally given productivity and plasticity of the biological energy.... The newborn child is first of all a piece of living nature (61,63).

Both Reich and Lawrence recognize that true sexual fulfilment is rare and not to be confused with, in Reich's words, "the various mechanical substitutes" (Boadella 41) that pass for normal in society. True sexuality is whole-person involvement, as well as whole-body involvement.[7]

Boadella also challenges Caudwell's assertion that Lawrence demands "we must *be* and no longer think," that "intellectualism and consciousness" (Caudwell 56) must be abandoned. Both Reich and Lawrence emphasize a different, more whole knowing than that offered by the western rational "intellectualism":

> Truth is not something to be learned or imparted to the organism. It is born as a crucial function within

[7] Myron Sharaf notes the criticism these theories of Reich's have received. One interesting comment is by James Baldwin: "There are no formulas for the improvement of the private, or any other, life – certainly not the formula of more and better orgasms (who decides?). The people I had been raised among had orgasms all the time and still chopped each other up with razors on Saturday nights." Sharaf rightly finds this criticism the usual misinterpretation of Reichian "orgiastic potency" (102).

> the organism, and it develops as long as the organism maintains its unitary functioning. (Boadella 50)

Boadella finds that Lawrence's perception of truth closely resembles this kind of knowing, when he quotes Lawrence's statements: "The profoundest of all sensualities is the sense of truth ... if you can't feel truth you can't have any other satisfactory sensual experience" (Boadella 50). Caudwell's intellectualism, however, "is mental, and reflects the rigidity of machine civilization. It is the kind of knowledge which kills the thing it is trying to know" (Boadella 51).

Scott Sanders notes that Lawrence's art focusses on the unconscious part of the human psyche, what Lawrence himself termed the "carbon" of humanity. Traditional personality portrayals are, for Lawrence, too manipulated, too contrived in their cerebral presentation of self. They confuse the truer issue of self-understanding:

> To use Freud's terms, he set the ego against the id. But the id is not an identity at all, rather a name for the unknown, a territory of obscure forces, the dark and silent basement of the self. All of Lawrence's works exhibit a greater interest in the shadowed basement than in the sunlit house. (16)

Lawrence's greatest contribution to literature may well be, as Anthony Burgess has asserted, his portrayal of the human unconscious, the underlying emotional states of being that comprise the essence of the human makeup. Burgess compares the respective approaches that Joyce and Lawrence take in their artistic representation of the unconscious:

> There is more "fine writing" in Joyce than in Lawrence (look at the first chapter of *Ulysses*), and Lawrence's exploitation of the ill-formed sentence – a high poetic

content qualified by a deliberate looseness of shape – is in the service of rendering the jerky illogicality of life. The poetic subject-matter itself is a deeper layer of human consciousness than fiction had previously been equipped to admit. Lawrence's contribution to the novel lies in his having found a technique for such deep-level mining. Joyce in *Ulysses* touches preverbal areas of consciousness and shows the naked libido at work. In *Finnegan's Wake* he dares to dive into the sleeping mind. But he is committed to human identity in a way that Lawrence is not, and it is probably fair to say that his experimentation has been acceptable only because of that solid traditional element in his work. Humphrey Chimpden Earwicker's initials are stitched into the fabric of Joyce's dream-prose like a desperate monogram, a gesture of fear of the loss of identity. Lawrence's characters sink easily into the world of "otherness," where human life accepts that it is also natural life, and identity – "the screaming of the ego," as Huxley puts it – is quelled. (208)

Lawrence's focus on the significance of the unconscious was, to some extent, coincidental with his milieu's growing fascination with psychoanalysis; there existed a growing recognition that the conscious mind, the "tip of the iceberg," was no longer adequate to understand human behavior. Lawrence's emphasis on human sexuality as the purest extension of the unconscious into daily life simultaneously imbues sexuality with positive, creative, life-enhancing power. Sanders thus finds Lawrence's portrayal of the unconscious as a positive force to parallel Wilhelm Reich's theory of sexual fulfillment as the source of creative living:

> Lawrence's ... view was closest to that of Reich, who considered the social self a crippling and vicious imposition upon the spontaneous, animal self....
>
> Lawrence, ... like the Romantics before him and like Wilhelm Reich and Herbert Marcuse since, held that man is not inherently corrupt, but is corrupted by his institutions, particularly by those which repress his sexual impulses.... men were capable of living much more freely and finely and peacefully than their present society permitted. (Sanders 68, 84)

Lawrence's art and Reich's theory remain very parallel until Lawrence enters his leadership novel phase, where Sanders criticizes Lawrence's inversion of the Reichian theory that the authoritarian state was based on the authoritarian-patriarchal family pattern. Sanders refers to "lower-middle-class and peasant families" (161-62) as being the most authoritarian in structure, and is concerned with the patriarchal authority Lawrence deems necessary in the home. Lawrence's extolling of a strong male image is not, however, only due to traditional patriarchalism; it also derives from the lack of authority and dignity in males in his own life and in the lives of many of his fictional characters. Walter Morel was not a dominant father figure in Paul's family, nor was Lawrence a dominant husband in his own marriage. Sanders agrees with Reich that authoritarian families produce authoritarian states and concurrently finds Lawrence at fault for wanting more male authority. Lawrence's own experience, however, had been that of too little rather than too much male authority. Admittedly Walter Morel is brutish at times, and a wife-batterer, but *Sons and Lovers* also presents a clear portrait of a father who skulks and cringes under his wife's morally indignant eyes.

This is not to say that the lot of the female in England in 1911 was enviable. Lack of education and profession did often make her home a prison, her life empty of ambition except for the goals of her children. Lydia Lawrence, when strapped for money, opened the front room of the family house as a crafts shop. Lawrence's emergence from a mother-oriented home helped him to be as resourceful and "domestic" as his own mother had been; Frieda Lawrence was bilingual, but Lawrence was the one who "translated" for money. Whether sexual discrimination or lack of status are connected to these facts of Lawrence's existence, one must appreciate the feminist viewpoint and also Lawrence's opposite view; had Lawrence come from a truly authoritarian household like, for example, that found in Samuel Butler's *The Way of All Flesh*, he might easily have condemned patriarchalism as heartily as Butler does.

The Plumed Serpent presents a portrait of the supposedly authoritarian leader who is also a father. Don Ramón is hardly very authoritarian in his fatherhood, and is certainly not a strict, puritanical disciplinarian. He shines more as a loving father than he does as a husband, leader, or friend. A truly authoritarian "paterfamilias" would have absolute obedience from his children, usually obtained through violent punishment. One cannot imagine one of his boys saying to him what Cyprian does: "Never, ... never can we love you, papa. You are our enemy. You killed our mother" (388). How does this authoritarian father respond? "'Come to me, little one!' said Ramón softly, holding out his hands" (388). A cornerstone of authoritarian fatherhood is to show no tenderness, no open declarations of caring or love; to do so is to risk jeopardizing the "masculinity" of the boy. Ramón certainly does not personify such an authoritarian pattern as a father.

The scholarship of Adorno, Arendt, Noltë and Reich, then, provide the multi-faceted approach to fascism that is essential to understand the fascist/authoritarian elements in Lawrence's work. The scholastic work done by Arendt and Noltë is necessary to understand the fascist and totalitarian ideologies and their relationships to each other. This ideological comprehension will be important when determining what the fascistic elements in Lawrence's works are, and how significantly they relate to the ideologies and to the actual events these ideologies led to. The work done by Reich and Adorno, especially that by Adorno, provides the tools that allow for a critical assessment of many of the characters in Lawrence's novels. One of Lawrence's remarkable strengths as a novelist turns out to be the sharpness and validity of the psychological portraits he creates; whether these characters prove to be "authoritarian" or "liberal" in their approach to life, they demonstrate a psychological integrity that says much for the author.

Chapter 3

"The Pathology of Cultural Criticism"

The previous chapter has established the ideological basis for an analysis of authoritarianism and fascism in Lawrence's works, and for the psychological profile that will be applied to some of Lawrence's fictional characters. When determining the nature of the "fascist personality," however, it is incumbent also to consider some of the "proto-fascist" ideological/artistic figures that preceded the period of National Socialism in Germany. The following analysis of the philosophies and personalities of three German theorists who led to the rise of fascism in that country therefore adds a practical element to the multi-faceted definition of fascism and authoritarianism that has so far been established.

Fritz Stern, in *The Politics of Cultural Despair*, examines the lives and works of Paul Lagarde, Julius Langbehn, and Moeller van den Bruck, and analyzes their contribution to the rise of the Germanic ideology of fascism. The discussion of these personalities will invite some comparisons between them and Lawrence, especially since none of these writers lived to witness the implementation of National Socialism; therefore, none of them have a retrospective vision. These comparisons between Lawrence and the German writers, where applicable, are included in the conclusion to this work. Lawrence's novels are certainly complete in themselves, and do not require a psychological analysis of the artist for clarification. However, a fuller perception of Lawrence's position as an artist and ideologist of the pre-World War II era may be achieved through these comparisons with the early German proto-fascists.

Stern's objective is to examine "the pathology of cultural criticism [in which] ... the dangers and dilemmas of a particular type of cultural despair" (1) are isolated. After the turn of the century in Germany, as in England, an intellectual rebellion is evident against the progress of science and commercialism, and the belief in rationality and intellect. This new *Weltanschauung* is characterized by a growing philosophy of despair and protest against the mechanized, decidedly rational character of the society of this period. The proponents of this philosophy "detested the growth of mechanization and equated it with arid intellectualism" (Harrison 20). Such a protest was not peculiar to Germany alone: D.H. Lawrence and W.B. Yeats, among others, also protested the growing mechanization of society (Harrison 20).

Stern considers Lagarde, Langbehn and Moeller van den Bruck as the philosophers of "cultural despair." Although Paul Lagarde began writing in the early nineteenth century, while Moeller van den Bruck's *Das Dritte Reich* was published in 1931, strongly similar motifs are evident amongst all three writers. Above all, they shared an intense hatred of "liberalism," which they blamed for all that was wrong in their time:

> They attacked liberalism because it seemed to them the principal premise of modern society; everything they dreaded seemed to spring from it: the bourgeois

> life, Manchesterism, materialism, parliament and the parties, the lack of political leadership. Even more, they sensed in liberalism the source of all their inner sufferings. Theirs was a resentment of loneliness; their one desire was for a new faith, a new community of believers, a world with fixed standards and no doubts, a new national religion that would bind all Germans together. All this liberalism denied. Hence, they hated liberalism, blamed it for making outcasts of them, for uprooting them from their imaginary past, and from their faith.... They sensed that liberalism was the spiritual and political basis of modernity and they sought to equate liberalism with...the acceptance of economic selfishness and exploitation, with the *embourgeoisement* of life and morals. They ignored – or maligned – the ideal aspirations of liberalism, its dedication to freedom, the hospitality to science, the rational, humane, tolerant view of man. For what they loosely called liberalism constituted little less than the culmination of the secular, moral tradition of the West. (Stern 10)

Moeller van den Bruck's *Das Dritte Reich* was extensively used by the Nazis, as were the works of Nietzsche and Wagner, as an endorsement of their political program. Stern emphasizes that "the red thread that ran through all [van den Bruck's] thought and wishes was his loathing for what he had come to identify as the decadent West, with its philosophy of right and reason, its liberalism, its dull and unheroic life" (295). From an examination of the lives of these three ideologists, Stern uncovers an emerging underlying philosophy which he calls the "Ideology of Resentment," and which is not only evident in recent German cultural history, but elsewhere in the

Western world. This "rebellion against modernity," states Stern:

> lies latent in Western society and its confused, fantastic program, its irrational and unpolitical rhetoric, embodies aspirations just as genuine, though not as generous or tangible, as the aspirations embodied in other and more familiar movements of reform. (13)

Hence McCarthyism, as well as Nazism, suggests Stern, may be viewed as an outcome of this prevalent resentment against weak moral and political principles that were identified under the all-encompassing banner of "liberalism."

Paul (Botticher) de Lagarde was born in 1827, and his writings, warning the German people of the doom they faced, became popular in the mid and later eighteen-eighties. Lagarde, a moralist as well as a scholar, was openly nationalistic in espousing his theories for Germany's rebirth.

Lagarde believed in the rebirth of Germany, and actively sought to bring to his people the vision of a Germany reborn. He himself would guide them to the new Germany. Only a national religion, a Germanic-Christian faith, could effect Germany's spiritual regeneration: "Only the extirpation of liberalism in all its guises, only the inclusion of the Austrian empire – a radical *grossdeutsche* solution – would permit Germany's continued life and growth" (Stern 26). Lagarde's early life is characterized by alienation from his father and dissatisfaction with his scholastic milieu; although intellectually brilliant, he was often erratic and arrogant, argumentative and suspicious of those around him. Lagarde's "loner" stance corresponds to a similar motif in the lives of Julius Langbehn and Moeller van den Bruck. Lagarde's personality cost him the chance of ever attaining the university positions that he desired as a scholar; he spent much of his professional life teaching at the secondary school level.

Lagarde viewed himself as the prophet of a Germany reborn, "of the *Volkstum* that was still unspoiled...":

> Lagarde believed man to be a creature of will and energy and sentiment, for whom reason was of secondary importance: "The core of man is not his reason, but his will.... For like everything that is good, knowledge also enters through the will, whose wings are sensibility and imagination, and whose driving force is love." ... When Lagarde insisted that he was the last defender of German individualism, he was not thinking of political rights at all; he thought of himself as the last champion of the German character. (Stern 53)

Lagarde idealized suffering and work: the threat of material comfort in the new commercial age was that it would make individuals self-indulgent and lazy. This idealization of adversity and hardship is not, of course, original to Lagarde; the whole traditional German "fusion of Protestantism ... and the Prussian ethos" (54) carries the same moralistic theme. Once established as a writer of repute, Lagarde carried this theme even further through his venomous critique of the German educational system. His proposed new curriculum is a forecast of Hitler's youth programs:

> The state would impose the most rigorous intellectual and moral standards. These schools were not to be polluted by the greatest evils of student life, smoking and drinking. This appeal to abstinence and hardiness underlines the similarity of conception and purpose between Lagarde's dedicated school for potential rulers and the later *Ordensburgen* which combined

National Socialist ideology and Spartan discipline to train National Socialist leaders. (Stern 108)

In a similar vein, Lagarde repeatedly reiterated the great need for an all-powerful *Führer*, who would unite the people and represent their united wishes so completely that his absolute command would simply be the expression of the people (Stern 88). The "people," in Lagarde's view, did not include the Jews, "who were a terrible misfortune for every European people" (Stern 91); in Lagarde's mind, the Jews increasingly came to represent everything that was wrong with the modern age and with liberalism itself. The beginning of Lagarde's career was marked by mild eruptions of anti-Semitism, but these hardly resembled the vicious rhetoric he developed as he grew older. Regarding this later anti-Semitism, Stern notes that "few men prophesied Hitler's work with such accuracy – and approval" (93).

All these themes found in Lagarde's writing recur one hundred years later in National Socialism; this phenomenon is not surprising, but rather shows that the growth of a particular frame of mind, a specific theory, develops gradually, if at times seemingly imperceptibly. Lagarde *was* popular and was therefore able to carry his ideas to the academic public first, and finally to the people themselves:

> After his death, the soft Lagarde began to appeal to a growing number of educated Germans. To invoke Lagarde in those years was to attest one's patriotic idealism, to prove one's hatred of everything un-Germanic, to take a stand for the 'yea-saying,' the irrational, the creative forces of culture against the negativism and materialism of mere intellectualism. (Stern 117)

Stern next examines the writer Julius Langbehn, whose book *Rembrandt als Erzieher* (1890), created a tremendous stir during the late nineteenth century. It was hugely successful, but for all the wrong reasons. The book is not a carefully thought out study of the wrongs of the age, but an erratic, emotional vision, for Langbehn saw himself as the prophet of the age. The 1890s were, in Germany as well as in many other countries, years of instablity and disquiet: the approach of the twentieth century, amidst all of the changes wrought by science and Darwinist theory, and in the newly urban environment of the machine age, led many European people to a premonition of disaster ahead:

> The decade was one of strife and unrest, when the cultural discontent which previously had been the complaint of a few artists and intellectuals became the faddish lament of the many. The revolt against modernity, the attack on civilization, gathered force, hundreds of voices inveighed against all sorts of evils and repressions, and multitudes of people everywhere were repeating these imprecations. Nietzsche, ignored during his creative period, was suddenly read and admired, Ibsen was played and praised, Nordau's *Degeneration* vehemently debated. Everywhere, and not only in Germany, sprang up the cry for greater freedom, for self-expression, for more experience and less theorizing, for a fuller life, for the recognition of the tortured, self-torturing individual. The intensity of this awakening in Germany can be gauged by the instantaneous success of Langbehn's book. The decade that ended with the exuberant fling of the German Youth Movement began with this wild book, this breathless tirade, this rhapsody of irrationalism. (Stern 131-32)

The book portrayed Rembrandt as Germanic, as what is finest in Langbehn's ideal of German character. It simultaneously attacked liberalism, science and rationality. Creativity would only be rediscovered with a return to the latent Germanic qualities of "childlike simplicity, subjectivity, individuality" (Stern 132). But it was primarily the intense, visionary style with which Langbehn wrote that captured the imaginations of his readers. It "provided the Germanic ideology at the moment of its widest appeal with a conservative, idealistic, and thoroughly acceptable guise" (Stern 199).

Langbehn lived alone for long periods of time, without a set of social contacts or a professional identity to secure his stability; at one point he cultivated an obsession with self, which became a morbid narcissism. Stern mentions that "he could sit for hours before his own portrait, caressing it" (138). While he might have been described as an egoist, his character is also embued with the kind of self-denying romanticism of the *Weltschmerz* or brooding despair of earlier periods. His loneliness led him to desire human relationships which he would then repudiate. He appears to have taken a perverse joy in cutting himself off from the mainstream of life. During the height of his later popularity, however, the German public compared him to Nietzsche, misunderstanding the few surface similarities as a deeper likeness. Stern refutes any resemblance between the theories of the two:

> Although Langbehn's intellectual relation to Nietzsche is obscure, there is no doubt that he felt a particular affinity for the lonely prophet. Langbehn expected to play a role analogous to Nietzsche's, only greater, purer, and more constructive. I think it probable that Langbehn thought his *culte du moi* and his idio-

> syncrasies of style were Nietzschean, just as later on young would-be geniuses mastered the gestures, but not the qualities, of Nietzschean greatness. (144)

Langbehn's revolt against a new age of science corresponded superficially to a wider, international anti-scientific stance as represented by such leading figures as Nietzsche, James, Bergson and Freud, and it was in this latter theoretical position that the narrow rationalism of the late nineteenth century was essentially defeated. But Langbehn had nothing in common with these men, save that all attacked late nineteenth-century science; Langbehn's intent, temperament, training, and above all, the quality of his mind, set him apart:

> Nietzsche attacked science because of the increasing narrowness of this particular generation of scientists. He was anti-Darwin because the Darwinists violated his view of human freedom, and he was critical of mechanistic, soulless science. But his roots were deep in the Western humanistic and scientific tradition, and he sought to preserve the freedom and intellectual vitality of that tradition from the dogmatism of an ephemeral aberration. Langbehn's attack, on the other hand, was the irritated gesture of a man unwilling to admit the validity of science, unwilling to recognize the supremacy of intellect, unwilling even to study the findings of science. His was the prototype of the modern antiscientific temperament, yearning for mystery and religion, and disdainful of intellectual effort. (Stern 163)

Langbehn used a mythical basis in his pursuit of the true Germanic character: he idealized the German peasant in his uncontaminated simplicity and subservience; this was where the genuine *Volk* could be found. Similarily, like Lagarde before him, he turned to the youth of the nation as the source of salvation. His book's publication and consequent popularity coincided with the beginning of various arts and crafts societies and youth organizations designed to strengthen and unite Germany's young. The German Youth Movement was headed by Karl Fischer, who was hailed by his students with "heil":

> [It] erupted like a great phenonmenon of nature. Out of unsuspected depths leapt forth defiance, hate, yearning, love, all the hopes and fears that for decades had been repressed, denied, forcibly sublimated. The movement was spontaneous, translating sentiment directly into action, with thought as a kind of intermittent and subordinate guide. Even the briefest description of the Youth Movement will demonstrate its close affinity, historical and psychological, to Langbehn. What he had confusedly articulated, the youths exuberantly acted out; they heeded his message, as they willingly acknowledged, and the few indispensable adults who helped and protected them, had also been followers of the Rembrandt-deutsche. (Stern 223)

Another central tenet of Langbehn's thought was the necessity of spreading German culture, which, in its innate superiority, could save other related *Niederdeutsche* countries. He writes of the necessity of annexing Holland and Denmark "for their own sake":

> "so that they will not dullen because of the narrowness of their horizons." Germany must establish an empire from Amsterdam to Riga, and "she must collect all her children around her. That is the best policy of state and spirit. It is a family policy." (Stern 194)

Some critics find that *Rembrandt als Erzieher* contains the first sign of the imperialistic policies that guided the Germans in the two world wars, but Stern finds the irony in Langbehn's policy to be that his book is devoted to a critique of present German culture, yet he proposes an annexation of other countries because of the superiority of German culture; thus, as Stern states:

> It seems incongruous for Langbehn to justify German imperialism by appealing to German culture when the rest of the book proclaimed the decline of that culture. To understand this apparent paradox, to understand this leap from despair to aggression, is to probe deeply into the roots of what I have here called the politics of cultural despair. (195)

Nevertheless, *Rembrandt als Erzieher* became the handbook of future German right-wing political movements, and the key tenets found within it relate directly to the development of National Socialism.

The third theorist Stern examines is Moeller van den Bruck, and Stern finds him "in some ways the most admirable of the Germanic critics" (231). Moeller began adult life as a drifter and rebel. He was expelled from school at an early age and broke away from his family. The isolationist position that he adopted was romanticized by him and many other young, rootless men:

> How many youths of his time dignified their retreat from life by invoking Zarathustra, as if that superb self-conqueror had preached resignation and passivity in the face of an uncongenial culture. (Stern 233)

Moeller personified what Stern calls "the familiar German theme, the *Generationsproblem*, the struggle of the young against the old" (233), and it is interesting to note that later in his life, at the height of his influence in forming a right-wing reactionary movement, he and his fellows "called themselves the *young* conservatives, the voice of the young..." (Stern 278). He produced an exorbitant amount of writing in his lifetime, which Stern says was characterized by "his relentless seriousness":

> ... in 1902 ... [he published] *Die Moderne Literatur*, an 800-page critique of contemporary prose and poetry. For a man so young – he began the book when he was 22 – this critical survey of German literature after Nietzsche was an impressive achievement. (235)

Much of Moeller's writing was concerned with "hero-worship" of leading figures in Germany's past, such as Goethe. Stern notes that both Carlyle's *On Heroes, Hero-Worship and the Heroes in History* and Emerson's "On Representative Man" were popular in Germany. One of Moeller's basic themes was to point to the "antithesis between civilization and culture" (246), of which Germany had too much of the first and too little of the second. Moeller viewed civilization – under liberalism – as mechanical mass-conformity – deadening to the senses and the soul. Stern comments that:

> [t]his antithesis between civilization and culture was a favorite subterfuge of German "idealists"; it expressed in an unexceptionally cultured manner their resentment against modernity, democracy, and the West. During both world wars German intellectuals pictured the Allied Powers as the protagonists of civilization, and as the enemies of culture, represented chiefly by Germany.... [I]t is beyond doubt that the idea of establishing a sharp dichotomy between civilization and culture was born at the time of German idealism, and has played an important and pernicious role in German thought ever since.... It is therefore disheartening to find the same vacuous antithesis prominently used in a recent American study, Amaury de Riencourt's *The Coming Caesars*. "Culture pre-

> dominates in young societies awakening to life, grows like a young organism endowed with exuberant vitality, and represents a new world outlook. It implies original creation of new values, of new religious symbols and artistic styles, of new intellectual and spiritual structures, new sciences, new legislations, new moral codes.... Civilization aims at the gradual standardization of increasingly large masses of men within a rigidly mechanical framework – masses of 'common men' who think alike, feel alike, thrive on conformism, are willing to bow to vast bureaucratic structures, and in whom the social instinct predominates over that of the creative individual." (Stern 246)

Such civilization is produced, in Moeller's view, by liberalism – the source for all that was wrong in the world. It is important to note that Moeller never actually defines liberalism. Christianity is similarly refuted, and Moeller, as a Darwinian, thanks science for the downfall of established religion. What Moeller fervently hoped for was a new religion, "a Germanic *Weltanschauung*," to fill the void created by liberalism and Christianity. Stern notes that "[i]n his uncritical critique of philosophy, as in his veneration for Dostoevski, Moeller anticipated the mood of modern existentialism" (249).[1]

Stern suggests that the three German writers, Lagarde, Langbehn and Moeller, share a highly similar countenance, that, in fact, they belong to the same "type" of personality:

[1] Moeller interpreted Dostoyevsky as a conservative revolutionary who hated western liberalism as much as he himself did. Stern states that "[n]o other modern writer save Nietzsche had as great an impact on German thought as Dostoevski, and the character of that impact was to some extent shaped by Moeller" (261-62).

"the portrait of this type emerges now with some clearness; certainly isolation, alienation, and self-hatred are the outstanding characteristics" (335). He examines their utter negation of any modern social, political or religious institution.[2] They "felt and were awed by a mysterious power, inexplicable and yet immediately real to them, which they believed to rule the fate of man and the laws of nature" (334). All of these characteristics correspond closely to the personality traits that Adorno has found to define the authoritarian personality.

It is interesting to find that Fritz Stern mentions D. H. Lawrence in the context of the "type" of personality that he is trying to define. Lawrence is not placed in the tradition, but one of his characters is:

> The type clearly emerged in the 1880's, and ranged from Charles Maurras, Maurice Barres, and Knut Hamsun to the poet Miguel de Unamunno. It thus included men of diverse interests and unequal talents who were linked by a feeling of alienation in the modern world and an attendant search for a new faith. The type was also depicted in a long line of fictional characters from *The Possessed* to D. H. Lawrence's James Sharpe in *Kangaroo* "who is half an artist, not more, and so can never get away from it or free himself from its dictates".... This type dominated the literature of the *fin de siecle* and of the German Expressionists. Philip Wylie's *Generation of Vipers* may be taken as a contemporary instance of the enduring quality of this genre. Note his bombast: "We have cancer – cancer of the soul. Religion has failed." (Stern 328)

---

[2] Langbehn's conversion to Catholicism is an exception, which it appears was accomplished only by his gross misunderstanding of the concepts involved.

Stern himself also acknowledges the resemblance of the three Germans he has analyzed to the authoritarian type propounded by Adorno: "I should also mention the similarities between my views of these men and the authoritarian personality as defined by T. W. Adorno and his collaborators" (335).

The following four chapters, then, will be devoted to an analysis of a number of characters from *Women in Love, Aaron's Rod, Kangaroo* and *The Plumed Serpent.* This analysis will not only consider the theories of Arendt and Noltë, or the psychological profile drawn by Adorno, but will also, in a number of instances, draw upon the study by Stern to further elucidate fascist and authoritarian elements in some of these characters. Once analysis of the fictional characters is completed, comparisons can also be made between Lawrence and three men that Stern analyzes. How closely do Lawrencian ideas resemble the ideological platforms proposed by Lagarde, Langbehn and Moeller van den Bruck? This analysis should, in turn, help to define the degree of fascism in Lawrence's thought.

Chapter 4

Authoritarian, Totalitarian and Utopian Elements in *Women in Love*

The passage in *Women in Love* that has most often been singled out for critical commentary regarding fascism is that in which Birkin, after Gerald Crich's death, contemplates the annihilation of the human species (538). This passage may, at the most extreme, be viewed as representative of the final, destructive urge that is an inherent part of the totalitarian ideology, where the need to purge supposed imperfections, through genocide, becomes so powerful that it ends in universal destruction. Birkin's reflections on the passing of mankind may, however, be viewed from other perspectives as well; certainly it is more a prophecy of doom than a call for human extermination. The other element that Birkin represents in this novel is the urge toward a utopian society. Birkin's love for Gerald was based on the need for more than one single satisfying relationship. He wants, as he tells Ursula, "a perfected relation between you and me, and others ... so that we are all free together" (356). Together with Lawrence's emphasis on rebirth, this indicates a strong feeling for a utopian community of some kind.

One of the strongest features of this novel, however,

is the thoroughly convincing and clearly-drawn authoritarian personality of Gerald Crich. The fact that Gerald dies because of his inadequacy as an individual, his inability to love in a reciprocal way, also indicates clearly that Lawrence views authoritarianism as a fatal flaw, not, as some critics have indicated, as a desirable trait.

Women in Love in many ways portrays the inhabitants of a wasteland, the most central metaphor for the twentieth century western world in literature. If there is an "antagonist" in the novel, it is Gerald, the exponent of mechanical order, who feels he must rigidly control all that is spontaneous in the human being. The novel portrays Gerald in strong contrast to his liberal-humanist father, who represents the old order of failed Christian and democratic idealism.

The portrait of Gerald is remarkable in its precise detail and far-sightedness from the perspective of 1915. Now, with modern hindsight, we can see the parallels between Gerald's streamlined, impersonal operation of the mines and the workings of capitalistic bureaucracies that culminated in the fascism of the '30s and '40s. Further, Gerald's psychological makeup is delineated so definitively that he resembles very closely the "type" of psychological authoritarian personality defined by Adorno and his collaborators in *The Authoritarian Personality.* After the early triumphs and subsequent defeats of some of the major authoritarian regimes of the twentieth century, various studies have been written assessing the kind of human personality most susceptible to authoritarian systems. As early as 1933, Wilhelm Reich produced his analysis of the authoritarian patriarchal family structure; he views the authoritarian family as the cornerstone of authoritarian society. Focussing specifically on fascism, he finds the ideology characterized by abstract, mystical, metaphysical irrationalism and produced by the repression of human spontaneity and creativity. The conclusions that Reich draws rest finally on the element of repression in authoritarian systems – where the human personality is not allowed freedom to be and to act spontaneously. An irrational compensatory gratification is substituted for spontaneity and a corresponding irrational self-image is projected by the individual within the system.

Adorno's study extends Reich's theory of repression (as productive of authoritarianism) by isolating specific personality traits that are more concrete and precise than the all-encompassing term "repression." Gerald Crich in *Women in Love* may be analyzed as a specifically authoritarian personality of the type suggested by both Reich and Adorno. While the term "repression" is symptomatic of the general malaise in Gerald's personality, the more specific qualities that Adorno works with help to analyze his character more precisely and fully. Gerald is recognizable at the end of the novel as a human being who can neither love nor wholely live a spontaneous, creative existence; instead, he substitutes his ideal of mechanized organization, creating for himself a mystical, abstract "harmony" that is his basic irrationality.[1] If repression of the whole sexual being is present here, which is what Reich means, Gerald's promiscuity is indicative of such repression:

> ... all forms of fascistic, imperialistic, and dictatorial mysticism can be traced back to the mystical distortion of the vegetative sensations of life, a distortion that

[1] This is similar to the stress within fascistic systems on the abstract ideal of "patriotism." Reich notes that "despite all hypocrisy, the ecstasy derived from the notions of 'honor' and 'duty' is genuine" (52).

> results from a patriarchal and authoritarian organization of the family and state.... In fact, it is precisely this *inhibition* of the capacity for orgastic experience that lies at the basis of many pathological manifestations that occur in later sexual life, such as indiscriminate choice of partners, sexual restlessness, proclivity to pathological extravagances, etc. (Reich 136)

Thus, Reich's central tenet is that an individual's "*authoritarian structure* – this must be clearly established – *is basically produced by the embedding of sexual inhibitions and fear in the living substance of sexual impulses*" (30). This may well be the cause of Gerald's stultification of inner growth.

Gerald is certainly repressed in terms of an instinctual, spontaneous being; this repression is described in detail throughout the novel. The element of stealth in his personality has often been noted, many critics relating this to the mythical northern wolf-imagery that Lawrence interweaves into Gerald's, as well as into Mrs. Crich's, character. A psychological interpretation of this quality, however, qualifies its "animalistic" connotation; the "significant, sinister stillness in [Gerald's] bearing" (15) suggests an inner emptiness that has developed through a fear of the surrounding world. Such hyper-awareness of the environment indicates a fear of one's surroundings, so that human nature is never really able to feel freely: "there was a strange stealth glistening through his amiable, almost happy appearance" (24). Gerald fears spontaneous emotion, perhaps more than any other single quality:

> "You think people should just do as they like... And I," said Gerald grimly, "shouldn't like to be in a world of people who acted individually and spon-

> taneously as you call it. We should have everybody cutting everybody else's throat in five minutes." (36)

His response here is far too vehement to be in proportion to the situation. A young couple about to be married have made a run for the church door; that is all. At another point in the novel, his stealth is described clearly as an abnormal suspiciousness:

> From time to time, in a manner characteristic of him, Gerald lifted his head and looked around. Even though he was reading the newspaper closely, he must keep a watchful eye on his external surroundings. There seemed to be a dual consciousness running in him. He was thinking vigorously of something he read in the newspaper, and at the same time his eye ran over the surfaces of the life round him, and he missed nothing. ... Gerald seemed always to be at bay against everybody. (58)

In a manner typical to the authoritarian personality, Gerald projects his internal fears onto his external environment:

> Projection of one's inner impulses, particularly of aggression, onto others will naturally lead to a conception of a dangerous and hostile world and consequently to a general suspiciousness of others.... a conception of people as threatening in the sense of an over-simplified survival-of-the-fittest idea. Feelings of victimization are often connected with such notions. (Adorno 411)

The authoritarian tends to perceive the environment around him as hostile, an attitude that represents the "'jungle-character' of the world ... in which one has to destroy others to prevent them from destroying oneself" (Adorno 411). In *Women in Love* Birkin chastizes Gerald for both his "cut-throat" philosophy towards others, and for his feelings of victimization, his suspiciousness toward other people:

> "That means *you* would like to be cutting everybody's throat," said Birkin....
>
> "It's a nasty view of things, Gerald," said Birkin, "and no wonder you are afraid of yourself and your own unhappiness."
>
> "How am I afraid of myself?" said Gerald, "and I don't think I am unhappy."
>
> "You seem to have a lurking desire to have your gizzard slit, and imagine every man has his knife up his sleeve for you," Birkin said. (36-37)

Gerald is not consciously aware of his own underlying aggression; nevertheless, it is that force that he fears in others. Ultimately Gerald's projection of his inner fear onto the external world, his fear of "letting go," results in a more global fear of society as a whole "letting go":

> "It's quite true," said Gerald, "it never is *quite* the same in England. But perhaps we don't want it to be – perhaps it's like bringing the light a little too near the powder-magazine, to let go altogether, in England. One is afraid what might happen, if *everybody else* let go." (444)

Gerald's readiness to react to a hostile environment distinguishes him as a character in this novel; it is an underlying suspiciousness and fear that neither Gudrun nor Birkin show.

The authoritarian personality exhibits a "moralistic condemnation" of other people or human groups. The need to morally condemn segments of humanity appears to be a means of reassuring oneself of belonging to the right group and having moral rightness on one's side. Alternatively, "while rejection of other people is more common in high scorers [authoritarians], low scorers [liberals] tend more toward self-rejection" (Adorno 409). Gerald's attitude was superficially shaped by his university training, but the "sociological ideas, and ideas of reform" do not really enable him to view humanity *en masse* in a sensitive manner:

> ...he found humanity very much alike everywhere, and to a mind like his, curious and cold, the savage was duller, less exciting than the European. So he took hold of all kinds of sociological ideas, and ideas of reform. But they never went more than skin-deep, they were never more than a mental amusement. Their interest lay chiefly in the reaction against the positive order, the destructive reaction. (249)

Other people assume the stature of playthings in Gerald's thought and in his life; only their oddities or inferiorities distinguish them enough to make them interesting to him. The excitement engendered by the more primitive African sculpture wanes because the primitive itself is no improvement over civilized humanity. Gerald finds that:

> There aren't many fierce things, as a matter of fact. There aren't many things, neither people nor animals, that have it in them to be really dangerous.... They are over-rated, savages. They're too much like other people, not exciting, after the first acquaintance. (73)

Civilization itself neither intrigues him, nor does he possess a healthy openness toward humanity. At one point he states that "every civilized body is bound to have its vermin" (180). Such a comment echoes an assumption of innate superiority over segments of the human mass, which closely parallels Adorno's authoritarian personality type, who exhibits "a great deal of indulgence in what is seen as 'righteous indignation' about people considered as inferior" (406).

Similarly, Gerald's strong sense of a "hierarchical conception of human relations" coincides with the authoritarian's belief in the "right kind of people" (Adorno 418), and in "accepted or even 'admired' social status" (419). The authoritarian personality must of necessity identify himself with the right group, the "winning side." Thus, when Birkin, deploring the plunder of Britain by industrialism, asks Gerald, "Don't you feel like one of the damned?" (67), Gerald replies "no." His denial of being any part of a losing or weakened group shows how constantly necessary it is for him to align himself with the powerful and the "righteous"; it exhibits a lack of compassion for the new urban poor, since Birkin and he are facing a "hideous great street" (67) when the remark is made.

Gerald's awareness of, and insistence on, his upper-class status is again evidenced when he meets the Brangwen sisters:

> "Who are those two Brangwens?" Gerald asked.
> …"Teachers in the Grammar School."
> There was a pause.
> "They are!" exclaimed Gerald at length. "I thought I had seen them before."
> "It disappoints you?" said Birkin.
> "Disappoints me! No – but how is it Hermione has them here?"
> "And what's the father?"
> "Handicraft instructor in the schools."
> "Really!"
> "Class barriers are breaking down!"
> Gerald was always uneasy under the slightly jeering tone of the other. (104)

Gerald is attracted to Gudrun on an unconscious level, because consciously he is reluctant to endorse his attraction to a "town girl." This social snobbery is further emphasized when Lawrence notes, of Gerald, that "In his world, his conscious world, she was still a nobody" (133). Gerald's insecurity leads him to rely on external order: the class system defines the individual's behavior and dress codes and simplifies life by the assertion of rigid levels of status. The fact that class snobbery is beginning to break down during Gerald's lifetime causes him insecurity, rather than a sense of true indignation, as when he asserts his social ascendency:

> "... because I don't think teachers as a rule are my equal." ... He did not *want* to claim social superiority, yet he *would* not claim intrinsic personal superiority, because he would never base his standard of values on pure being. So he wobbled upon a tacit assumption of social standing. (235)

This is not intrinsic snobbery; rather, it is the need of an insecure individual to have an external order within which to define himself; his inner emptiness is incapable of providing him with a sense of self-definition.

In a similar vein, Gerald also rejects the liberal-Christian humanism of the Victorian era, which is exemplified in the older Mr. Crich's idealism. Possibly Gerald is only more honest here than his father, since the old, monied class system inherently denied true equality and humanism. Mr. Crich's efforts to placate the poor are in no measure an equalizing force: his benevolence is finally hypocritical. Gerald merely makes his upper-class managerial position more blatantly powerful:

> Gerald ... did not care about equality. The whole Christian attitude of love and self-sacrifice was old

> hat. He knew that position and authority were the right thing in the world, and it was useless to cant about it. They were the right thing, for the simple reason that they were functionally necessary. (255)

Another trait exhibited by the authoritarian personality is a strong emphasis upon conventionality:

> Conformity is one of the major expressions of lack of an internal focus in the high scorer. One of the most outstanding characteristics … is the adoption of conventional values and rules. (Adorno 476)

Gerald's concern with a conventional self-image is carefully underlined by Lawrence. Beginning with the young couple's race to the church door in chapter one of *Women in Love,* Gerald's disapproval of spontaneous or uncustomary behavior is manifest: "Birkin told him about the race of the bride and the bridegroom. 'H'm!' said Gerald, in disapproval. 'What made you late then?'" (34). After the ceremony, the guests gather at Shortlands to celebrate; the usual gaiety and banter common to weddings is highlighted in a specific scene between Gerald and one of the brothers-in-law, Marshall, who jokingly ridicules the abstract nature of the conversation he overhears: "'You don't want a soul today, my boy,' said Marshall [to the young bridegroom]. 'It'd be in your road'" (35). Gerald immediately recoils, conventionally puritanical about his sister's wedding night and her honor being joked about in a ribald manner: "'Christ! Marshall, go and talk to somebody else,' cried Gerald with sudden impatience … staring after him with angry eyes" (35). There is a lack of self-knowledge here that is astonishing: Gerald's treatment of women clearly indicates their pure instrumentality for him; consequently, his squeamishness over Marshall's teasing is hypocritical.

Gerald, throughout the novel, embodies a rigid sense of decorum, of what is "correct" for the occasion. Birkin asserts, at one point, that "Gerald stickles for convention," to which Gerald retorts: "'I don't stickle for it.... But if you'd got as sick as I have of rowdy go-as-you-please in the house, you'd prefer it if people were peaceful and conventional, at least at meals'" (259). The elder Crich notes the same quality in his son; Gerald sits with his dying father, the appropriate behavior of a son, but feels no real compassion or grief. Gerald will perform his duties in accordance with conventional behavioural formulas, but he resembles Eliot's "hollow men" because he is "form without essence." Mr. Crich, acutely assessing his son's lack of essence, of the ability to care, "... would have liked to cry aloud to Gerald, so that his son should be horrified out of his composure" (321). After Crich dies, the family assembles together to mourn, praising their father as a worthy man. While Gerald cannot feel sorrow over his father's death, or enough love to want to praise him posthumously, he feels secure and relieved that the appropriate behavior for such an occasion is being carried out: "Gerald acquiesed in all this. It was the right conventional attitude, and, as far as the world went, he believed in the conventions" (380).

Gerald also feels annoyance at Gudrun's attire when she arrives at Shortlands shortly after the funeral. She "came dressed in startling colours, like a macaw, when the family was in mourning. Like a macaw she was!" (269). An individual's choice of dress is an indication to Gerald of how well they fit in with the established order. Gudrun clearly has no desire to be a part of custom and predictability. Her colourful stockings reflect the avant-guarde bohemian lifestyle she has come to identify with;

she is conforming as well, but to a different, "anti-establishment" sub-group; hence her stockings symbolize, to Gerald, the disruption of convention. It is not only the colliers and their wives who are shocked by the brazen colour of Gudrun's stockings; Gerald especially finds that "[h]er stockings always disconcerted him" (266). Gudrun's colorful bohemian style contrasts sharply, in his mind, to the dress style of the French governess, whose correctness of apparel pleases him, even as he recognizes it's ugliness:

> She was like some elegant beetle with thin ankles, perched on her high heels, her glossy black dress perfectly correct, her dark hair done high and admirably. How repulsive her completeness and her finality was! He loathed her. Yet he did admire her. She was perfectly correct. (268-69)

Gerald's own attire is meticulously chosen; his rigid sense of what is fitting for his station in life is reinforced in expansive detail. The luxurious apparel is not so much indicative of a sensuous love for silk finery in Gerald as a symbol of the class to which he belongs: "... how scrupulous Gerald was in his attire, how expensive too. He wore silk socks, and studs of fine workmanship, and silk underclothing, and silk braces" (308). His clothing symbolizes externally what Gerald feels inwardly; it defines him, and places him in a specific class of people, which for him is the "right" class. An earlier exposure to liberal education and theories of reform cause him to superficially and temporarily embrace "liberal" traits, but even this seeming openness and flexibility finally prove too frightening and insecure for him.[2] Gerald reverts to ideologies that are commonly considered safe, supported by the *status quo,* and unlikely to cause disruption or change. He finally wants "to go back to the dullest conservatism, to the most stupid of conventional people. He wanted to revert to the strictest Toryism" (249). Gerald's inflexibility is reflected in his emphasis on conventionally appropriate behavior, a rigidly simplistic political-social philosophy and strictly correct style in dress and personal appearance.

Thus, it is understandable that, upon meeting Halliday and his fellow bohemians in London, Gerald experiences a sense of release from the self-imposed strictures of his conventional existence. Such a sense is all the more violent because of the enormous repression which precedes it. At Halliday's flat, he self-consciously walks nude from his bath:

> He was so conventional at home, that when he was really away, and on the loose, as now, he enjoyed nothing so much as full outrageousness. So he strode with his blue silk wrap over his arm and felt defiant. (88)

But such defiance is not usual in Gerald's life, and when dressed for breakfast, he once again reverts to a "correct and *comme il faut* ... appearance and manner" (88). Together with the correctness of manner and dress, an overwhelming desire exists in Gerald to be identified as a member of the right group, to belong to the strongest side. The

[2] Gerald's switch from left-wing radicalism to a right-wing reactionary attitude is typical of Kreml's assertion that this psychological type may be determined on the basis of "the ideological differences between politically Left-wing or politically Right-wing authoritarianism" (87). Hans Eysenck suggested in 1954 that "English Fascists and Communists, the parties at the two extremes of the British political system, would both be more tough-minded than members of the more centrist parties" (209).

handsome, powerful figure he portrays is at times undercut by pathos: his strength is external only. Here is a gentleman whose managerial power in the England of the time is awesome, yet he does not know how to dance the new ragtime:

> Gerald was marvellously exhilarated at finding himself in motion, moving towards Gudrun, dancing with feet that could not yet escape from the waltz and the two-step, but feeling his force stir along his limbs and his body, out of captivity. He did not know yet how to dance ... their convulsive, rag-time sort of dancing. (102-3)

Here too, is a man who delights in "loose" women, but afterwards feels soiled by them, someone who sleeps with a pregnant Minette while simultaneously withdrawing in horror and indignation over an African statue depicting a female in the throes of childbirth: "He hated the sheer barbaric thing ... Gerald resented it. He wanted to keep certain illusions, certain ideas like clothing" (87).

Conventional individuals like Gerald do not simply decide to adopt such an attitude midway through their lives: such conventionality is the external enactment of a set psychological personality structure, formed in childhood and carried into adulthood. For Gerald, conformity is all or nothing. Wilhelm Reich and Adorno both analyze the nature of the authoritarian family structure. Adorno notes the emphasis on discipline within an authoritarian family. While affection and even love may exist within this structure, it is generally "conditional" on the "approved behavior" of the child. Interrelationships within the family structure are based on well-defined role playing, with specific responses indicating acceptance and fulfillment of the various roles, which are in turn based on a hierarchical structure of dominance and submission: "Faithful execution of prescribed roles and the exchange of duties and obligations is ... given preference over the exchange of free-flowing affection" (Adorno 482). Adorno further indicates that for an authoritarian:

> The functioning of his superego is mainly directed toward punishment, condemnation, and exclusion of others, thus mirroring the type of discipline to which he himself was apparently exposed.... The difficulty which children growing up in such an environment ... seem to have in developing close personal relationships may be interpreted as one of the outcomes of the repression of hostile tendencies, which are not integrated or sublimated, but which become diffuse and free-flowing. (483)

This more or less describes Gerald's early experience at school, presumably an upper class boys' school, in which both discipline and competition are encouraged.[3] Well-integrated children will form friendships that overcome or compensate for the harshness of such an environment. But it seems that Gerald was unable to establish such relationships; Birkin deftly pinpoints this flaw when he asks: "You never really mixed, did you?" (230). Gerald's experience of school was a painful one, yet he is unable to view it with the appropriate bitterness, substituting instead a belief in the necessity of a life of discipline:

> School had been torture to him. Yet he had not questioned whether one should go through this torture. He seemed to believe in education through subjection and torment.

---

[3] Mary Eagleton and David Pierce define such an atmosphere as representative of "the repressive and philistine middle class, quintessentially expressed in the English public school, whose key characteristics are dogged industry, respectability and narrow snobbery" (94).

> "I hated it at the time, but I can see it was necessary," he said. "It brought me into line a bit – and you can't live unless you do come into line somewhere." (230)

Gerald's belief in rigid discipline is common to the authoritarian personality. The inability to be at all introspective or to analyze problems within the self leads the authoritarian to project much of his fear and hostility onto the outside world. This tendency, combined with the inability to connect to other human beings in a direct, meaningful way, forces him to cope with situations and experiences in an indirect, often tortuous manner. The rigidity of the personality structure precludes the development of close bonds to others; the authoritarian's "comparatively impoverished potentialities for interpersonal relationships may exhibit themselves either in a relatively restricted, conventional, but dependable approach to people … or in a ruthless, manipulative approach" (Adorno 475). Gerald certainly utilizes both methods in his dealing with others: hosting his sister's wedding dinner would be indicative of the rigidly conventional code in a leadership role, while his treatment of the colliers and of Minette illustrates his more extreme manipulative kind of approach.

The two characters in the novel who become most involved with Gerald are Birkin and Gudrun; both describe the underlying rigidity and inflexibility of Gerald's character. Birkin attempts to pledge love and life-long loyalty to Gerald, but is rebuked; Gerald evasively pretends not to understand what such a pledge means. And these two male characters are subtle contrasts to each other throughout: Birkin's spontaneity and anti-conformity are capsulized in his belief that, "Instead of chopping yourself down to fit the world, chop the world down to fit yourself" (230).

Birkin's spontaneous, "off-the-cuff" visit to the Brangwen home to propose marriage (and the incredulity with which Ursula's father receives the proposal) is singularly amazing to Gerald, who would never approach a marriage proposal in so haphazard and impulsive a fashion himself. He is open-mouthed at the unconventional oddity of both Birkin's approach and Ursula's lackadaisical reception.

Lawrence's artistic portrait of Gerald has an uncanny truthfulness and recognizable reality: he exudes an assertive, confident, man-of-the-world air: "…his eyes with their humorous kind twinkle, which was so deceptive," or "… his voice, sudden and mechanical and belonging to the world of man" (203), and "… the decisive, instrumental voice that was full of the sound of the world" (204). The stealth of his stance has already been noted as an indicator of the underlying fear with which Gerald approaches the environment around him, but the same quality may also be seen as indicative of the strong-willed competitiveness of the successful power figure. The projection of power and insularity is further enhanced as Gerald looks "fixedly into the darkness, very keen and alert and single in himself, instrumental" (200). Gudrun, however, recognizes the inconsistent and repressed nature of this image:

> … the Geralds of this world. So manly by day, yet all the while, such a crying of infants in the night. Let them turn into mechanisms, let them. Let them become instruments, pure machines, pure wills, that work like clockwork, in perpetual repetition. Let them be this, let them be taken up entirely in their work, let them be perfect parts of a great machine, having a slumber of constant repetition. (524)

Such a strongly-controlled will, coupled with such underlying hostility, leads to highly rigid, if at times unpredictable, behavioral patterns. The unpredictability results from the inability of the individual's superego to maintain tight control over all free-flowing emotion:

> In order to keep unacceptable tendencies and impulses out of consciousness, rigid defenses have to be maintained. Any loosening of the absoluteness of these defenses involves the danger of a breaking through of the repressed tendencies.... Greater rigidity of defenses is necessary to cope with such increased threat. In this vicious circle, impulses are not prevented from breaking out in uncontrolled ways. (Adorno 480)

Gerald *appears* to function rationally and powerfully in his world, the outside, everyday world of enterprise and profit. When emotional demands are made, however, in the few interpersonal relationships he has tried to establish, a lack of reciprocal sensibility is evident. Birkin loves Gerald, but is clearly aware of this dearth of spontaneous feeling in his friend:

> It was the insistence on the limitation which so bored Birkin in Gerald. Gerald could never fly away from himself, in real indifferent gaiety. He had a clog, a sort of monomania. (233)

Gudrun's contempt for Gerald is finally due to the predictability of his responses:

> Gerald is so limited, there is a dead end to him. He would grind on at the old mills for ever. And really, there is no corn between the millstones any more. They grind on and on, when there is nothing to grind – saying the same things, believing the same things, acting the same things. Oh, my God, it would wear out the patience of a stone. (521)

Gerald enacts the correct forms, but there is no "corn" left to grind; the forms so rigidly enacted are without essence or life. Instead the surrounding universe is perceived by Gerald as hostile and threatening; his sharpened wits, rather than his ability to introspect and understand self, or even to approach the unknown with concrete rational logic, are kept in readiness: "...he always kept such a keen attentiveness, concentrated and unyielding in himself.... He had been so insistent, so guarded, all his life" (199).

Lawrence draws a portrait of a character who on the surface is powerful, authoritative, highly energetic and resourceful, the world's "successful man," yet this character is subtly but repeatedly shown to embody an inner psychological vacuum. Like the authoritarian personality, Gerald is characterized by a "compulsive drive for power, strength, success, and self- determination" (Adorno 474). Gudrun's early impression of Gerald's remarkable force and energy are ominously qualified as she begins to realize how undirected and eruptive Gerald's force is:

> "Certainly, he's got go," said Gudrun. "In fact I've never seen a man that showed signs of so much. The unfortunate thing is, where does his *go* go to, what becomes of it?" (53)

Gerald originally directs his force, his "go," to refining the efficiency and production of his father's business, but the energy he expends so successfully on the business might as easily have been applied elsewhere; ambitiousness on the scale of Gerald's efforts would usually indicate a love of wealth or position. Such, however, is not his goal:

> It was not for the sake of money that Gerald took over the mines. He did not care about money, fun-

> damentally. He was neither ostentatious nor luxurious, neither did he care about social position, not finally. (251)

What Gerald wants to achieve is a compensation for the inner emptiness in soul or psyche with which he is burdened. By achieving power in the outside environment, he attains a sense of self-worth, of meaningfulness and accomplishment, where only confusion and emptiness reigned internally and hostility and fear was represented externally.

The authoritarian personality shows a similar emphasis on the aspects of power and success, while he views the nature of the actual work as arbitrary or indifferent. "Work," wherever it may be directed, is the means to success and power: "To succeed in the struggle of competition by roughness and by 'out-smarting' the competitor seems ... an important component of the ego-ideal" (Adorno 420). The individual case study of "Mack" is a portrait of what the authors of *The Authoritarian Personality* call a typical high scorer, or a typical authoritarian. Mack, like Gerald, is practical and efficient:

> His emphasis upon practicality, efficiency, and diligence as ends in themselves, his tendency to ignore social and psychological determinants of human characteristics and human events, his failure to take into account possible inner sources of his opinions, the discrepancies between his expressed values and what appears to be his real motives, were outstanding features of his interview. (Adorno 273)

Gerald's ideal of efficiency finally translates into power; he considers the resulting ugliness and inhumanity as: "The sufferings and feelings of individuals did not matter in the least. They were mere conditions, like the weather.

What mattered was the pure instrumentality of the individual. As a man as of a knife: does it cut well? Nothing else mattered" (251). The ugliness produced by mining, the stripping away of the natural forests and vegetation, was "hideous and sordid, during his childhood they had been sores in his consciousness" (250), but now they cause him no qualms or ambivalence; in fact, "he saw them with pride" (250), because they have come to symbolize the power of the system he has so successfully inaugurated.

Lawrence adeptly shows Gerald's growing sense of purpose in refining the management of the mines, and his enormous satisfaction with the new mode of efficiency and centralized power. Suddenly, however, in the midst of his apparent success, he falls into fits of despondent inertia, of confused restlessness. Birkin observes Gerald's desperate attempts to fill this void within himself and quite correctly criticizes Gerald's superficial grasp of psychological reality. There is a dearth of self-knowledge, of self-sufficiency in Gerald's character that contrasts sharply with the magnetically powerful figure he cuts in the outside world. He is almost childlike in his confusion over Birkin's critical attitude toward him:

> "I can't see what you will leave me at all, to be interested in," came Gerald's voice from the lower room. "Neither the Minettes, nor the mines, nor anything else.... What am I to do at all, then?" came Gerald's voice. (108)

Gerald is incapable of realizing that his approach to "the Minettes" and "the mines" is so coldly and objectively instrumental that they afford no genuine emotional engagement of his self. His narrow approach to living affords him little satisfaction, a temporary reward at best, because so little of his self is involved with such human activities as interacting with other human beings and finding fulfillment in creative labour. Lawrence frequently describes the automaton quality of Gerald's existence; the *mechanical* wilfulness evident in his forceful personality simultaneously attests to his lack of introspection and self-examination. Like a human animal in whom some central sensibility has failed to develop, Gerald swings between obsessive, mechanized wilful activity and a crippling psychological atmosphere of boredom, emptiness, and meaninglessness. The latter extreme is always underlying and latent in Gerald:

> "Sometimes I think it is a curse to be alive," said Gerald, with sudden impotent anger.
>
> "Well," said Birkin, "Why not! Let it be a curse sometimes to be alive – at other times it is anything but a curse. You've got plenty of zest in it really."
>
> "Less than you'd think," said Gerald, revealing a strange poverty in his look at the other man. (234)

While Birkin exhibits a spontaneous tolerance of the vicissitudes and joys of human existence, evincing an immediate sense of his involvement in all experience, Gerald's reaction is mechanical, tired and characterized by a sense of emptiness, of the poverty of his involvement with living experience. Lawrence describes him elsewhere in the novel as "completely and emptily restless, utterly hollow" or "suspended motionless, in an agony of inertia" (300). A momentary self-realization of this lack of emotional involvement in life does occur to Gerald himself at one point, although he views it as a familial trait, rather than a psychological quality within himself. He says of the Crich family that "We're all of us curiously bad at living. We can do things – but we can't get on with life at all" (229).

Gerald's relationship with Gudrun is based on a contest

of wills, but it is finally Gudrun who dominates; while Gerald is master of force, Gudrun has the artist's advantage of standing apart from the life around her, of remaining independent of other individuals. Although Gerald and Gudrun's relationship is not successful in fulfilling either partner, it is all Gerald has to cling to and identify with at the brink of a psychological void. Once more, he is quite satisfied to substitute "form" for essence – the outwardly conventional "couple" in appearance and behavior for the fulfilment of a truly intimate interpersonal relationship. Gudrun's gradual rejection of Gerald compounds his already desperate, pathetic sense of loneliness. When they look at the alpine scene from their hotel window, Gudrun is transported into a separate world of her own. Gerald finds being left alone behind insufferable:

> Already he felt he was alone....
>
> "Do you like it?" he asked in a voice that sounded detached and foreign. At least she might acknowledge he was with her. (451)

Gudrun's increasing involvement with Loerke forces Gerald to realize that the relationship is ending between Gudrun and himself. He knows that for his own survival he should leave her, yet to be utterly alone again is what he fears most: "But then, to have no claim upon her, he must stand by himself, in sheer nothingness.... Why did she leave him standing there, with the ice-wind blowing through his heart, like death ...?" (501-2).

Lawrence is compassionate and sympathetic toward Gerald at this point in the novel: loneliness such as this is a horrible phenomenon to contemplate. It is possibly the "do or die" situation in which Gerald finds himself that prompts compassion for him: he is destroyed if he stays with Gudrun, and he is annihilated into loneliness and finally death without her. Yet one must assess Gerald's personality acutely before allowing compassion for him to blind one to his flaw; the most overwhelmingly negative trait that flaws Gerald's personality is his inability to genuinely love or care for another human being.

How is it possible to be unable to love? References to Gerald's infancy and childhood carry hints of both neglect and abuse, despite the privileged luxury of the upper class setting. The passage in the novel in which Gudrun talks with Mrs. Kirk, the Crich children's old nurse, has a curious resemblance to certain parts of *Wuthering Heights*, perhaps especially where Nelly Dean and Mrs. Earnshawe are forced to accept the orphan, Heathcliff, into the family. Nelly refers to the small waif as an "it" and treats him cruelly: it is hard to believe that the motherly soul presented as narrator throughout Brontë's book can be as coldly cruel to a child as this. She remembers that:

> [h]e seemed a sullen, patient child; hardened, perhaps, to ill-treatment: he would stand Hindley's blows without winking or shedding a tear, and my pinches moved him only to draw in a breath and open his eyes, as if he had hurt himself by accident and nobody was to blame. (36)

It is worth noting that Nelly's malicious abuse (as well as Mrs. Earnshawe's) has been attributed to the possibility that Heathcliff is, in fact, the bastard offspring of Mr. Earnshawe. But whatever actually does occasion such malice, it is paralleled here in the portrait of Mrs. Kirk, as she tells Gudrun:

> "I nursed three of her children. And proper little terrors they were, little fiends – that Gerald was a demon if ever there was one, a proper demon, ay,

> at six months old!" A curious, malicious, sly tone came into the woman's voice. "...Kick, and scream, and struggle like a demon. Many's the time I've pinched his little bottom for him, when he was a child in arms." (231)

When she describes whippings the children received from the elder Mr. Crich (saintly liberal-humanist Mr. Crich?), she adds: "And didn't we used to be thankful when one of them caught it" (231). Catherine Earnshawe was similarly viewed as an innately "bad" child, the "changeling" superstition of Victorian times. But what such a view, and treatment, finally results in is child abuse: rebellious children rebel for a reason; they are not simply born that way. According to Mrs. Kirk, Mr. Crich's whippings were in contrast to Mrs. Crich's attitude of ultra-leniency: "she wouldn't have them corrected – no-o, wouldn't hear of it" (239). But Mrs. Kirk also states that Gerald's mother was otherwise totally disinterested and neglectful of the children: "she wasn't going to be bothered with them herself. No *she* took no trouble for them" (239). Mrs. Crich's behavior towards her son appears cold and yet intuitively knowledgeable of his nature. Early on she declares that Gerald is "... the most wanting of them all" (28). As the elder Mr. Crich lies dying, she warns her son to keep himself in control; her words once again refer to some psychological flaw or imbalance in Gerald:

> "You mind *yourself* – ... You mind yourself, or you'll find yourself in Queer Street, that's what will happen to you. You're hysterical, always were." (369)

Knowledgeable of her son's nature she may well be, but her tone toward him is neither warm, affectionate nor loving. The element of human warmth appears to be curiously lacking in both Gerald's parents. Regarding the relationship between Gerald and his father:

> [t]here had always been opposition between the two of them. Gerald had feared and despised his father, and to a great extent had avoided him all through boyhood and young manhood. And the father had felt very often a real dislike of his eldest son, which, never wanting to give way to, he had refused to acknowledge. He had ignored Gerald as much as possible, leaving him alone. (245)

Perhaps the most damning comment Gerald's mother makes about Gerald is when she notes to Birkin that "[h]e has never had a friend" (28). The inability to connect, or the lack of desire for contact, for human companionship is a paralyzing psychological flaw in a child. In Gerald's case, the cold, uninvolved familial atmosphere in which he grew up could be responsible for his inability to form close bonds with others. He certainly carries this trait into adulthood; the closest union he forms appears to be with Birkin, but even this relationship remains on the brink of real liking: one can never feel certain that they become "friends" reciprocally. The relationship could not develop because Gerald was unable to truly care for another human being. He tells Birkin that he does not understand it just yet, but Gerald will *never* fully understand the nature of a committed relationship:

> There ... seems to be relatively little enjoyment of sensuality or of passive pleasures, such as affection, companionship, or art and music on the part of the typical high scorer [authoritarian]. Instead of these internalized pleasures, there is an inclination toward mobility and activity, and a striving for material benefits. (Adorno 475)

Gerald's involvement with women before meeting

Gudrun was largely mercenary: his life centers around the running of the mines; he occasionally finds relief from the intensity of work and pressure with an easily available female, paralleling here the behavior of the Prussian Officer in Lawrence's story of that name. Gerald's ties to women have been temporary and emotionally uninvolved. The brief heterosexual interactions he indulges in appear to signify no more to him than a good meal or the imbibing of some other sensual pleasure. Such an encounter offers a temporary release and a tranquillizing effect against the daily tensions he has accumulated. Thus, Gerald's attitude toward women is established at the novel's outset; it is their instrumentality in his life that matters; their function is to provide him with a sense of release: "After a debauch with some desperate woman, he went on quite easy and forgetful" (262). This "lack of … real object relationship,… the relative isolation of sexual impulses from the rest of the personality, the paucity of affection, and the somewhat exploitive, manipulative approach in the choice of a mate" (Adorno 404) are all aspects of those possessing an authoritarian nature. Adorno becomes even more precise about the role of the female as viewed by the authoritarian male:

> The role of the woman … is one of passivity and subservience. She … offers … man the much needed opportunity of asserting his superiority. There is, however, *ample evidence that the high-scoring [authoritarian] man wants to be on the receiving end in his relation to women*; from them he wants material benefits and support more than he wants pure affection, for it would be difficult for him to accept the latter.… On the whole, sex is for him in the service of status, be this masculine status as achieved by pointing toward conquests, or be it social status as achieved

by marrying the "right kind" of woman. (477) [italics mine]

Gerald's treatment of women resembles very closely the attitudes Adorno describes here. The character of Minette is introduced early in the novel at least partly to illustrate what Gerald's attitudes are. Minette is not a fully developed, complex character; she is a typical "loose" female who catches Gerald's imagination and makes "his blue eyes … [light] up with a flame of curious desire" (66). After his involvement with Minette is over, Gerald projects the feeling of uncleanliness he experiences, possibly due to a hidden sense of guilt, onto the woman:

> "… she strikes me as being rather foul.… I liked her all right, for a couple of days," said Gerald. "But a week of her would have turned me over. There's a certain smell, about the skin of those women, that in the end is sickening beyond words – even if you like it at first." (106)

The odour that Gerald feels he recognizes is not a concrete physical odour; it is psychologically a part of Gerald's own psyche, the surfeited sensual appetite that now brusquely turns to other interests, momentarily ashamed of its self-indulgence.

Gerald's anxiety over his negligence about paying Minette further illustrates his tendency to project self-disgust onto someone outside of himself: Minette needs to be placed into a perspective that he can handle; once paid, she assumes the role of an instrument in life. Ostensibly he pretends to follow a conventional social rule when he claims that "'[it] seems to me the right thing to do, you know, with the Minettes, is to pay them'" (106). But it is really a means of externalizing his own self-disgust or salving his guilt.

The authoritarian personality thus views the female as a useful, functional instrument at his disposal. Love as a concept is tossed back and forth between the Brangwen sisters and Birkin and Gerald, and all four seem to acknowledge what is meant by the term, although two of these characters, Gerald and Gudrun, have never really experienced love. The most apt definition of what *is* meant by love could be the realization or awareness of another as a human being in all his uniqueness and individuality outside of oneself; this would be equivalent to achieving Birkin's "star-polarity" of two individuals together and yet separate. Loving as a process, then, rescues and absolves one from the prison of the self – something that neither Gudrun nor Gerald are able to do. Without loving, these two characters live existences totally centred toward their individual self-gratification; other human beings, all of the surrounding environment, are mere instruments for their use. Gerald acknowledges to Birkin that he has never felt love for a woman, and by this admission, simultaneously implies that he understands what is meant by love:

> "I've never felt it myself – not what I should call love. I've gone after women – and been keen enough over some of them. But I've never felt *love.* I don't believe I've ever felt as much *love* for a woman as I have for you – not *love.*" (310)

Gerald's later involvement with Gudrun parallels Birkin's relationship with Ursula, at least superficially. Birkin reaches the decision to marry, however, while Gerald's attitude toward Gudrun has not encompassed any such far-reaching commitment. But he is influenced by Birkin's decision to marry; it seems the right thing, the correct behavior at this stage of their lives. Yet the underlying difference in each man's attitude to marriage is clear. Birkin is hit suddenly with an illumination of the other individual's uniqueness:

> She was really so marvellously gentle and sensitive. Why did he ever forget it? He must go to her at once. He must ask her to marry him ... so to make a definite pledge, enter into a definite communion. (287)

Gerald consequently also entertains the idea of marriage, but only because it is the customary behavior of an English gentleman in his early thirties:

> But he would not make any pure relationship with any other soul. He could not. Marriage was not the committing of himself into a relationship with Gudrun. It was a committing of himself in acceptance of the established world, he would accept the established order, in which he did not livingly believe, and then he would retreat to the underworld for his life. (398)

By the novel's end, it is clear that neither Gerald nor Gudrun cares deeply enough to marry. In a devastating passage, Gudrun coldly, cruelly exposes Gerald's incapacity to feel love for another human being; the reader's compassion must in some measure go to Gerald here, though Gudrun is equally bereft. Nevertheless, she proceeds to strip away his assumed conventional guise as her "lover," until he is exposed as humanly and psychically barren:

> It was the statement "It was never love," which sounded in his ears with madness.
>
> "Why must you repeat it so often, that there is no love?" he said in a voice strangled with rage. (497)

At another time, Gudrun analyzes his "Don Juan" stance towards women. She concludes that he wants women to "be in love with him," while "[h]is very ignoring of the women is part of the game" (521).

The "ignoring" of the other human being is not really as egotistical and self-willed as Gudrun asserts. In the very depths of his being, Gerald is unable to recognize the validity of other human existence outside of his own: as soon as he catches a hint of this void within himself he reacts to hide it, but it is the abyss of his life and soul. Yet compassion for Gerald at this point is mitigated by the memory of how he earlier exhibited the same unfeeling qualities towards others that he now experiences at Gudrun's hands; it is at these times that the unflinching cruelty of such a personality is most clearly in evidence. Consider Minette's appeal to Gerald:

> He felt an awful, enjoyable power over her, an instinctive cherishing very near to cruelty. For she was a victim. He felt that she was in his power.... He would be able to destroy her utterly in the strength of his discharge. (71)

It is the qualities of vulnerability evinced in her slight frame, childish round eyes and baby-ish lisp, including "her fingers [which] were fine and seemed very sensitive in the tips" (76), that attract Gerald; Lawrence variously describes her as "naive," "slave-like," "delicate" and "soft, unfolded like some fair ice-flower." Such an attraction on Gerald's part parallels the authoritarian personality's urge to bully: "The very sight of a powerless person may lead to the urge to attack, dominate, or humiliate them" (Adorno 414).

Gerald's reaction to Minette's vulnerability is repeated in his handling of the mare in the "Coal Dust" chapter, where he coldly and cruelly subjects her to the noise of the passing train, despite her terror. It is only when a spirit is broken, when a woman like Minette is fully humiliated and subdued, or the horse brought to blind and complete obedience, that Gerald is finally satisfied. As long as they retain their own freedom, their instrumentality for him is limited. Gerald's attitude here may be contrasted to Lawrence's own admonitions on child-rearing in *Fantasia of the Unconscious*, where he comments:

> don't neglect [the child], don't have a negative attitude to it. Play with it, tease it and roll it over as a dog her puppy, ... and when it makes you genuinely angry, spank it soundly. But always remember that it is a single little soul by itself; and that the responsibility for the wise, warm relationship is yours, the adult's. (115)

Where Minette and the mare were individual entities, Gerald's colliers are many, and it is in these manifold lives that he sows the greatest destruction:

> Terrible and inhuman were his examinations into every detail; there was no privacy he would spare, no old sentiment but he would turn it over. The old grey managers, the old grey clerks, the doddering old pensioners, he looked at them, and removed them as so much lumber.... He had no emotional qualms. (257-58)

Such a lack of caring is not indicative of a truly unemotional character: there is a feeling self in Gerald, although it remains largely primitive and repressed. Because of the concentrated wilfulness he expends upon controlling such primal energy, his exterior personality appears cold and objective. He himself notes that "I feel that if I don't watch myself, I shall find myself doing something silly" (302). "Silly" is a poor word to describe the kinds of perverse destructiveness into which repressed emotion erupts, but the point is that Gerald senses the high tension within himself. Adorno notes that in the authoritarian personality, "… to keep the balance under these conditions, a simple, firm, often stereotypical, cognitive structure is required. There is no place for ambivalence or ambiguities" (480). At another point in the novel Gerald finds "that sooner or later you'll *have* to let go. Do you understand what I mean? And so something's got to be done, or there's a universal collapse – as far as you yourself are concerned" (367).

Gerald's external manner rarely indicates how close to a breaking point he really is. Lawrence at times refers to the tension within him, but it is doubtful that much of this would be externally observable. Yet Lawrence provides us with many acute physical reactions that are typical to Gerald, while, in contrast, he describes Birkin reacting intellectually or emotionally to situations. Gerald possesses a great deal of pent-up violence and instantaneous inner aggression that continually threatens to take over his being:

> Gudrun saw Gerald's body tighten, saw a sharp blindness come into his eyes.… The man's body, strung to its efforts, vibrated strongly. Then a sudden sharp, white-edged wrath came up in him. (270-71)

This state of sharpened hostility is brought about by a rabbit frightened into a frenzy. Gerald is aware of his underlying violence, and recognizes it as a similar form of primal/primitive passion to that which the rabbit exhibits:

> "God be praised we aren't rabbits," … [Gudrun] said in a high, shrill voice. The smile intensified a little on his face. "Not rabbits?" he said, looking at her fixedly. (273)

Not primal/primitive? Gerald understands clearly the force at work, although he is not clear about how to control it, except with enormous will power. Gudrun and Gerald share this underlying violence and primal sensation and both are strongly attracted to it: "...they both felt the subterranean desire to let go, to fling away everything and lapse into a sheer unrestraint, brutal and licentious" (323).

The attraction to the extremity of human sensation and the underlying aggression in Gerald are different sides of the same primal bed of emotion. Gudrun slaps Gerald across the face at the beginning of their relationship, and the action both excites him to a challenge and evokes a fierce anger in him:

> He recoiled from the slight blow on his face. He became deadly pale, and a dangerous flame darkened his eyes. For some seconds he could not speak, his lungs were so suffused with blood, his heart stretched almost to bursting with a great gush of ungovernable emotion. It was as if some reservoir of black emotion had burst within him and swamped him. (190-91)

He later describes the incident to Birkin, and comments: "Furious? I should think I was. I'd have murdered her for two pins" (227). It is inevitable that such a beginning to a relationship – a degree of anger reaching such extreme proportions – leads to the desire to annihilate the other, and so it does in Gerald. A world of repressed anger erupts in him at the end, and his one resulting desire is to murder Gudrun. Lawrence's description of this desire is consistently couched in the use of semi-erotic terminology, so the act of murder represents a consummation, an ecstatic sensual gratification:

> A blinding flash went over his brain, his body jolted.

> His heart had burst into flame. His consciousness was gone into his wrists, into his hands. He was one blind, incontinent desire to kill her. His wrists were bursting, there would be no satisfaction till his hands had closed on her. (520)

If the import of the repressed violence within Gerald's psyche is still not sufficiently evident, Lawrence further makes it clear that Gerald is set apart, like Cain, right from early childhood by his propensity towards aggressive attack. Gerald murdered his brother by "accidentally" shooting him; Lawrence uses Ursula, the most pacifist of his major characters, to make clear the fact that such a murder cannot be said to be truly accidental. She knows that she "… couldn't pull the trigger of the emptiest gun in the world, not if someone were looking down the barrel" (54). Lawrence presents Gerald as tainted from the beginning, to differentiate Gerald's violent nature from that of a more balanced personality. Human aggression exists in everyone; Gerald, however, represents the extreme type of repressed wilfulness which neither knows nor understands itself. Such aggressiveness, because so strongly held in check for so long, and so little understood because of a complete lack of introspection and ability to self-examine, is all the more violent and destructive when it finally breaks through the controlled surface behavior.

Gerald's peak moments of violent emotion and behavior in the novel contrast sharply with Birkin's more introspective, flexible nature. One thinks of Ursula screaming in rage at Birkin and the cyclist approaching, much to Birkin's embarrassment – conscious of the fools they must look to him. Or Birkin running *from* Hermione's physical attack – running away from perverted contact such as this, rather than fighting back as surely Gerald would have been impelled to do. Birkin has glimpses of himself as others must see him, of the ridiculousness of some of life's situations. Gerald's lack of self-exploration limits him to stern external control and strictly conventional responses; very little autonomy really exists in such a personality.

Gerald's lack of introspection leads to a final quality that distinguishes the authoritarian type. Adorno calls this quality "suggestibility," but in general it is the tendency, within such a personality, to approach situations from an emotional, vague, unquestioning perspective, rather than in a rational manner. This personality tends to view himself and others in black and white terms, so that the world is seen as predictable and consequently easier to handle, and even manipulate.[4] This is the "easy way out" and, through fear, avoids closer examination of stereotyped premises. Consequently authoritarians are not only suggestible, but also gullible; because of their dependence on church and social institutions, and on conventional authority and values, they fall "easy prey to ... unsound and destructive political propaganda" (Adorno 467). Non-authoritarians, on the other hand, act independently, and often in opposition, to established forms of authority.

Lawrence deftly pinpoints the lack of rational, objective thinking in Gerald's premises. This is only slightly ironic,

---

[4] It is interesting to find Reich supporting this analysis by showing how Hitler was well aware of the emotional responses of people: "Without really divining it, Hitler was building upon this lower middle-class attitude when he wrote: 'The people in their overwhelming majority are so feminine by nature and attitude that sober reasoning determines their thoughts and actions far less than emotion and feeling.... And this sentiment is not complicated, but very simple and all of a piece. It does not have multiple shadings; it has a positive and a negative; love or hate, right or wrong, truth or lie, never half this way and half that way, never partially, or that kind of thing'" (Reich 53).

because while both Lawrence and Birkin overtly *deplore* the rational approach, they both use it extensively and very sensitively, as many critics have noted. Birkin points out Gerald's lack of reasoning when he states: "Without bothering to *think* to a conclusion, Gerald jumped to a conclusion" (255). The conclusion that Gerald reaches is that "[w]hat mattered was the great social productive machine," and Birkin is admonishing him because this is an unquestioned premise. Surely it would be an "establishment" priority; nevertheless, to really "think" in Lawrence's terms, is to question and weigh the true value of assumptions, and Gerald fails to do this. Further in the novel, Lawrence reiterates Gerald's incapacity for sound thinking:

> He did not define to himself at all clearly what harmony was. The word pleased him, he felt he had come to his own conclusions. And he proceeded to put his philosophy into practice by forcing order into the established world, translating the mystic word harmony into the practical word organization. (256)[5]

Fritz Stern, in his analysis of Langbehn, Lagarde and Moeller van den Bruck, reaches the conclusion that the three men personify an authoritarian personality-type that coincides with Adorno's findings. The relevance of Stern's study is that the thought patterns of the three writers, like Gerald's thought patterns in *Women in Love*, were emotional rather than rational and objective:

> These men ... have to be understood as a cultural

[5] Gerald's mistake here is accurately summarized by George Orwell in his classic essay "Politics and the English Language." Orwell here makes the point that such thinkers "usually have a general emotional meaning – they dislike one thing and want to express solidarity with another – but they are not interested in the detail of what they are saying" (Orwell 2267).

> type, a type moreover that made its simultaneous appearance in all Western countries.... [They were] intellectuals whose work was emotional and seldom reflective.... Having abjured reason, they could not expect a natural human evolution toward the community they sought. The goal, consequently, was a mystique, and the means, though left obscure, suggested violence and coercion. (328-29)

This type of personality inculcates emotional rather than rational thought. Such types are recognized "not by their intellectual force but because they were suffused with passion..." (Stern 331).

Gerald personifies this type uncannily: it is astonishing to see such a clear fictional portrait of an authoritarian personality emerging as early as 1915. Virtually all the qualities that Adorno has found to be indicative of the authoritarian personality are also convincingly evident in Gerald. Gerald envisions "harmony" as an ideal, but the harmony that he translates into his own personal life and into the practical "organization" within the mines is what Orwell cites as a fallacy, "an idealistic abstraction." Stern could be summing up Gerald's existence in his following description of Lagarde, Langbehn and van den Bruck: "their political imagination grasped lifeless abstractions and the petty details of their proposed reforms. The middle range of practicality was foreign to them" (327). Like these three men, Gerald has the vision of harmony, and the psychological force to implement this vision successfully within the mines. But again, like the three writers Stern describes, Gerald's vision of harmony is a "lifeless abstraction" to be imposed upon a mass of people without consideration for their individual rights, concerns, or identities (which constitutes the "middle range of practicality"). It is in this imposition of an ideology without concern for the people that the danger of fascism becomes so evident.

Lawrence, then, clearly recognized, or created, Gerald as an authoritarian personality. The lack of real development in Gerald's character, combined with the important position he holds as a fictional character in the novel, indicate that Lawrence not only recognized authoritarianism, but condemned it, realizing it for the powerful, negative force it later turned out to be. Adorno's summary of an extreme authoritarian, the "manipulative type," describes Gerald perfectly:

> ... the break between internal and external world, in this case, does not result in anything like ordinary "introversion," but rather the contrary: a kind of compulsive overrealism which treats everything and everyone as an object to be handled, manipulated, seized by the subject's own theoretical and practical patterns. The technical aspects of life, and things *qua* "tools" are fraught with libido. The emphasis is on "doing things," with far-reaching indifference towards the content of what is going to be done. The pattern is found in numerous business people and also, in increasing numbers, among members of the *rising managerial and technological class who maintain, in the process of production, a function between the old type of ownership and the workers' aristocracy*. Many fascist-political anti-Semites in Germany showed this syndrome: Himmler may be symbolic of them. Their sober intelligence together with their almost *complete absence of any affections* makes them perhaps the *most merciless* of all. Their organizational way of looking at things predisposes them to totalitarian solutions. Their goal is the construction of gas chambers rather

> than the pogrom. They do not even have to hate the Jews; they "cope" with them by administrative measures without any personal contacts with the victims. Anti-Semitism is reified, an export article: it must "function." (Adorno 767-68) [italics mine]

The emphasis in the preceding passage on the "sober intelligence" of the manipulative authoritarian, or his "organizational way of looking at things" does not really contradict the point made earlier regarding the authoritarian's lack of rational, objective thinking. The authoritarian, the Gerald of the world, tends to be rational and objective with regard to detailed work, the revamping of the mines or the construction of gas chambers. On large, moral issues, however, he lacks the reason to make objective, individual decisions.

In analyzing Gerald Crich as an authoritarian type, we have all the hindsight of modern psychology and political-historical analysis to aid us; this only makes it all the more remarkable that Lawrence was able to draw this portrait in such precise, exact detail seventy years earlier. Certainly the authoritarian personality existed in England at that time, but an acute and prescient prophetic insight is required to recognize the type as being as ominously destructive as Lawrence views it.

While Gerald Crich is the authoritarian personality-type in *Women in Love*, it is nevertheless Rupert Birkin who prophesies human annihilation. Anticipating racial extinction, and possibly human annihilation, can be viewed as a totalitarian motif. It is remarkably perceptive of Lawrence, once again, to bring into the novel issues that twenty years later were so catastrophic to the entire world. Such issues are, of course, "in the air," being talked about, argued, long before they become set theories.

Nevertheless, Lawrence read his milieu sensitively, finely enough to incorporate them in *Women in Love*. It is important to determine precisely what Lawrence's own attitude was toward the possible annihilation of mankind.

An important point to make here is that Birkin displays none of the authoritarian characteristics that define Gerald Crich. Birkin makes decisions based on reason rather than on emotion, as pointed out earlier. He does not view his environment as hostile, is open rather than guarded in his relationships with others, and above all, is able to love fully. So why is this individual, who according to Adorno's study would be a "liberal" personality, making pronouncements of doom for the human species?

Lawrence emphasizes the theme of rebirth throughout his writing: the old order is giving way, and we must discover a new form of consciousness to rejuvenate mankind. This emphasis on the decline and possible extinction of mankind is not unique to Lawrence alone; he does, however, often use aggressive verbs such as "break," "wipe out," and "destroy," to describe the passing of the older traditions. In *Women in Love*, Lawrence conceptualizes the universal failure of man to develop creatively, a conception of failure that is certainly due, in part, to the world war he experienced during the writing of this novel. It is also, however, a conception that extends beyond any specific historic event. His characters at times almost appear to endorse the elimination of the people of the decadent order. Birkin tells Mrs. Crich, "people don't really matter ... it would be much better if they were just wiped out" (27). Gudrun's bitterness over the small town colliers' ridicule leads her to "have liked them all annihilated, cleared away" (14). Birkin thinks to himself:

> Well, if mankind is destroyed, if our race is destroyed like Sodom, and there is this beautiful evening with the luminous land and trees, I am satisfied. That which informs it all is there, and can never be lost. After all, what is mankind but just one expression of the incomprehensible. And if mankind passes away, it will only mean that this particular expression is completed and done.... Let mankind pass away – time it did. (65)

In the essays, "The Crown," and "The Reality of Peace," Lawrence discusses the need for a balance of pure opposites which he variously calls life/death, lamb/tiger, or unicorn/lion, and does not advocate a total death or annihilation: the process of dissolution is one side of the coin; the other is the process of creation. In these essays, death is a psychological force, an experiential form of being, necessary to undergo in order to emerge *into* life. Still, even here, Lawrence rhapsodizes on death's hygenic power: "smash, beautiful destructive death, smash the complete will of the hosts of man, the will of the self absorbed bug" ("Reality" 686). But he is talking of the annihilation of the *will*, the superimposed ego of western civilization.

One may accept such a psychological dissolution more readily than the more extreme form presented in *Women in Love*, where Birkin not only prophesies human extinction, but almost seems to welcome it as the inevitable culmination of the totalitarian order:

> "God cannot do without man." It was a saying of some great French religious teacher. But surely this is false. God can do without man. God could do without the ichthyosauri and the mastodon. These monsters failed creatively to develop, so God, the creative mystery, dispensed with them. In the same

> way the mystery could dispense with man, should he too fail creatively to change and develop. The eternal creative mystery could dispose of man, and replace him with a finer created being. Just as the horse has taken the place of the mastodon ... the timeless creative mystery would bring forth some other being, finer, more wonderful, some new, more lovely race, to carry on the embodiment of creation.... Races came and went, species passed away, but ever new species arose, more lovely, or equally lovely, always surpassing wonder.... It could create utterly new races. (538)

Given Birkin's non-authoritarian nature, his commentary here is a prophetic statement, rather than a statement of individual preference. Both an objective view of the prophetic tradition, as found in Norman Cohn's *The Pursuit of the Millenium*, and the more subjective understanding of the prophetic voice, as described by Abraham J. Heschel in his two volume work, *The Prophets*, help to shed some insight on Lawrence's use of the annihilation themes expressed by Birkin in the novel.

Alongside the bitterness and finality of the vision of human annihilation which Birkin preaches, lies another impulse coincidental to it. Birkin's approaching marriage to Ursula has awakened new hope and belief in the possibility of human contact as a salvation. Birkin reiterates the need "'to be free, in a free place, with a few other people.... It's a perfected relation between you and me, and others – the perfect relation – so that we are free together'" (356). This defines his longing for a utopian existence apart from the masses, which he feels are doomed. Cohn emphasizes in his study that "revolutionary millenarianism flourishes only in certain specific social situations" (281), which occur "[a]gain and again ... against millenarianism flourishes only in certain specific social situations" (281), which occur "[a]gain and again ... against a background of disaster" (282). Cohn defines the term "revolutionary millenarianism" as an unqualified and absolute attempt at self-transformation:

> It is characteristic of this kind of movement that its aims and premises are boundless. A social struggle is seen not as a struggle for specific, limited objectives, but as an event of unique importance, different in kind from all other struggles known to history, a cataclysm from which the world is to emerge totally transformed and redeemed. This is the essence of the recurrent phenomenon – or, if one will, the persistent tradition – that we have called "revolutionary millenarianism." (281)

Lawrence's dream of a utopian coterie of caring people, "Rananim," appeared in his writings during this period, and coincides with Birkin's desire for "further fellowship ... being really happy with some few other people – a little freedom with people" (409). Similarly, Lawrence's Rananim comes to mean the only chance for human salvation in a sinking world. Cohn characterizes millenarianism as collective, terrestrial, imminent, a "total transformation of life," and "miraculous, in the sense that it is to be accomplished by, or with the help of supernatural agencies" (13).

Lawrence's Rananim satisfied most of these conditions, except that Lawrence, like Wilhelm Reich, would have pointed to the inner, sensual life as the "miracle" for rebirth. Birkin emphasizes that the group of people he wishes to bring together would share a "perfect freedom," always a utopian cornerstone, although finally a contradiction in terms. Cohn's delineation of the prophet of millenarianism throughout history also, in many ways, parallels the thought of Birkin and of

Lawrence himself. Cohn finds "the *propheta* as a social type" to have been an intellectual rather than a manual worker, and to have been acquainted with the tradition of apocalypse. Further, such a *propheta* possessed personal magnetism through which he established himself as having "a special role in bringing history to its appointed consummation":

> What the *propheta* offered his followers was … the prospect of carrying out a divinely ordained mission of stupendous, unique importance. This phantasy … [offered] an escape from their isolated … condition … so it quickly came to enthrall them in their turn. (285)

Parallels exist between Lawrence and Joachim of Fiore, whose three stages of history recur in Lawrence's ages of the Father (or Law), Son (or Spiritual) and finally, a third new age of freedom on earth:[6] "If the first age had been one of fear and servitude and the second age one of faith and filial submission, the third age would be one of love, joy and freedom" (Cohn 109).[7]

Lawrence presents a theory of history, in his "Study of Thomas Hardy," that essentially encompasses two different

---

[6] Frank Kermode, in *The Sense of an Ending*, also finds Joachite influence in Lawrence's theory: "Joachite speculation … was condemned in 1260, and subsequently thrived best in unorthodox contexts.… Some aspects of this brand of apocalypse survive in D.H. Lawrence. More dangerously, the ideology of National Socialism incorporated Joachite elements; 'the Third Reich' is itself a Joachite expression."

[7] Cohn states: "it is unmistakably the Joachite phantasy of the three ages that appeared in the … theories of historical evolution expounded by the German Idealist philosophers … in Auguste Comte's idea of history as an ascent from the theological through the metaphysical up to the scientific phase; and again in the marxian dialectic of the three stages of primitive communism, class society and a final communism which is to be the realm of freedom.… [T]he phrase 'the Third Reich,' first coined in 1923 by the publicist Moeller van den Bruck and later adopted as a name for that 'new order' which was supposed to last a thousand years, would have had but little emotional significance if the phantasy of a third and most glorious dispensation had not … entered into the common stock of European social mythology." (109)

stages, the age of the Father, who represents Law and Nature, and the age of the Son, who symbolizes Love and Knowledge. The third, coming age, will "reconcile the two" (510). Birkin's theory of star-equilibrium would be the beginning of such a reconciliation, as would Lawrence's real-life dream of Rananim. Lawrence's utopian ideal of this third age embodies "the final reconciliation, where both are equal, two in one, complete" (516):

> Law is the law of the body, the personal body that has arrogated to itself divinity. Love is the recognition of the limitations of the personal self, the recognition that there are other selves that have different, even hostile, laws. (Goodheart 94)

Goodheart agrees that the third age will, in Lawrence's view, effect a reconciliation rather than a complete fulfilment: "[s]ince fulfilment cannot occur completely either in the spirit or in the flesh, both the spirit and the body must be regarded as 'Complementary Absolutes'" (94).

Cohn also traces the growth of the millenial movement of the brethren of the Free Spirit from medieval times to Cromwell's England. This movement carries motifs that have possibly evolved into themes in Lawrencian theory. Emphasis on the pantheistic, erotic nature of self, can be interpreted as similar to Lawrence's stress on the anti-rational, spontaneous centres of life, but also, as Cohn notes, such themes might equally have been absorbed by the Romantic tradition: "one can already recognize in this medieval heresy that blend of millenarianism and primitivism which has become one of the commoner forms of modern romanticism" (181). Cohn realizes that such an incorporation of Free Spirit trends culminates in modern times with the '60s "Hippie" movement:

> For the ideal of a total emancipation of the individual from society, even from external reality itself – the

> ideal, if one will, of self-divinization – which some nowadays try to realize with the help of psychedelic drugs, can be recognized already in that deviant form of medieval mysticism. (286)

In any case, the simple desire to find "a little freedom with people" on Birkin's part, can be viewed as the utopian impulse to detach a select group from the destructive masses of men and together find salvation in the ideal of collective, earthly "freedom."

That Birkin can prophesy the annihilation of man and simultaneously hope for the utopian fellowship of a deserving few, is part of the same tradition. The finality with which he dispenses with mankind as a failed species may be more easily understood by a look at the prophetic tradition as outlined by Heschel in his study of *The Prophets*. Heschel helps us to understand the nature of prophetic anger, and underlines the fact that anger is not always evil; rather, at times it is the only response strong enough to combat evil. He refers to the biblical quotation: "For everything there is a season, and a time for every matter under heaven … a time to keep silence, and a time to speak, a time to love, and a time to hate" (Ecclesiastes 3:1, 7, 8).

Birkin's premonition of disaster is so strong as to make him appear lacking in compassion; this has encouraged critics to cry "élitist." But the kind of anger exhibited here may be viewed as "a scream in the night" (Heschel, I, 16). Heschel says of Jeremiah that "[h]e terrified in order to save" (I, 16). Anger such as Birkin's over the destruction of the human spirit under industrialization parallels Lawrence's rage against humanity in the throes of the first world war. Such anger may be seen *as* the only possible response to dehumanizing evil and inhumane suffering. Heschel attempts to differentiate this kind of prophetic anger from a hatred that is ego-centred and productive of evil:

> Nothing is so sweet to the heart of man as love. However, for love to function, the suppression of sympathy may be necessary. A surgeon would be a failure if he indulged his natural sympathy at the sight of a bleeding wound. He must suppress his emotion to save a life, he must hurt in order to heal. Genuine love, genuine mercy, must not be taken to be indulgence of mere feeling, excess of sensibility, which is commonly called sentimentality.... The end of sentimentality is the enfeeblement of truth and justice.... There are moments in history when anger alone can conquer evil. It is after mildness and kindness have failed that anger is proclaimed. (II 76-77)

Women in Love is a rich, complex novel that expresses not only Lawrence's disillusionment with humanity during the period of the first world war, but also his hope for a future, utopian, environment. In his definitive characterization of Gerald, Lawrence has indicated how thoroughly he understands the authoritarian personality and the destructive nature of an authoritarian society. Through Birkin's perceptions, he evokes both the despair and the hope he feels for the future of humanity. The novel therefore encompasses strong utopian, as well as authoritarian and totalitarian aspects.

Chapter 5

The Search for a Leader in *Aaron's Rod*

Aaron's Rod (1922) and *Kangaroo* (1923), while not finished works of art like *Sons and Lovers* or *Women in Love*, are nevertheless significant novels in terms of the development of Lawrence's thought. A contempt for mass conformity and a fear of mob rule are presented in Richard Somers' view of democratic Australians, who, he feels, are "like a full river of life, made up of drops of water all alike" (*Kangaroo* 16). Somers soon decides that such an equalizing political force renders men "irresponsible," that there must be "the categorical difference between the responsible and the irresponsible classes. You cannot fail to admit the necessity for *rule*" (17).

Lawrence seems to echo Ortega y Gasset's theory that "culture" could be drowned by the rise of the the masses, when he speaks of the necessity of salvaging and protecting the "élite" from the mass. In both *Aaron's Rod* and *Kangaroo*, however, Lawrence's final preoccupation is not with an improved liberalism such as Ortega favored, but with finding a strong, enlightened, all-encompassing leader, though, in this quest too, he appears ambivalent at times. In the following exchange between Lilly and Levison in *Aaron's Rod*, Levison expresses the obvious drawback to a rule by the strong leader or by an élite:

> [Lilly] "You've got to have a sort of slavery again. People are not *men*: they are insects and instruments, and their destiny is slavery.... But ultimately they will be brought to agree – after sufficient extermination – and then they will elect for themselves a proper and healthy and energetic slavery."
> [Levison] "I should like to know what you mean by slavery. Because to me it is impossible that slavery should be healthy and energetic. You seem to have some other idea in your mind, and you merely use the word slavery out of exasperation –"
> [Lilly] "I mean it none the less. I mean a real committal of the life-issue of inferior beings to the responsibility of a superior being."
> [Levison] "It'll take a bit of knowing, who are the inferior and which is the superior," said Levison sarcastically.
> [Lilly] "Not a bit. It is written between a man's brows, which he is."
> [Levison] "I'm afraid we shall all read differently."
> [Lilly] "So long as we're liars!" (327)

Lilly's stance throughout this exchange could certainly be termed totalitarian. But it *is* only one side of an exchange, and as usual with Lawrence, one finds a reversal on the next page, of the too-extreme pose indicated above:

> "Why, I'll tell you the real truth." said Lilly. "I think every man is a sacred and holy individual, *never* to be violated. I think there is only one thing I hate to the verge of madness and that is *bullying*. To see any living creature *bullied* in *any* way, almost makes a murderer of me. That is true. Do you believe it?" (328)

At the same time that Lawrence wrote *Aaron's Rod*, he was also writing *Movements in European History*, in which he restates his antipathy to "mere Force" and "bullying" during Mussolini's takeover in Italy. It is interesting to note that he equates bullying with both the fascists and the socialists:

> A certain group of men in Italy intend to *force* their will on all other men. Earlier, socialists tried to force *their* will. In Russia, the Communists succeed in forcing their will.
>
> The forcing of one man's will over another man is bullying. We know what it is, we experienced it during the War. It is a bad, degrading thing. It degrades both the bully and those who are bullied. (317)

Aaron's Rod is not, however, intentionally about fascism, as is so commonly thought, even though the strong, charismatic leadership qualities Lawrence appears to be looking for are often identified with fascism. And in *Kangaroo* Lawrence's overriding concern is the fear of violent mob rule; the alternative he looks for is a beneficent sort of leadership within a socialistic environment. While Lawrence was repelled by the actual political systems – both fascist and socialist – that were implemented in Italy and Russia, he nevertheless felt that "there must be *power*.... Because if there is not power there will be force.... A man invested with power has a profound responsibility. Force is irresponsible, unless controlled by the higher power" (*Movements* 317). In fact, realistically implemented forms of socialist, fascist and even many democratic governments have *never* been without strong leadership. George Watson, a notably conservative critic, goes so far as to assert there has been no great difference between the implementing of socialist and fascist regimes, that Hitler's National Socialism *was* socialism all along

(93-94), and that the distinction made by Noltë, for example between socialism and National Socialism, is really non-existent.

In *Aaron's Rod*, Lawrence deals extensively with socialism as a viable program for the future, but the ideal of socialism as he envisions it would have a strong leader who uses power with "profound responsibility." This Lawrencian concept is certainly distinct and different from the actual enactment of Communism in Russia. The novel illustrates his extreme ambivalence toward the doctrine. Near the end of the book, Aaron has two dreams that defy reason when he awakes, and so he pushes them aside. The first dream depicts a threat against Aaron's "self" from the lower classes. Tin-miners are about to devour a man who – in dreamlike credibility – is really "a man's skin stuffed tight with prepared meat, as the skin of a Bologna sausage" (332). Symbolically, this cannibalism may be viewed as the self being engulfed and destroyed by the rise of the lower classes (tin-miners). Ultimately, the dream symbolizes the victory of a socialist revolution. Aaron's second dream is equally fearful, although it seems to contradict the first one. Here Aaron's "self" travels by boat amongst unknown people without sensing the danger of stakes in the water. But in this dream the people *try* to help, to communicate with him and warn him, although in vain – the self seems locked in perpetual isolation. Further, it is interesting to note that in each dream the self is divided into two selves: the "invisible, *conscious* self, what we have called his second self, hovered as it were before the prow of the boat, seeing and knowing, but unseen. His other self, the palpable Aaron, sat as a passenger in the boat" (333). The second, invisible self might be viewed as a function much like Freud's Superego – attempting to caution and guide the ego. In the first dream the second self fears the masses of men, while in the second dream, it senses the community of all people and tries in vain to join with and understand them. The symbolism of these dreams focuses the basic ambivalence of the novel towards socialism as a proposed program.

If the theme of *Aaron's Rod* is ambivalence towards socialism, then one of the strongest and most repeated motifs running through the novel is that of patronage and class distinctions, especially where patronage is obviously condescending, for this type of unjust and discriminatory treatment results in the longing for equality. Lawrence's frequent use of the patronizing motif in *Aaron's Rod* arises out of his own working-class background and the condescension and patronage he himself experienced. But the persistent use of the class motif also functions to accentuate Lawrence's ambivalence. On the one hand, having been a member of the lower classes, he would welcome an overthrow of the dominant culture that he relied on for – at times – condescending patronage. There *is* a just anger within the lower classes towards the rich. On the other hand, Lawrence also fears such an overthrow and the ascendence of socialism. He is educated and individualistic enough to fear the violence and the mediocrity that an overthrow of the monied classes by the lower classes could bring in its wake. One of Lawrence's concerns at this time seemed to be the need to implement some kind of a socialistic program without the mediocrity that often accompanies equality.

Aaron's Rod begins with Aaron Sisson deserting his wife and children; critics have attempted to exonerate Aaron's desertion on grounds of either a moral escape from female domination or as being simply the next stage in a picaresque novel. Julian Moynahan, however, harshly condemns the irresponsibility of Aaron's behavior:

> On a hard view, and in the end the novel forces this view on all except the most incompetent of Lawrence's readers, Aaron, like the majority of the twenty thousand American men who take the option of a poor man's divorce each year, deserts his family simply out of boredom. He becomes a plaything of the idle rich, peddling his musical talent and sexual magnetism to neurotic upper-class wives and mistresses in exchange for more or less luxurious lodgings, fees, and sensations. He exploits the appetite of a jaded social set for queer birds and can be expected to go on drifting until his luck runs out with the onset of age and the decline of his novelty value. It is hard to imagine what he might be doing in twenty-five years' time. Perhaps if Italy continued to suit his indolent disposition he might be found improvising a musical background to speeches delivered over the Italian radio by Ezra Pound. (Yudhishtar 79)

Such a view is countered, however, by both F.R. Leavis and Eugene Goodheart, who insist that Aaron's behavior cannot be judged so superficially; Aaron's behavior is a microcosmic view of a larger macrocosm: something is dreadfully wrong within a society that produces deadlocks and desertions in marriage. Goodheart asserts that Lawrence's portrayal of Aaron is "his *radical* vision of the generic failure of the erotic connection between man and woman" (138). He agrees with Leavis that the reader should ask himself: "What is wrong here? *What laws of life* have been ignored that there should be *this* situation, this dreadful deadlock between a man and a woman?" (Goodheart 139). Lilly pinpoints the dilemma when he says: "There's something wrong with marriage altogether, I think. *Egoisme a deux* –" (122). Goodheart even suggests that *Aaron's Rod* exemplifies a contemporary dilemma which de Rougemont has analyzed in *Love in the Western World*. Perhaps, after all, romantic passion is not the force the western world has believed it to be: it is unable to sustain a life-long relationship because it "could no longer obtain the ingredients necessary to sustaining its myth..." (Goodheart 139). Lawrence is sincere in his portrayal of the bitter conflict of wills between Aaron and Lottie, so much so that one believes a deadlock is indeed present. Lawrence is furthermore fair-minded in his presentation of guilt and blame. Aaron acknowledges to himself that "both he and Lottie had been brought up to consider themselves the first in whatsoever company they found themselves" (192). Goodheart's point regarding the failure of the social system is well taken; Aaron is in fact "deserting" more than a wife and children, for the nature of the heterosexual relationship itself often ends in frustration and deadlock in our society.

Certainly Lawrence is not the first – nor the last – artist to write of husbands leaving wives. Two later novels that may be readily compared to *Aaron's Rod* are George Orwell's *Coming Up For Air* (1950) and John Updike's *Rabbit Run* (1970). Although we might wish that Orwell's George Bowling had had the courage to leave his wife permanently, while we condemn Updike's immature Rabbit Angstrom for his desertion, there are some strikingly parallel characteristics in all three attempts at desertion. Goodheart's analysis of modern marriage as a "generic failure" plays a role in all three cases. Marriage in western society is an established conventional institution that assumes, ostensibly, fulfilment for both partners. Yet it is curious to find that first Aaron, then George Bowling and finally Rabbit Angstrom, react to their actual physical residence – not their wives directly – as places of captivity and stultification. Aaron returns to his home in order to get his flute; as he quietly waits in the garden for a chance to enter the house, the picture of his home amongst all the others like it in a row repels him; they seem like "dark little blocks ... the whole private life of the street was threaded in lights. There was a sense of indecent exposure, from so many backs.... So many houses cheek by jowl, so many squirming lives, so many back yards, back doors giving on to the night. It was revolting" (51-52). George Bowling experiences remarkably similar feelings of suffocation in his view of his home:

> Down below, out of the little square of bathroom window, I could see the ten yards by five of grass, with a privet hedge round it and a bare patch in the middle, that we call the back garden. There's the same back garden, same privets and same grass, behind every house in Ellesmere Road. Only difference – where there are no kids there's no bare patch in the middle. (Orwell 1)

The same sense of unending sameness and a dreary claustrophobic atmosphere is found in Rabbit Angstom's perception of his "home":

> The frame homes climb the hill like a single staircase. The space of six feet or so that each double house rises above its neighbour contains two wan windows, wide-spaced like the eyes of an animal, and is covered with composition shingling varying in color from bruise to dung. The fronts are scabby clapboards, once white. There are a dozen three-story homes,

> and each has two doors. The seventh door is his. The wood steps up to it are worn; under them is a cubbyhole of dirt where a lost toy molders.... Rabbit pauses in the sunless vestibule, panting. Overhead, a daytime bulb burns dustily. Three tin mailboxes hang empty above a brown radiator. His downstairs neighbor's door across the hall is shut like a hurt face. There is that smell which is always the same but that he can never identify; sometimes it seems cabbage cooking, sometimes the furnace's rusty breath, sometimes something soft decaying in the walls. He climbs the stairs to his home, the top floor. (Updike 6-7)

Each man is overly conscious of his neighbours; their close vicinity, their similarly monotonous lot in life emphasize the emptiness and predictability of his own. While Goodheart's thesis about the inadequacy of erotic heterosexual bonds is valid, so too is the negative perception of the physical "hearth and home" indicative of each man's disillusionment. And this inability to perceive one's home with the required conventional idealism, leading as it does to desertion or the contemplation of desertion, embodies overtones of social and political protest. For a protest is being made here against the deadly conformity and automatism of contemporary life. Richard Somers and his wife confront this same element of conformity immediately after their arrival in Australia:

> ... there went the long street, like a child's drawing, the little square bungalows dot-dot-dot, close together and yet apart, like modern democracy, each one fenced around with a square rail fence. (*Kangaroo* 5)

Through Aaron's life, then, Lawrence identifies conformist mediocrity as a product of modern democracy. Lawrence's own life mirrors a similar memory. During a visit back to Eastwood he recalls: "...The Breach, which is the house I first remember – an end house of hideous rows of miners' dwellings..." (*Phoenix II* 261). Lawrence continues throughout his writing to protest against the ugly mediocrity of lower-middle-class life styles. Democracy, he feels, is the underlying cause of this mediocrity because the mass of people are not able to discern with taste and judgment, and on this point Ortega y Gasset agrees with him. Ortega, however, would like the existing form of democracy to be improved so that élitist tastes could dominate. Lawrence does not really feel that democracy can be rescued; instead, he looks at times to a form of socialism for his ideal, although, like Ortega y Gasset, he feels that the ideal socialism will be impossible to enact: "Myself, personally, I believe that a good form of socialism, if it could be brought about, would be the best form of government" (*Movements* 315).

Peter Scheckner argues that Lawrence's earliest predilection was for socialism and that he "never entirely abandoned this point of view" (12). Certainly, critics and patrons during his lifetime expected him, as a son of the working class, to be a voice for that class. Whether or not his voice does this at all times – and Lawrence was never one to lend himself to any absolute type of identification – his works are certainly permeated throughout with a consciousness of class structures.

At this point it becomes significant to mention some of the discriminatory attitutes of others toward Lawrence himself, and to enumerate some instances of the patronage that he experienced, since many of these instances are paralleled in *Aaron's Rod*. And Lawrence's own experiences help to set the focus of the social issues that form part of the framework of the novel, as well as reflecting some of the humiliations that Aaron experiences.

T.S. Eliot, himself Harvard educated, snobbishly referred to Lawrence – a product of the British Education Act – as "an untrained mind" (59). Although Aldous Huxley later became a close supporter of Lawrence, his earlier portrait of Lawrence as Kingham in *Two or Three Graces* is one in which this character is hyper-snobbish about his lower-class origins, and takes offence at imagined slights: "I know that my father was a plumber, ... and that I was educated at the expense of the State and by scholarships for the encouragement of clever paupers..." (13). This is a rather malicious caricature to come from the mouth of an offspring of the well-born Huxley family. Norman Douglas perhaps catches the most patronizing upper-class tone of all in his descriptions of Lawrence in his autobiography *Looking Back*. He comments on Lawrence's "menial" humility: "Lawrence was never happier than when scrubbing floors or peeling potatoes: how frequently in his books are the men portrayed as doing the work of women or servants" (283-87).[1] Douglas also finds Lawrence "one of the most envy-bitten mortals I have known. He was envious of other men's social rank, of their reputations and natural gifts, their health, and chiefly of their bank-balances... he was a 'provincial' without 'poise' or 'reserve'" (283-87).[2]

Ford Madox Ford's memories of Lawrence are permeated with the distanced, amused tone of upper middle

[1] This directly contradicts Barbara Hardy, who criticizes Lawrence's portrayal of Clara Dawes as a working woman in *Sons and Lovers*: "Here are traces of that peculiar Victorian perversion, the gentleman's excitement at the woman's hard drudgery" (120).

[2] John Galsworthy also refers to Lawrence as "that provincial genius" (Page, I, 147).

class contempt. Having never been as poor as Lawrence's class, Ford finds Lawrence:

> ... expressing a satisfaction that seemed to me to be incomprehensible over the fact that his mother's house – which seemed to me to be like any other miner's cottage – had something – a double passage or an alcove on the stairs, I could not quite understand what, that none of the other miners' cottages had. But it ceased to seem incomprehensible when I understood that that satisfaction was not merely because that special appendage raised him above the other miners' sons; it was that it was, as it were, a proper homage that destiny paid to his suffering, exiled patrician mother, infinite satisfaction as marking her off from the other miners' wives. (57)

This is a fairly patronizing commentary, since Ford is essentially ridiculing the poor – whether mother or son – for their naive pleasure in the little they have achieved, and the status they have attained within their own class. Ford further heightens the contrast between his own status and Lawrence's by describing his own quarters in proud detail:

> I launched out into a defence of my room. I pointed out the beauty of its long, low, harmonious proportions; the agreeable light that fell from windows at both ends with trees beyond one half of them; the pleasant nature of the Chippendale chairs and bureaus that had been in my family for several generations; the portrait of myself as a child by my grandfather, and his long drawings for stained glass. (55)

Lawrence is considered one of the greatest novelists of the twentieth century because of the sensitivity and acute perception he brings to his examination of human needs and interrelationships. He would certainly have been aware – resoundingly so – of being patronized. Because of the well-entrenched class consciousness in England during his lifetime, he could expect such patronizing from even those who were well disposed toward him. David Garnett's first impression of Lawrence appears honest and affectionate, yet is again insidious in pegging even his physical appearance so definitively as a "mongrel" or lower-class product:

> His hair was of a colour, and grew in a particular way, which I have never seen except in English working men. It was bright mud-colour, with a streak of red in it, a thick mat, parted on one side. Somehow, it was incredibly plebian, mongrel and underbred.... He looked like a mongrel terrier among a crowd of Pomeranians and Alsatians, English to the bone. He was the type of the plumber's mate who goes back to fetch the tools. He was the weedy runt you find in every gang of workmen: the one who keeps the other men laughing all the time; who makes trouble with the boss and is saucy to the foreman; who gets the sack; who is "victimized," the cause of a strike; the man for whom trade unions exist; who lives on the dole; who hangs round the pubs; who bets on football and is always cheeky, cocky, and in trouble. He was the type who provokes the most violent class-hatred in this country: the impotent hatred of the upper classes for the lower. (91)

A sensitive writer like Lawrence could not possibly remain ignorant of the impression he was making. Lawrence certainly felt the patronizing, even from people like David Garnett who honestly liked him. Anthony Burgess, many years after Lawrence's death, recognizes this element clearly, since he also experienced it in his own life. He finds that:

> Virginia Woolf praised *Sons and Lovers* but, with the rest of Bloomsbury, was to reject Lawrence as she rejected Joyce: that phrase she used of *Ulysses* might also have been applied to any of Lawrence's works: "the book of a self-taught working man ... of a queasy, undergraduate scratching his pimples." It is unworthy language, and variants of it are still to be heard in reference to both writers. (209)

Virginia Woolf assumes that products of the Bloomsbury group possess a greater depth and sensitivity than Lawrence could either produce or understand, due to his working-class origins. This is clearly expressed in her comment, the first one made, on *Lady Chatterley's Lover* in her novel *Orlando*:

> And then she will write him a little note ... and make an assignation for Sunday dusk and Sunday dusk will come; and the gamekeeper will whistle under the window – all of which is, of course, the very stuff of life and the only possible subject for fiction. (190)

This ridiculing tone towards gamekeepers as fit subjects for fiction is directed at the class from which gamekeepers come: the implication is that they are not suitable lovers for upper-class ladies and that they are neither complex nor interesting enough as human beings to be fictional heroes.

The patronizing attitudes that Lawrence experienced in the artistic milieu of the '20s was constant and at times hurtful; he occupied the anomalous position of living beside and at times with the upper classes, while constantly being reminded that he did not really belong there. His expatriate existence can be explained partly by the discomfort and lack of definition he and his aristocratic

German wife experienced in English society, which meant being sometimes accepted and sometimes not. Terry Eagleton has argued that Lawrence's working-class origins were what enabled him to perceive the injustices in, and offer a devastating critique of, the national English culture. More middle-class writers were too enmeshed in the dominant culture to criticize it, but Lawrence's "milieu ... was in certain ways ... ambivalently related to the national culture..." (*Exiles* 17). By "national culture," Eagleton means the tradition of modern western democracy, of English liberal humanism. Lawrence's perception and vision is therefore political, and based to a large extent on his own background, though he never waves any particular banner. It is this vision that Eugene Goodheart finds both so radical and so subversive of the dominant culture.

Lawrence's portrayal of Aaron Sisson is a protest against the exploitation of the working class. Aaron's marriage breakup is a statistic rather than an action to be judged on moral grounds. Given enough pressures, such as poverty and unemployment, and enough bleakness in life, such as row housing and mass conformity, marriages break down. Yet Aaron has *life;* his is a questioning mind on a quest for self-understanding, as well as escape. He resembles many of Lawrence's male characters, as Diana Trilling asserts:

> ... he always entrusts his doctrine to men of similar body and inclination, also to men of more or less the same class as his: his leading male characters are regularly thin, wiry, fierce, home-centered men of the working class. (303)

Fiction that is written, then, through the perceptions of someone from the working class will portray the dominant culture ambivalently – at times subversively, at times a part of it, and the political solutions proposed may be equally ambivalent and at times contradictory.

David Schoenbaum has indicated that National Socialism originally had its strongest support from the middle and lower-middle-classes in Germany. These are the people who form the "dominant" strata of society; their values are conventional, and since they represent and make up the "national culture," it follows that they become the strongest proponents for nationalism and at its more extreme end, for fascism (44).[3] Lawrence, however, is far more concerned with equality than with national culture – he despised the smug, dominant culture of his native England – and though he does, during this phase of his life, focus strongly on the leader/follower issue, this is not in and of itself a fascist trait. Socialist movements certainly required and had strong leaders as much as did fascist movements. Lawrence was more concerned with how power could be used responsibly by the leader who held that power. It is also interesting to note that in *Women in Love*, *Aaron's Rod* and *Kangaroo*, the apocalyptic statements are not made by characters who fit the type of an authoritarian personality. Rather, they are made by the protagonists, the people like Birkin, Lilly and Somers, who prove to be sensitive, thoughtful and, above all, rational individuals. The authoritarians, Gerald Crich, Jim Bricknell and Jack Callcott, show through their actions that they fit into an authoritarian mold, a repressed pattern of life which, as Reich and Adorno have pointed out, leads easily into fascism and totalitarianism.

[3] Adorno and Reich emphasize the middle-class support for fascism as well: "fascism is most characteristically a middle-class phenomenon" (Adorno 229). Reich supports this with his comment: "National Socialism was a lower middle-class movement" (41).

George Watson's study, *Politics and Literature in Modern Britain* (1977), asserts that Lawrence's working-class origins are a myth, that in fact he rightly belongs to the middle class, because "Lawrence's early life had in fact been sheltered by an exceptionally protective mother ... [who created a] superior existence ... for the sons who, as she successfully resolved, would never work in a mine" (113). Watson supports his theory of Lawrence's middle-class origins by asserting that Marxist critics "were unimpressed ... Lawrence was a bourgeois artist, in their view" (115). Watson implies that a true artist from the working class would inevitably have been Marxist. A more realistic view might be to suggest that the ambivalence in Lawrence's writings toward class structures is caused partly because he never fully belonged to either the working or middle class. This left him at times outside of the dominant culture, and possibly at such times more in identification with his father's class, while at other moments, his mother's aspirations and his own education would allow him to feel a part of the larger culture. For all Lawrence's supposed extremism, he managed to balance opposites and contraries in his life much as characters like Lilly do, finding it necessary to "oscillate between north and south" (*AR* 337). Lawrence's erudition and sensitivities were certainly more than comparable to those of the middle class, but that class made it clear to him in subtle and not-so-subtle ways over and over again that having a working-class member as his father disqualified him from complete acceptance into the middle class.

Although *Aaron's Rod* is resoundingly emphatic in recognizing money as western democracy's controlling force, it is also a novel permeated with a consciousness of class distinctions and the patronizing of the lower classes by the upper. John Harrison, in *The Reactionaries*, likewise states that the monied class is the controlling influence:

> The most convincing political argument against democracy as it exists today seems to me to be Pound's, that the men who possess the real power are not the elected delegates, but the men who control the purse strings, the financiers and the controllers of big business. (207)

Aaron Sisson, a member of the working classes, finds the same power in wealthy people such as Lady Franks:

> Aaron wondered at her assurance. She seemed to put him just a tiny bit in his place, even in an opinion on music. Money gave her that right too. Curious – the only authority left. And he deferred to her opinion: that is, to money. (165)

The sense of helplessness under the manipulation of a system based on money overcomes him shortly before he decides to walk out on his family; he realizes balefully that:

> "When you work it out, everything comes to money. Reckon it as you like, it's money on both sides. It's money we live for, and money is what out [sic] lives is worth – nothing else. Money we live for, and money we are when we're dead: that or nothing. An' it's money as is between the masters and us. There's a few educated ones got hold of one end of the rope, and all the lot of us hanging on to th' other end, an' we s'll go on pulling our guts out, time in, time out." (29).

Aaron's desertion is a leave-taking of more than wife and children. He is turning away from the established system, a way of life that has become empty and purposeless. His decision leads him to a migratory existence which, of necessity, needs patronage from the rich to keep it going. The irony is that Aaron leaves a stultifying system only to return to it for sustenance in his newly established freedom. That money equals power is a formula that is accepted throughout the novel, and in 1922 the rich are more often than not the upper class. Although the word "money" is sprinkled liberally throughout the work, and ostensibly appears to be one of the novel's primary concerns, an even more pervasive preoccupation with class distinctions and the condescending patronage that results from such distinctions also becomes evident. If Lawrence had come from the solid middle class stratum that George Watson claims he did, he could not have been as sensitive to condescension as he proves to be through Aaron in this novel. He would scarcely have understood such class discrimination from a personal point of view, yet his portrayal of Aaron amongst upper class people is "felt" as if it had been lived. Aaron's background is solidly working class, and to some extent parallels Lawrence's own:

> His father had been a shaft-sinker, earning good money, but had been killed by a fall down the shaft when Aaron was only four years old. The widow had opened a shop: Aaron was her only child. She had done well in her shop. She had wanted Aaron to be a school teacher. He had served three years' apprenticeship, then suddenly thrown it up and gone to the pit.... He had a curious quality of an intelligent, almost sophisticated mind, which had repudiated education. On purpose he kept the Midland accent in his speech. He understood perfectly what a personification was – and an allegory. But he preferred to be illiterate. (82)

Later in the novel, Lawrence establishes that Lilly as well is from the working classes; the rapport between Aaron and Lilly is explained by the fact that "[t]hey came from the same district, from the same class" (129). Aaron's first meeting with Jim, Josephine and their group draws a curious contrast between the portrayal of Aaron and the reaction of the group to him. They see "a man in a bowler hat, with a black overcoat buttoned to his throat, a pale, dazed, blinking face. The hat was tilted at a slightly jaunty angle over the left eye..." (44-45). While their hysterical laughter appears to be prompted by the incongruity of Aaron's dress and demeanor, it nevertheless constitutes the ridicule of the lower by the upper class. Robert's manner from the beginning of the meeting is peremptory and condescending; it is very evident that Robert is addressing what he considers to be an inferior. Aaron's dress style and hat are pretentious for a working man. His lack of taste, combined with the blankness of his expression, makes him a comical figure and cause for laughter. The bowler hat that Aaron affectedly wears is again cause for derision later in the novel. The group of friends look for Aaron at the opera in London:

> At last Aaron was found – wearing a bowler hat. Julia groaned in spirit. Josephine's brows knitted. Not that anybody cared, really. But as one must frown at something, why not at the bowler hat. (72)

This irony of Aaron's not being quite up to their class standards is heightened by Lawrence's simultaneous presentation of Jim as an ostensible supporter of the working classes:

> Jim was leading Aaron, holding him by the arm and slightly pinching his muscles. It gave him great satisfaction to have between his fingers the arm-

> muscles of a working man, one of the common people, the *fons et origo* of modern life. Jim was talking rather vaguely about Labour and Robert Smillie and Bolshevism. He was all for revolution and the triumph of Labour. (72)

This is prejudicial discrimination, even though Jim is behaving kindly toward Aaron; over-kindliness and solicitation are just as discriminatory as open hostility and condescension. The main thrust of both reactions is to tell the working-class person that he is different in some irretrievable way. Lawrence's personal exposure to lower-class life enables him to perceive this class realistically; he portrays the miners as rough and uncouth in speech, but emphasizes their physical grace. Jim's attempt to idealize the working classes parallels Frieda's early approach to sexuality; it is "all in his head." He focusses on an indiscriminate ideal and attempts to apply it to an individual human being, thus conveniently "labelling" Aaron. This simplistic stereotyping of a complex individual is again a clear form of condescension:

> "She!" said Jim, rising and pointing luridly to Clariss, "she's Love. And *he's* the working people. The hope is in these two –" He jerked a thumb to Aaron Sisson, after having indicated Mrs. Browning.
>
> "Oh, how awfully interesting. It's quite a long time since I've been a personification. I suppose you've never been one before?" said Clariss, turning to Aaron in conclusion.
>
> "No, I don't think I have," he answered. (80)

Jim is the supposed friend of the down-trodden, the man with ideals, yet when he chooses a girlfriend, she is "a nice girl, well-to-do middle class" (98); in other words, conventionally "safe."

Aaron must survive as a musician, so he must necessarily seek employment amongst the upper classes. This is hardly different from Lawrence as a young artist trying to make himself known amongst the London literati. Such a position entails patronage, much of it of the condescending kind. Aaron is picked up as a curiosity, examined, and then tossed aside:

> It pleased the young men musically inclined and Bohemian by profession to patronize the flautist, whom they declared marvellous. Bohemians with well-to-do parents, they could always afford to squander a little spasmodic and self-gratifying patronage. And Aaron did not mind being patronized. He had nothing else to do.
>
> But the party broke up early in September. The flautist was detained a few days at a country house, for the amusement of the guests. Then he left for London. (148)

Aaron is detained "for the amusement of the guests"; when they are no longer amused, he leaves: they have lost interest; he has lost support. This manipulative use of people, of the artist especially, is symbolic of twentieth-century western society. Because money is the dominant power in this culture, artists, like clergymen, remain poor, since they depend to such an extent on patronage. No wonder Aaron develops a "certain fretful dislike of the patronage of indifferent young men, younger than himself" (148).

Another opportunity for employment presents itself to Aaron as "one of an odd quartette" (157) which goes to perform for the aristocratic, aged "Lady Artemis Hooper, when she lay in bed after her famous escapade of falling through the window of her taxi-cab" (157). That Artemis is mythically an archer focuses Lawrence's ridicule more firmly on this high society dilletante, since the shaft she sends through a window is herself. Aaron is drawn out, exposed, becomes a confidante – only to be dropped, once again manipulated as a plaything of the upper classes: "Having got him a few steps too far upon the personal ground, she left him to get off by himself" (158). The parallel to Robert Burns is unmistakable here: the Scottish poet was invited to perform for the gentry, but was later sent to the back kitchen to be fed with the servants.[4] Aaron performs for Lady Artemis Hooper – on his flute, and as a curiosity from the lower classes, and then she loses interest. Like Burns, Aaron finds that:

> Among the musical people he frequented, he found himself on a callow kind of equality with everybody, even the stars and aristocrats, at one moment, and a backstairs outsider the next. (158)

Aaron's stay with the Franks evolves into another case of supercilious patronizing. "Sir William," states Lawrence, tongue-in-cheek, "was a self-made man, and not in the least a snob. He liked the fundamental ordinariness in Aaron, the commonness of the common man" (166). Yet Aaron is cross-examined in the same peremptory manner that Jim and his friends, and later Lady Artemis Hooper, had inflicted on him. Lawrence manages to suggest the atmosphere of an almost "royal audience" in their assumption that they have the right to know the facts of Aaron's personal life, almost as if this is their repayment for food and board. It is inevitable that Sir William criticizes Aaron's, and Lilly's, unconven-

[4] Catherine Carswell details how Lawrence himself was patronized in a similar manner in her write-up of "The Cafe Royal Episode," in *D.H. Lawrence: Interviews and Recollections* (Page, II 193).

tional, "hand-to-mouth" existence, since their apparent lack of fiscal responsibility casts an unspoken aspersion on his greatest accomplishment, his wealth. Sir William especially cannot comprehend why Lilly, as an artist, refuses to write books tailored for public taste, and guarantee himself some commercial success. Instead, as he complains, Lilly writes "never with any eye to the market" (173). Sir William warns Lilly that such a position is irresponsible financially and that "he will have to fall back on charity" (174). Lilly's reply is to assert the artist's role in society as truthteller; he maintains that people like Sir William will finally be dependent on the artist: "the men who work and make provision, will have to fall back on him [the artist]" (174). Sir William clearly does not accept a role as a simple patron of the arts; instead, he demands respect as a captain of industry. He is well aware that he has power in twentieth-century society:

> The old man who had made a fortune: how he expected homage: and how he got it! Homage, like most things, is just a convention and a social trick. Aaron found himself paying homage too to the old man who had made a fortune. (187)

Sir William is not ungenerous with his wealth; obviously both Aaron and Lilly have benefitted from it. But Sir William's generosity is self-righteous; it can only be called charity. It is a self-congratulatory form of giving, and Aaron, with a working-class background, immediately perceives it as such: "It was evident the Franks had dispensed much hospitality: much of it charitable. Aaron felt it" (162). It is worth noting from Adorno's study of the authoritarian personality that "charity often has the function of keeping the underprivileged in their place, kindness acting in effect as a humiliating factor" (307). In this context the dispensing of charity is actually a trait of the authoritarian, one who keeps people in their place, or maintains the *status quo,* through supposed beneficence. Such beneficence is really "a possible manifestation of atonement which, in turn, is known to be a reaction to aggression" (Adorno 307).

Aaron's Rod is a novel that is critical of charity and critical of a society that maintains a structure of superiority/inferiority through the dispensing of charity. Aaron and Lilly depend on patronage throughout the book, and Lawrence needed it throughout his life. Lawrence suggests, however, that a social order that makes charity the means of support for certain sectors of the populace is inherently wrong. Charity in this context is *not* beneficent; rather, it robs the recipient of his pride. Lawrence's view of charity and patronage is, like Adorno's, based on social and economic equality rather than on class patronage:

> From the "liberal" point of view charity is mainly a soothing of conscience and a means of maintaining an unjust state of affairs. The causes of poverty are seen, not in the innate stupidity of the poor, but in the politico-economic organization which, by virtue of its concentration of economic power, creates poverty as a symptom. And the answer is seen, not in ineffectual though often well-intentioned charity, but in the elimination of poverty through modification of its societal causes. (Aorno 155)

Lawrence has been criticized for the fact that he often attacks the very people who have helped him. This may be pettiness on his part, but a society that forces an artist to survive on the kindly patronage of the rich is stating quite clearly what its value system is. Lawrence also might have felt condescension due to his lower-class background. It is more difficult to accept help from wealthy people outside one's own social strata than from those who are socially one's equal, as was the case, for example, between Yeats and Lady Gregory. Douglas Goldring recalls some advice he received from Koteliansky regarding a proposed donation to Lawrence:

> As soon as I displayed my eagerness to be of use to Lawrence, Koteliansky uttered a salutary warning. "If you don't want to lose Lawrence's friendship," he said, "you must be very careful never to let him guess that you are doing anything for him." (Page 149)

Another curious parallel between Aaron's position in the novel and Lawrence's own experience is when Aaron dines at the restaurant in the Hotel Britannia in Milan. The waiter sizes him up immediately as someone who can be patronized, since he does not possess the socially required knowledge of wines:

> "What should I drink?" said Aaron, whose acquaintance with wines was not very large.
>
> "Half-litre of Chianti: that is very good," said the waiter, with the air of a man who knew only too well how to bring up his betters, and train them in the way they should go. (226-27)

Upper and middle class people do not allow themselves to be patronized by waiters; they patronize the waiters instead. They are conscious of being "the right sort of people" and coolly expect the world to recognize them as such. Lawrence himself never exhibited such social assurance, partly due to his background and, no doubt, partly due to his own individualistic non-conformity. A highly similar scene that occurred, involving Lawrence himself, is recorded by Brigit Patmore in 1917:

> We arrived at the restaurant. The waiters were shocked in their vulgar consciousness of Lorenzo's unconventional clothes and they did not disguise it. I refused table after table with the nonchalant impertinence they take for good manners. Lorenzo did not seem to notice their rudeness, but I felt like a watch-dog. (143)

Later Lawrence related the event to Frieda in the following manner:

> "Brigit took me to the Elysian Fields. Think of that. And the waiters didn't approve of Brigit's guest so she turned very haughty and great lady." (Patmore 144)

The incident illustrates that Lawrence was very conscious of being patronized, however much he pretended not to notice. Coming from the lower classes is cause for condescension, but such condescension is further accentuated by a very overt consciousness of poverty.

Aaron's Rod exhibits an emphasis on the necessity of "paying one's way." If the upper classes aid him financially or even deign to keep his company, the patronized individual must repay the debt by entertaining them. Aaron travels to Florence with Angus and Francis:

> Angus enjoyed the novelty, and the moderate patronage he was able to confer. And Aaron felt amused and pleased, and hoped he was paying for his treat. (235)

Aaron is with them, and yet separate and distinct from them. He travels third class while they are first class, that is, until he loses his seat in the third-class section and Angus rescues him. The Italian peasants on the train view Angus and Francis as nobility, while Aaron is conscious that they probably imagine him to be a servant of the two gentlemen. Aaron is invited to have lunch in the first-class carriage, and when the time arrives, is "summoned" by Francis. Aaron attempts to be clear-sighted about these differences in class; they are external differences only and in no way indicate the individual beneath the class label:

> Aaron had lived long enough to know that as far as manhood and intellect went – nay, even education – he was not the inferior of the two young "gentlemen." He knew quite well that, as far as intrinsic nature went, they did not imagine him an inferior: rather the contrary. They had rather an exaggerated respect for him and his life-power, and even his origin. And yet – they had the inestimable cash advantage – and they were going to keep it. They knew it was nothing more than an artificial cash superiority. But they gripped it all the more intensely. They were the upper middle classes. They were Eton and Oxford. And they were going to hang on to their privileges. In these days, it is a fool who abdicates before he's forced to. (236)

This passage is based on a premise – that class distinctions are external and not indicative of the individual's true worth – that the novel does not bear out. Aaron wants to believe that his "intrinsic nature" and "life-power" are valued by his benefactors and even elicit "an exaggerated respect" from them, yet the respect dies quickly. Much like the Franks and Lady Hooper, Angus and Francis pick Aaron up, examine him playfully and then, tiring of him, they drop him:

> By the tone of the young men, he now gathered that they would prefer it "if he took himself off to

> a cheaper place." They wished to be on their own.... It was as if both young men had drawn in their feelers now. They were afraid of finding the new man an incubus. They wanted to wash their hands of him. (246)

Aaron perceives the snub as economical in origin. Perhaps, but this rationale is also kinder to his self-image. Rejection of this nature, however, implies a disrespect for the individual himself; Aaron's "life-power" is not so charismatic that it is indispensable to his patrons. This pattern of condescending patronage and rejection is portrayed throughout the novel by Jim Bricknell and his friends, by the Franks, and by Angus and Francis. Far from exhibiting the conventional attribute of social snobbery and superiority that claims membership with "the right people," which Adorno cites as intrinsic in the authoritarian personality, Aaron is treated consistently as the "wrong sort."

Although Lilly at one point rejects Aaron, as well as Jim Bricknell, Lilly's own position in the same society is also precarious. His poverty (he has thirty-five pounds in the bank, and a sauterne is all there is in the house to offer the Major) and his lower-class origin define his social status as similar to Aaron's.

Another quality exhibited by authoritarians is conventionality and conformity. Once again, Aaron and Lilly are not the conformists; they actively protest *against* unthinking conformity. Lilly's tirade against institutionalized marriage shows a repugnance towards conventional life styles, but does not indicate an inability to love or to interact sensitively with others, which is again an authoritarian attribute. Lilly despises "married people who are two in one – stuck together like two jujube lozenges"

(111). But he confesses that, with regard to his wife Fanny, away in Norway, he "missed her horribly.... I felt my heart was broken" (121).

Aaron's protest *against* the mechanical conformity of the Italians around him is a critique of conventional rigidity:

> the verbal and the ostensible, the accursed mechanical ideal going day by day over the spontaneous life – dynamic, so that Italy becomes as idea – bound and as automatic as England: just a business proposition… the one world triumphing more and more over the many worlds, the big oneness swallowing up the many small diversities in its insatiable gnawing appetite, leaving a dreary sameness throughout the world, that means at last complete sterility. (184-85)

To this increasing trend of mechanical conformity, Aaron contrasts the Italian peasant's "looseness," his spontaneous naturalness. It is in the "third class carriage" that Aaron discovers "no tight string round every man. They were not all trussed with self-conscious string as tight as capons" (239). This perception of Aaron's is characteristic of the liberal rather than the authoritarian, since it involves a degree of self-examination. Aaron recognizes that the conventional self (Reich's character armor is another term for the same concept) which he projects on the surface does not represent the human being underneath:

> This ready-made and very banal idea of himself as a really quite nice individual: eyes blue, nose short, mouth normal, chin normal: this he had insisted was really himself. It was his conscious mask.
>
> Now at last, after years of struggle, he seemed suddenly to have dropped his mask on the floor, and broken it. (197-98)

One primarily conformist character in the novel is Robert, Julia's husband. An army man, he always performs the proper, expected social action. One wonders whether or not a real self that loves and hates can exist underneath the conventional exterior. In this sense Robert strongly resembles Gerald Crich. He reminds the women authoritatively to dress warmly before going outside for the tree-decoration (43). He also peremptorily confronts the intruder, Aaron. His military manner is both authoritative and condescending:

> "Are you a miner?" Robert asked, *de haut en bas*....
> "Won't they be expecting you?" said Robert, trying to keep his temper and his tone of authority....
> "Then, you'd better be getting along, hadn't you?" (48).

Robert remains solicitously polite to his wife, who is openly debating whether or not to leave him for another man. Fanny pinpoints the flaw under his socially conventional exterior when she states that "Robert can't love you *really*, or he'd want to keep you" (65). Defined by his stereotyped personality, Robert, like Gerald, cannot relate to others in a complete way, cannot share that "reciprocity of tenderness" (Zaslove 62) that is so characteristic of Lawrence's work.

The other example of social conventionality portrayed in the novel is revealed in the apparent military bravery of Captain Herbertson. Lilly disclaims this as the action of an unthinking conformist automaton, and indeed, the horrors of war embedded in the captain's soul are related in "the same animated, chatty fashion" (141) that conventional social intercourse demands. Herbertson's rigidly conventional behavior is supplemented with an appropriate social snobbery – he shares the authoritarian's desire to belong to the "right" people: "Awfully queer lot down there. Not my sort, no.... Not the right sort of people" (137). His anecdotes are sprinkled with royal names in an attempt to impress Lilly and show him that he belongs to the "right sort."

Robert's inability to care for others is paralleled in Jim Bricknell, who is again reminiscent of the portrait of Gerald Crich. Bricknell, like Gerald in his university years, spouts high-flown idealism without really believing in it. He idealizes Aaron as a working-class representative and therefore savior of the world. Jim is described as "a sort of socialist, and a red-hot revolutionary of a very ineffectual sort" (91). He advocates Love as an ideal, but has clearly never realized the ideal himself. Shortly after proclaiming that "...Christ's the finest thing time has ever produced.... Don't you think love and sacrifice are the finest things in life?" (96), he violently hits Lilly in the stomach. His muddled idealism is quickly undercut and shown up as hypocritical. Both the lack of clear thinking and the repressed violence he exhibits are attributes of the authoritarian personality. Shortly after hitting Lilly, Jim hypocritically asserts: "'I like the man ... never liked a man more than I like him.' He spoke as if with difficulty" (103). The "difficulty" arises because Jim attempts to deny his underlying hostility and violence in the name of ideal love, but he is unconvincing. The destructive emotion underlying his surface personality becomes apparent on numerous occasions, as when he discusses a socialist revolution under the banner of "freedom and liberty":

> "So should I [love it]," said Jim, in a luscious sort of voice. "What price machine-guns at the end of the Strand! That's a day to live for, what?" (77)

Lilly recognizes the hostility behind Jim's idealism and the enormous self-control and will power Jim must exert to keep it repressed:

> Jim eyed the letters.s
>
> "It's right," he said, "Quite right when you love, your soul breathes in...."
>
> "Breathing out is a bloody revolution," said Lilly.
>
> "You've hit the nail on the head," said Jim solemnly.
>
> "Let's record it then," said Lilly. And with the blue pencil he printed:
>
> WHEN YOU LOVE, YOUR SOUL BREATHES IN.
>
> And on the next Line:
>
> WHEN YOUR SOUL BREATHES OUT, IT'S A BLOODY REVOLUTION.
>
> "I say, Jim," he said. "You must be busting yourself, trying to breathe in." (79)

Lilly appears to sense the huge demand that repressing such violence has on Jim.

At another point in the novel, Jim's behavior supports Freud's view expressed in *Civilization and Its Discontents*, that the cost of repression can become too great to bear; the individual either becomes so repressed as to be void of creative individualistic life, or primal violence breaks destructively through the civilized surface (90-92). Lilly states something very similar when he says that the "anarchist, the criminal, the murderer, he is only the extreme lover acting on the recoil. It flies back, the love-urge, and becomes a horror" (342).

Such is the case when Jim's will relaxes momentarily: "He suddenly sprang to his feet, and brandished his fists. 'I'll pitch the lot of you over the bloody rail,' he said. He glared at them" (68). This is his response to being teased about his frequent liaisons with women. Jim resembles once again Gerald Crich – and portrays another authoritarian attribute – in his use of women as tools or instruments to relieve his feelings of nullity and boredom. He constantly needs someone to love him and makes the process of such loving sound like a game. Loving, he says, gives him "a great inrush of energy" (79) and restores life in him again. Fanny pinpoints the instrumentality of this pseudo-loving, since he is not really aware of the different women he dallies with: "'You should try loving somebody, for a change … You've been loved too often. Why not try and love somebody?'" (68). She implies that Jim is incapable of loving, of recognizing someone else's identity and worth. Like Gerald, Jim Bricknell exhibits the authoritarian personality's inability to love, to show true affection and awareness of another person. Lilly remonstrates with him over his coldly instrumental approach to women:

> "You haven't been here a day but you must telegraph for some female to be ready to hold your hand the moment you go away. And before she lets go, you'll be wiring for another." (101-2)

But Jim needs the distraction that heterosexual entanglements afford him. This is a superficial view of human interaction; it resembles, in fact, the consumption of an object to restore one's sense of well-being, rather than a sensitive appreciation of human interchange. Jim does in fact compare love to wine:

> "Only love brings it back – and wine. If I drink a bottle of burgundy I feel myself restored at the middle – right here! I feel the energy back again. And if I can fall in love – But it's becoming so damned hard." (99)

Even love is failing as a restorative in Jim's life.

Neither Lilly nor Aaron view love or women as instrumentally as Jim does. Aaron has left Lottie, but is not uncaring about her, rather the reverse. When he looks through the window of his house on his second visit back, he sees his wife feeding the baby: "She looked lovely. Wild emotions attacked his heart" (149). Lawrence here does not distort Lottie's attraction for him, as he so easily could have done. In *Rabbit Run,* Updike presents an unattractive portrait of Janice as seen through Rabbit's eyes, as does Orwell of Hilda in *Coming Up For Air*. The intensity of Aaron's feelings toward his wife indicate immediately that he does not see her as an object; instead, he *fears* her precisely because he does find her beautiful:

> She took the apron from her tear-stained face, and looked at him. It was true, in her moments of roused exposure she was a beautiful woman – a beautiful woman. At this moment, with her flushed, tear-stained, wilful distress, she was beautiful. (151)

Aaron loves his wife, but is afraid of being manipulated or coerced into a submissive position. Here the female appears to manipulate, or at least Aaron shares with Lilly the fear of being *used* as an instrument. This is the opposite of Gerald Crich's use of women; Aaron feels that women "look on a man as if he was nothing but an instrument to get and rear children" (123). Lilly is fond of Fanny, misses her when she leaves for Norway and worries about her being anxious about him after the bomb explodes (331). But he too sees the female as manipulative, capriciously using the male of the species for her own satisfaction: "'A woman is like a violinist: any fiddle, any instrument rather than empty hands and no tune going'" (131). Both men, then, feel love and affection for their wives, a very ant-authoritarian trait.

Both women appear to be strong, independent females, a quality that the authoritarian husband would hardly allow and would certainly not be attracted to. Anthony Burgess has pointed out that women always get the "last word" in Lawrence's fiction. He finds that "the effect of all these fictionalized rages is nearly always the confirmation of female sanity and male, or at least Laurentian, dementia" (126). This is certainly true in the episode where Jim Bricknell hits Lilly. It ends wryly: "'You shouldn't try to make a little Jesus of yourself, coming so near to people, wanting to help them,' was Fanny's last word" (105).

Lilly does talk of the necessity of women submitting to men. According to the pattern of the authoritarian personality as established by Adorno, however, this demand for submission, although reprehensible, is not in itself indicative of the authoritarian personality. It is not, in this instance, the result of viewing the female as an object or instrument, placed on earth for men's use. Rather, Lilly's demand for submission appears to be an attempt to provide a bulwark against the threat of female domination and manipulation. The theory of the female as devouring mother is capably analyzed by Judith Ruderman, who shows that the Lawrencian male hero's ambivalence toward women is partly made up of fear (148-50). This fear is evidenced in *Aaron's Rod*, for example, in Lottie's remark to Aaron that "'You're too weak to love a woman and give her what she wants'" (152). The comment has a grasping, mercenary tone to it. The authoritarian male, then, views women as instruments – insignificant and uninteresting other than in their use to him, not as dominant devourers of their masculinity.

Another characteristic of the authoritarian personality is an unwillingness to depend on rational thought as a means of solving problems in life. Rather, the authoritarian tends to a belief in the supernatural as a means of avoiding or side-stepping personal decisions. Implicit in this belief is the assumption that there is much in life that cannot be explained rationally, a superstitiousness which:

> ... indicates a tendency to shift responsibility from within the individual onto outside forces beyond one's control; it indicates that the ego might already have "given up," that is to say, renounced the idea that it might determine the individual's fate by overcoming external forces. (Adorno 236)

Jim Bricknell's sloppy idealism and his underlying desire for violence have already been noted. His espousal of the Christian ideals of love and self-sacrifice are an example of a lack of clear thinking. Lilly and Fanny reproach Jim for his blind adulation of an abstraction; Lilly questions the effect of Christian idealism and, like Freud, he despises the repressive morality that accompanies this idealism. Lilly stands back from the conventionally accepted institution of Christianity and evaluates it rationally; Jim cannot do so.

During Captain Herbertson's monologue on war horror stories, he implies that a soldier experiences a kind of psychic presentiment of his coming death before it happens. Such superstitions seem to abound, especially around crisis situations like war and death; nevertheless, Lilly once again questions the validity of such recourse to the supernatural and reasons instead that "Surely life controls life: and not accident" (141).

The most clear-cut example of an individual's belief in an irrational providence is found, however, in the character of Lady Franks. Sir William chides Aaron and the absent Lilly for their irresponsible belief in "providence" or "fate," rather than in a bank balance. But what Aaron and Lilly mean when they talk of fate is very different from what the captain and Lady Franks mean. Aaron and Lilly believe in a fate that is concretely grounded in their own ability to provide for themselves on a day-to-day basis. Lady Franks views "fate" as a belief in a supernatural sense of special guidance:

> "And I do feel that there is something in one's special fate. I feel that I myself have a special kind of fate, that will always look after me!"
>
> "And you can trust to it?" [Aaron asks]
>
> "Yes, I can. It *always* turns out right...." (203)

She tells Aaron how, after losing a fur coat, she experienced a premonition that she would get it back, which indeed happened. The incongruity of a supernatural power working on her behalf to retrieve a fur coat never occurs to her as ludicrous. It is worth noting also that, despite her belief in a supernatural providence, she, like Sir William, is firmly grounded in an appreciation of "things" – the possessions that money can buy. The incident regarding the fur coat simultaneously illustrates her confusion of spiritual and monetary values:

> "Something prompted me not to give it up: quite distinctly, I felt something telling me that I should get it back.... And that has happened to me almost every time. I almost *always* get my things back. And I always feel that something looks after me, do you know: almost takes care of me."
>
> "But do you mean when you lose things – or in

> life?"
>
> "I mean when I lose things – or when I want to get something I want – I am very nearly always successful. And I always feel there is some sort of higher power which does it for me.... And I always feel, as I say, that there is some higher power which helps me. Do you feel the same?" (203-4)

Aaron's reply contains a wry note of realism as he tells Lady Franks of the batch of music he had lost and which never has been replaced. He wishes ruefully that "some power would trace my music: but apparently we aren't gifted alike with guardian angels" (204).

One may argue that Lady Franks exhibits a certain depth of personality through her love of music. We could make the same argument for Mussolini and for Hitler, as both of these leaders also appreciated certain kinds of music. The authoritarian personality rarely appreciates the value of artistry, lacking the necessary self-examination and relaxation of will to understand how art can express the full range of human experience. This is not to say, however, that he cannot appreciate certain aspects of music, and even use its emotive power, as Hitler did so well, for political purposes. Lady Franks can play music, but is finally too practically involved with the concrete social world around her to be truly liberated or entranced by the piece she is playing:

> There sat the woman playing music. But her inward eye was on the spy-hole of her vital affairs – her domestic arrangements, her control of her household, guests and husband included. The other eye was left for the music, don't you know. (211)

Knowing music and how to play it does not necessarily indicate an artistic nature; it may be nothing more than a socially correct attribute for upper-class ladies. Lady Franks's perception of art is limited to the social milieu from which she comes.

Later in the novel, Aaron defines his idea of "fate" as "fight"; there is nothing providential and beneficent about it:

> "I don't want my Fate or my Providence to treat me well. I don't want kindness or love. I don't believe in harmony and people loving one another. I believe in fight and in nothing else. I believe in the fight which is everything." (307)

There is a lot of implied human decision-making and action in such a "fight"; there is nothing supernatural about Aaron's concept of providence as something the individual must fight for.

Similarly, Lilly cautions against the total abdication of human volition to a supernatural ideal. He admonishes Aaron to become self-reliant, rather than believing that an outside force will rescue him:

> "You thought there was something outside, to justify you: God, or a creed, or a prescription. But remember, your soul inside you is your only Godhead." (344)

Lilly emphasizes self-responsibility and self-reliance much more than an idealistic hope for providence from some outside agency. There is little self-congratulation in this emphasis on self, only a recognition of the individual's need to fight through to an answer.

In contrast, the Franks are portrayed as very smug. Love of power is, as has been noted, an authoritarian quality, and the Franks both exhibit an awareness of the monied power they have accumulated. Lady Franks states casually that "We have succeeded with almost everything" (204). Sir William is smug about the iron wilfulness he has applied to his work – the accumulation of wealth – throughout his life: "I have had to keep myself hard at work, all my life, choosing between this or that" (207). Indeed, Lawrence's portrait of Sir William parallels that of an aged Gerald Crich: the benevolence and amiability on the surface is occasionally undercut by the iron will of the true character underneath:

> Sir William lifted his glass with an odd little smirk, some touch of a strange, prim old satyr lurking in his oddly inclined head. Nay, more than satyr: that curious, rather terrible iron demon that has fought with the world and wrung wealth from it, and which knows all about it. The devilish spirit of iron itself, and iron machines. (205)

Gerald Crich, Sir William and Sir Clifford Chatterley are analogous portraits of the consummate capitalist. The impetus that drives these magnates of western industrial society is the need to accumulate wealth, which, in turn, gives them the power to be decision-makers in this society. If Lady Franks may be partly exonerated from authoritarianism for her appreciation of music, Lawrence is quite clear about Sir William: "He seemed not to care for music" (212).

Lawrence has included most of the qualities of the authoritarian personality in several of his minor characters in the novel. Many of these characters, such as Jim Bricknell and Sir William, are simultaneously patronizing in their attitude toward Aaron and Lilly. Further, the novel contains numerous references to socialism and uprisings and revolutions in the socialist cause. There is a clear ambivalence toward socialism expressed throughout. At one point, the reader is invited to share with the narrator a feeling of justification when Lady Franks dreams that the Italian peasants are about to revolt and overtake the Franks's estate. Yet, at another point, one sympathizes with Aaron in his dream of the tin-miners about to consume a kind of sacrificial victim; this is a revolution of the masses in all its horror and ugliness. Indeed, Aaron watches a socialist march and is struck with fear, as well as awe, when he perceives "a strange male slashing sound. Vicious it was" (219).

Lawrence's attempt to resolve such fear and still improve on what he calls this "democratic washerwoman business" (324) leads him to the conclusion that it is necessary to yield "to the peculiar mastery of one man's nature" (337). The need for a strong leader has commonly been thought to represent fascism, although why it is not associated with the practice of socialism as well is mystifying. Lawrence would have had the examples of both Lenin and Mussolini in mind. Although *Aaron's Rod* mentions socialism on numerous occasions, however, there appears to be only one suggestion of Mussolini's ascendence to power in 1922, nebulous though it is: "Ten months would steal imperceptibly by, and the mysterious revolution would be effected" (240). There is no approbation in the narrator's use of "mysterious." George Watson argues convincingly that there was little awareness of fascism in England prior to the 1930s:

> In Britain, as in other Western democracies, an awareness of fascism hardly began until after Hitler's accession to power in January 1933. The March on Rome in October 1922 had not seemed to demand much analytical attention from intellectuals, and had only occasionally received it. Italy was not thought a vital force in European affairs, in any event, and there was no reason to see Mussolini for what, in

> the event, he proved to be – the first in a long line of new leaders who by 1940 would subjugate almost all of Continental Europe.... The most Mussolini could hope to stand for abroad in those early days was a joke in the best style; Cambridge undergraduates in the Twenties, so Isherwood reports, might call their terriers "Musso" if they were rugger or rowing men. But as a political phenomenon, fascism was simply not felt in the Twenties to be of European significance. And even if D. H. Lawrence, who died three years before the advent of Hitler, held views that could be seen to stand in a startling relationship to the new tide of thought on the Continent, nobody could seriously suppose him an admirer of any existing dictator. Before 1933 intellectual fascism is scarcely to be seen or heard in Britain. (72)

While Watson's statement regarding the lack of awareness of fascism in England may be correct in general, Lawrence has certainly proven to be an exception. Living in Italy during the period of the revolution, he experienced the fascist phenomenon much more clearly than did his British counterparts. As noted earlier in this chapter, his *Movements in European History* was published in 1921, before Mussolini even came to power, yet in that book Lawrence clearly recognizes the "force" behind both fascism and socialism (316-17).

Lilly's fear of a socialist revolution, "the vicious, derisive crowd, that marched and clotted ... having its own way" (220), is contradicted by his desire for change. The existing political order based on economical power is unproductive. Just as liberal humanism uses banners such as "equality" and "freedom," so socialism's "brotherhood" and "freedom" slogans are equally suspect, since mass socialist uprisings are crude and violent in nature.

Lilly's proposal at the end of *Aaron's Rod* for "a sort of slavery" in a military state, on the other hand, is a blatant call for autocratic government; unlike fascism, however, Lilly's program emphasizes the Christ-like qualities of the leader, who must be disinterested and responsible, for the mass of men are "no pretty gift, after all" (327). Lawrence wants, like Wilhelm Reich, a *complete* change within man, a transformation of human nature that recalls into being the hidden, deeper layers of man's latent ability or potential. Boadella points out that "many anarchists still believe in the possibility of social revolution, whereas Lawrence's conception is of a deeper and more far-reaching change: what Reich has referred to as a 'biological revolution'" (55). *Aaron's Rod* expresses such a desire most clearly in Aaron's psychic perception of the hidden human potential:

> As in clairvoyance he perceived it: that our life is only a fragment of the shell of life. That there has been and will be life, human life such as we do not begin to conceive. Much that is life has passed away from men, leaving us all mere bits. In the dark, mindful silence and inflection of the cypress trees, lost races, lost language, lost human ways of feeling and knowing. (309)

The recovery of these lost "ways of feeling and knowing" will come about in the individual, rather than in the state. While Lawrence desires such transformation in the individual human psyche, fascism under Hitler – as well as socialism under Stalin – demanded little change in the individual human nature, being more a reductive force into blind obedience. The transformation under both fascism and socialism was to be a transformation of the state, and the power of the state, rather than of the individual.

It is interesting to note here that George Watson asserts that Lawrence, among other British intellectuals in 1922, would not have seen socialism and fascism as opposite camps of left and right. That polarization, he says, simply did not exist at the time:

> In Britain, at least, the polarization of Left and Right was late, and belongs to the mid-Thirties. Documents earlier than that do not naturally see socialism and fascism as opposites. The clarity or crudity of Left and Right was to come later; and the myth of fascism as a conservative force, being fundamentally a marxist myth, had to wait to be heard until marxism itself was widely accepted. (94)

Watson's thesis is essentially that Marxism and Nazism are the same kind of "state capitalism" and that the terms "left" and "right" are redundancies. He suggests "liberal" and "illiberal" as polarities instead. Ernst Noltë's definition of fascism, on the other hand, that:

> Fascism is anti-Marxism which seeks to destroy the enemy by the evolvement of a radically opposed and yet related ideology and by the use of almost identical and yet typically modified methods, always, however, within the unyielding framework of national self-assertion and autonomy. (20-21)

An obvious disagreement exists here between Noltë and Watson who, we might say, are occupying "left" and "right" positions regarding their different definitions of fascism. Watson asserts:

> D.H. Lawrence, in one of the last essays he ever wrote, speaks of Lenin and Mussolini as if they were distinct but by no means opposite cases, and as

> together illustrating the 'miracle, mystery and authority' that mankind will forever demand: "Russia destroyed the Tsar to have Lenin and the present mechanical despotism, Italy has the rationalized despotism of Mussolini, and England is longing for a despot." (95)

Now, with Hannah Arendt's definition of totalitarianism at our disposal, we are able to categorize two leaders like Stalin and Hitler together as totalitarians, despite the fact that their politics are assumed to be the original "left" and "right" polarities.

Lawrence's own perception of fascism appears to contradict Watson's thesis that socialism and National Socialism are essentially the same program. Lawrence asserted in 1921 that "Fascism ... was an anti-socialist movement" (*Movements* 316), yet Watson feels that "the polarization of Left and Right was late, and belongs to the mid-Thirties" (94). Lawrence finally identifies both the socialist and fascist rebellions he has witnessed as examples of negative, destructive force:

> This was the beginning of Fascism. It was an anti-socialist movement started by the returned soldiers in the name of Law and Order. And suddenly, it gained possession of Italy. Now the cabs had a fixed charge, a fixed charge for railway porters was placarded in the railway stations, and trains began to run punctually. But also, in Fiesole near Florence the Fascisti suddenly banged at the door of the mayor of the village, in the night when all were in bed. The mayor was forced to get up and open the door. The Fascisti seized him, stood him against the wall of his house, and shot him under the eyes of his wife and children, who were in their night dresses. Why? Because he was a socialist.

> This is Fascism and Law and Order. Only another kind of bullying.
>
> Now one *must* have Law and Order, because lawlessness and disorder in our great communities is hell. We *must* have authority, and there *must* be power. But there must not be bullying, nor the worship of mere Force. A certain group of men in Italy intend to *force* their will on all other men. Earlier, socialists tried to force *their* will. (*Movements* 316-17)

Lawrence saw neither system as encouraging the transforming of human nature in the way that he himself viewed as essential; both systems strive to transform the state as a mode of power, rather than the individuals that comprise the state.

Lawrence was not positively inclined toward any of the current political leaders; the temporal absolutism of either Lenin's or Mussolini's regimes would have transgressed against Lilly's dictum that "every man is a sacred and holy individual, *never* to be violated. I think there is only one thing I hate to the verge of madness and that is *bullying*" (328).

Throughout the novel, Lawrence has consistently created minor characters, such as Jim Bricknell, with authoritarian attributes. These then are the characters that could have dangerous fascist or totalitarian leanings. Lilly and Aaron are not irrational in their approach to life, nor do they conform to the profile of the authoritarian personality. It is incongruous, then, to find Lilly at the end of the book offering his infamous theory:

> "People are not *men*: they are insects and instruments, and their destiny is slavery ... ultimately they will be brought to agree – after sufficient extermination

> – and then they will elect for themselves a proper and healthy and energetic slavery." (327)

Firstly, the horror of this statement for the modern reader lies in its prophetic parallel with the two totalitarian experiments of Stalinist Russia and Nazi Germany. But Lawrence did not have the benefit of having seen these regimes in practice. In any case, the fascism espoused by Mussolini, which was the only kind in existence during Lawrence's lifetime, was *not* totalitarian. Where could Lawrence have heard of a theory of slavery and extermination as a means of governing? Once again, Watson cites the fact that the first concentration camps occurred in the Soviet Union:

> The Soviet process began as early as 1918, and the general brutality of the Leninist regime was noticed and reported almost at once; what is more, the existence of extermination camps in the U.S.S.R. was reported in English books at least as early as 1931, before the literary vogue for communism had begun. (49)

Lawrence's close friend Koteliansky emigrated from the U.S.S.R. to England, but he still had family members in the Ukraine. Even if Lawrence did not hear of actual extermination policies under Lenin, there is, Watson asserts, another source for these theories, and that is Marxism itself. Intellectuals during Lawrence's time, from the late 1800s onward, were engrossed with socialism: Fabianists, the General Strike, the Suffragette movement, the Bolshevik revolution in 1917, and the horror of WWI, made Marxism "the logically inevitable next step" (325), as Lilly admits. *Aaron's Rod* is a novel that is permeated with ambivalence toward such a step. Lawrence, like his heroes Lilly and Aaron, comes from a working-class milieu and cannot help but identify with the lower classes' desire to rise and to improve their lot in life. Simultaneously, however, Lawrence – as artist and individual – feels threatened by the revenge and chaos such an uprising necessarily brings in its midst. His view of the mass of men as "insects and instruments" is directly contradictory to his view that "every man is a sacred and holy individual, *never* to be violated." If this is the central core of his ambivalence, the first view of men as instruments may well derive, according to Watson, from Marxist theories and from socialism itself: "Marx did believe in extermination, and often boasted of that belief" (128). Marx and Engels advocated terrorism and annihilation in their articles on "Hungary and Panslavism," and "Democratic Panslavism":

> Among all the nations and petty ethnic groups of Austria there are only three which have been the carriers of progress, which have played an active role in history and which still retain their vitality – the Germans, the Poles and the Magyars. For this reason they are now revolutionary.
>
> The chief mission of all the other races and peoples – large and small – is to perish in the revolutionary holocaust.... [T]his ethnic trash always becomes and remains until its complete extermination or denationalization, the most fanatic carrier of counter-revolution, since its entire existence is nothing more than a protest against a great historical revolution. (Marx 59-64)

If Lawrence did not read Marx himself, Watson's study shows that many British writers of Lawrence's time did read him and absorb theories of extermination. One example he cites among many others is that of H.G. Wells, who, "in *Anticipations* (1902) made in the bluntest terms a case for socialist extermination in the cause of racial fitness"

(132). Lawrence's conceptualization of extermination policies was more likely derived from certain strains of socialist theory than from fascism. Compare, for example, Birkin's reflection on annihilation in *Women in Love* to the following comment by Marx, again with respect to the Slavs: "The next world war will cause not only reactionary classes and dynasties but also entire reactionary peoples to disappear from the earth. And that too would be progress" (Marx 67). But the fact that an artist (or a political theorist, in Marx's case), incorporates statements of this nature into his work is not in itself indicative of a totalitarian personality. Lionel Trilling sums this up very well in his discussion of the role of the artist within his cultural environment:

> A culture is not a flow, nor even a confluence; the form of its existence is struggle, or at least debate – it is nothing if not a dialectic. And in any culture there are likely to be certain artists who contain a large part of the dialectic within themselves, their meaning and power lying in their contradictions; they contain within themselves, it may be said, the very essence of the culture, and the sign of this is that they do not submit to serve the ends of any one ideological group or tendency. (9)

Lawrence's ambivalence toward socialism is that, in an idealistic view of individual man as "sacred and holy," socialism is a threat and fearsome simply because it subjects the individual to the power of the masses, who are "insects and instruments." Masses of men, as Lawrence saw them, exhibit the irrational cruelty of a "mob mentality," a theme that Lawrence reiterates over and over throughout the novel. There is hope only for the individual personality:

> To concentrate on social revolution is therefore no solution. "What's the point of a revolution?" Lawrence asks. He knows that "there's nothing to blame but ourselves, and there's nothing to change except inside ourselves." Everything else follows of its own accord from that. So that "a revolution is really the birth of a new baby, a new idea, a new feeling, a new way of feeling, a new feeling pattern. It is the birth of a new man." ... Those who want a revolution, he explains, must first "beget and conceive the new baby" in their own bodies. (Boadella 754)

The parallel to Christ's assertion, one that Lawrence would certainly have been very familiar with, that, "Except a man be born again, he cannot see the kingdom of God" (John 3:3), is evident here as well. A political program can never achieve the transformation of the "reborn" individual. Thus Lawrence concludes, in this same essay, that "Russia is a collapse, not a revolution" (*Phoenix* 754).

Chapter 6

Leaders and Followers in *Kangaroo*

If Lawrence is attracted to socialism as a possible program in *Aaron's Rod* – even implemented in a totalitarian fashion – he is simultaneously afraid of such absolute curtailment, what he calls "bullying," of individual freedom. This ambivalence is common to utopian idealism. History and literature have provided many examples of attempted utopias that have failed disastrously; at the same time, the need for hope, the striving for a perfect solution, has kept the utopian dream alive. Man must not give up hope, but neither should he attempt to enact an absolute utopia that inevitably deprives him of individual freedom. Lawrence reaches this contradictory conclusion at the end of *Aaron's Rod*. His next novel, *Kangaroo*, represents an attempt to enact two different kinds of programs; both are presented as absolute demands on individual freedom. Lawrence defines these two programs along the two definitive human possibilities of "being" and "doing" or, in his terms, "love" and "service." Willie Struthers represents the typical workers' movement of the time. Kangaroo is presented as the autocratic leader of a more theoretical absolutism based on a more complete transformation of human nature. But Kangaroo's authoritarian approach to a new mode of being is finally as as the workers' revolution would be under Struthers.

Lawrence's move to Australia at this time is also a move away from the structured class distinctions and social patronage that he had experienced in Europe and described in *Aaron's Rod*. Australia is presented as a new kind of democracy – the "colonial" kind – in the first chapter of the book. Both Somers and his wife Harriet criticize the mass conformity they encounter, and the insolence of the lower classes, the workers. Lawrence – like Somers, the Lawrencian main character of *Kangaroo*, is very conscious of the fact that Australians sense his non-conformist image, although he realizes that they interpret it as one of two extremes, the reactionary German of the Kaiser period or, alternatively, a Bolshevist:

> "A comical-looking bloke! Perhaps a Bolshy." (1)
> ..."Fritzies, most likely." (2)
> ...Because he had a beard and wore a little green house-jacket, he was probably a socialist. (14)
> "... Somers – he might be a German, he might be a bolshevist...." (32)

It is important for Lawrence to establish Somers as the outsider, as someone who can stand apart from the conformist flavor of Australian democracy. It is also important to establish Somers as a political figure of a decisive sort, since this is a politically questing novel. Similarly, Somers, like Aaron and Lilly before him, evades firm class distinctions because "...he was different, a gentleman and not a gentleman" (32). The weakened position which Aaron occupies as half-in-half-out-of the upper classes is transformed in Somers into a strength. Here Somers is surrounded by the working classes who revere him for his educated opinions and European worldliness, while being able to identify with his working class origins. Somers states:

> "My father was a working man. I come from the working people. My sympathy is with them, when it's with anybody, I assure you." (42)

But his working class identification does not ensure his absolute sympathy with socialism in this novel. Somers states concretely at one point: "...you can't put the brotherhood of man on a wage basis" (59). In the latter stages of the novel, Jaz and Somers discuss the possibility of a successful socialist revolution; their fear of violence following the revolution leads them to consider, as an option, replacing the leaders of the proposed new party with Kangaroo, who would exercise a more autocratic control. By the end of the novel, however, Somers, the intrinsic outsider, has rejected the absolutism of both the socialists and Kangaroo's party. Neither would accomplish the transformation of human nature that he feels is essential:

> "Sometimes I feel I'd give anything, soul and body, for a smash up in this social-industrial world we're in. And I would. And then I realize people – just people – the same people after it as before – why, Jaz, then I don't care any more, and feel it's time to turn to the gods." (162)

This transformation that Somers considers essential revolves around the definition of the liberal's attitude towards charity, already looked at in the examination of *Aaron's Rod*. Somers, too, denounces charity because it does not eradicate the basic problem of poverty:

> "You've got to *have* no poor that can be saved just by possessions." (97)
>
> "They cry, 'We are not pure in heart. We are too selfish. Let us educate the poor. Let us remove the

> slums. Let us save the children. Let us spend all we have on the noble work of education.' So they spend a bit more than before, but by no means all they have, with the result that by now everybody reads the newspapers and discusses world politics and feels himself most one-sidedly a bit of the great Godhead of the sacred People." (303)

Adorno's study indicates that, for the authoritarian personality, charity is desirable because it "... often has the function of keeping the underprivileged in their place" (307). Lawrence is critical of charity for this reason throughout *Aaron's Rod* and *Kangaroo*: it is merely a temporary measure to placate the poor. No real change will result from it. Lawrence's perception of the function of charity in western democracies is a liberal's viewpoint, from the perspective of Adorno's definition of a "liberal." The desire to eradicate poverty altogether is a utopian vision, one that hopes and believes in the possibility of a transformation of human nature, an erasing of the commercial basis of human interchange. Authoritarians, defined by their underlying pessimism, hostility, èlitism and repressed violence, would be unable to envision a utopia. Their conformist attitudes emphasize *status quo* stability at all costs. Lawrence presents the basic polarity of utopianism and authoritarianism succinctly in *Kangaroo*:

> So there they are, between the rocky Scylla of the fixed, established ideal, and the whirling Charybdis of the conservative opposition to this ideal. Between these two perils they must pass .... So the monster of humanity, with a Scylla of an ideal of equality for the head, and a Charybdis of industrialism and possessive conservatism for the tail, howls with frenzy, and lashes the straits till every boat goes down, that tried to make a passage. (303)

Lawrence's utopian vision recognizes both extremes; the "ideal of equality" is a Scylla because its utopian, absolute demands on individual freedom allow no more individuality than does the reactionary side. Lawrence here suggests the necessity to steer a course between the two extremes. Elsewhere in the novel, he clearly states that leadership is destructive when it relies solely on power, rather than a balance of "power" and "love." Power inculcates fear and obedience, but no love, reducing human nature to a function of the state. Stalin and Hitler would represent this kind of force and thus would be condemned by Lawrence:

> First, the great influence of shadow of power, causing trust, fear and obedience: second, the great influence of protective love, causing productivity and the sense of safety.... In Caesar and Napoleon the vertebral influence of power prevailed – and there was a break of balance, and a fall. In Lincoln and President Wilson the vertebral influence of love got out of balance, and there was a fall. There was no balance between the two modes of influence: the mind ran on, as it were, without a brake, towards absurdity. (*Kangaroo* 306)

Lawrence's conclusions are always emphatic about the need for a balance between extremes, whether utopianism versus conservatism or love versus power. This last passage, however, exhibits confusion over the term "trust," which is supposedly inspired by power, and "the sense of safety," which is created through love. Power alone cannot inspire trust; the more total the power is, the less capable the individual is of assessing it, and, as recent totalitarian regimes witness, the trust, if there is any, is only at the beginning, and it is blind trust without rational assessment to support it. Power alone in the state asks very little of the individual, reducing his potential to instrumentality. Lawrence may identify the masculine "power" of the patriarchal home as producting a sense of trust; superficially, at least, discipline ensures a sense of order, as Reich has illustrated in *The Mass Psychology of Fascism*. But Lawrence credits man's inner growth and creativity – what he calls "productivity" – to the power of love. Lawrence cites historical examples of the imbalance of power and love: with Caesar and Napoleon there was too much emphasis on power, while Lincoln and President Wilson erred on the side of love. A more contemporary example of imbalance on the side of love might be the insecurity of Americans under their liberal president Jimmy Carter, while, in contrast, Ronald Reagan's stronger patriarchal image might be more indicative of the power imbalance. Allende's fall in Chile would again appear to be a result of the "love" mode remaining too idealistic and ending tragically. So history supports Lawrence's conclusion that ideal leadership constitutes a balance between the polarities.

Lawrence's demand for a strong leader is not in itself fascistic. His fear, albeit naive, was that socialism would result in chaotic and violent mob rule, but socialist governments have certainly had leaders every bit as strong and dominating as those of the fascists. Lawrence was disillusioned by the violence of the socialistic activity he observed in Italy, and by the bullying of the new working classes in Europe and Australia; he saw trade unions as representative, in a miniscule way, of what a socialist government could become: "They're just the nastiest profiteering side of the working man – they make a fool of him too" (*Kangaroo* 127). Lawrence feared that socialism would be undirected, violently chaotic and finally immeasurably destructive. The goal of equality could not be achieved through mass confusion and violence: "it is a question with us today whether the masses will degenerate into mobs, or whether they will still keep a spark of direction" (*Kangaroo* 307). A "spark of direction" can hardly be termed totalitarian rule. Freud's fear of the amount of repression needed to keep twentieth-century man's primal aggression from erupting destructively is precisely what Lawrence fears in a socialist uprising – that rather than the brotherhood of man being achieved, "the great mass uprisings [would be] acts of vengeance against the dominant consciousness of the day" (*Kangaroo* 307).

Jaz's suggestion that Kangaroo might provide the sense of direction needed *after* a socialist revolution is achieved brings back to mind Noltë's definition of fascism, which uses a "radically opposed and yet related ideology and ...almost identical and yet typically modified methods" (20-21). Somers in this novel flirts with two extremes, both of which he finally admits are destructive: the bloodthirsty mob or Kangaroo's military state are "... a choice of evils, and I choose neither" (310). From the vantage point of the 1980s, we tend to identify storm troopers with Kangaroo's military diggers; such are the emotional connotations surrounding fascism in modern times. Would we be as intimidated if we could see the diggers as R.C.M.P. or marines? Yet all of these groups have similar military training.

Attracted to Kangaroo at the beginning, Somers indicates a decided preference for socialism at the novel's end because "Bolshevism is at least not sentimental." Throughout, Somers emphasizes reason and clear thinking.

High-flown idealism and impractical goals are suspect. What else *except* reason and analytical skepticism is Richard Somers praising here? This is the novel's clearest statement in support of rational consciousness and liberal self-questioning:

> "I won't give up the flag of our real civilised consciousness. I'll give up the ideals. But not the aware, self-responsible, deep consciousness that we've gained. I won't go back on that, Jaz, though Kangaroo did say I was the enemy of civilisation."
>
> "You don't consider you are, then?" asked Jaz, pertinently.
>
> "The enemy of civilisaiton [sic]?" Well, I'm the enemy of this machine civilisation and this ideal civilisation. But I'm not the enemy of the deep, self-responsible consciousness in man, which is what *I* mean by civilisation. In that sense of civilization, I'd fight for ever for the flag, and try to carry it on into deeper, darker places." (356)

In other words, Somers denies the hypocritical commercialism and Christian charity idealism of our society, but he *is* supportive of the rational self-questioning and objective skepticism that constitutes clear thinking. It is worth noting that Somers identifies with reason and logic at another point in the novel, when he tells Kangaroo that Willie Struthers' speech "seemed to me logical" (330): "'Logical!' Even Kangaroo flickered with surprise. 'You and logic'" (331). The socialist labour meeting he attends "was straightforward and sensible." But to attach himself finally to either absolute polarity is impossible, as he ruefully admits, "I can't be on either side" (323).

Somers' admiration of the utopian idealism of socialism, then, is tempered by his recognition that the idealism also needs to be directed. Nowhere is he given to impractical idealism; on the contrary, he voices skepticism and contempt when he finds these characteristics in others.

While Somers is characterized by clear thinking and other anti-authoritarian traits, the authoritarian personality can be found in the character of Jack Callcott. Jack exhibits the same strongly-willed stealth in human relationships as witnessed earlier in Gerald Crich. Somers, playing chess with Callcott, notes that "Jack had been silently, secretly accumulating his forces; there was a silence, almost a stealth in his game" (35). At another point, Somers sees Jack as "a long-faced, smooth-faced, strangely watchful kangaroo" (103). Even at his warmest, Jack remains willfully controlled and somewhat hostile, echoing Gerald's lifelong inability to form genuine friendships. Somers notes that:

> He only didn't understand Jack's way of leaving seven-tenths of himself out of any intercourse. Richard wanted the whole man there, openly. And Jack wanted his own way, of seven-tenths left out. (37)

Jack's approach to human relationships is superficial and conventional. He is "the manly man, the consciously manly man" (33), who conforms to the established masculine image that colonial society has invented. Adorno points out that the authoritarian personality "tends to think of himself as active, determined, energetic, independent, rough, and successful in the competitive struggle. There is no room in this ego-ideal for passivity and softness" (476). Somers exhibits greater self-awareness of his own image and understands Jack's necessity to be tough and masculine; he sees "contempt on Jack's face, the contempt of the confident he-man for the shifty she-man" (296). Adorno also notes that "An ego-accepted admission of passivity, softness, and weakness … is found predominantly in low-scoring [liberal] men" (428). Somers' admission of himself as a "she-man" is, then, *liberal*. Jack's conventional approach towards other human beings is assumed camaraderie, highly superficial and fickle:

> That scene of last evening: what right had a fellow like Callcott to be saying these things to him? What right had he to put his arm round his, Richard's, shoulder, and give him a tight hug? Somers winced to think of it. And now Callcott had gone off with his Victoria in Sunday clothes to some other outing. Anything was as good as anything else, why not! ... Yet the easy way Callcott flung a flimsy rope of intimacy across the gulf, and was embracing the pair of his neighbours in mid-air, as it were, without a grain of common foothold. (62)

Jack's world is black and white, with little room for shades of meaning. He feels contempt for Somers' anti-conventionality as a writer, "slightly despising the man who had no job, and therefore no significance in life" (38). His masculine image is contrived, however, as Somers senses a fear in Jack of Harriet and the upper-class European culture she represents:

> Because Harriet *really* disapproved, and he didn't know what was inside that rose-and-brown-purple cloud of her. The ancient judgement of the Old World. (185 6)

Jack's fear implies his strong sense of needing to belong to "the right sort" and causes him to react very conventionally, as, gazing at Harriet on top of the hill, he says to Somers: "'Well, I suppose we'd better be going up?' The curious note of obedience in the manly twang" (185). Jack's compulsive conventionality and sense of righteousness and power in being part of the élite or "right sort" is again evidenced in his vituperative description of the socialist movement:

> "...when it comes to going to bed with a crowd of niggers and dagoes, in an International Labour Combine, with a pair of red sheets so that the dirt won't show, I'm absolutely sure I won't have it." (189)

These sentiments resemble Gerald Crich's belief that every society has its "vermin," a trait consistently exhibited by the authoritarian personality whose "values form the basis of a hierarchical order in which the powerful are seen at the top and the weak at the bottom" (Adorno 476). Jack wants to be numbered with the powerful, as Harriet so acutely observes:

> "He's a returned war hero, and he wants a chance of keeping on being a hero." (96)
>
> "...he's chiefly jealous because other people run the show, and he doesn't have a look-in. Having once been a Captain with some power, he wants the same again, and more."
>
> ..."He wants to have his finger in the pie, that's what he wants ... to be bossy. To be a Captain once more, feeling his feet and being a boss over something." (98)

Jack's goal is power in itself; he is not really concerned with mankind or with the special ideals he espouses to justify his assumption of power. Harriet also accuses Somers of wanting "just power," but Somers analyzes the need for and uses of power, both within himself and within the social structure. He tries to work toward the requisite balance of power and love, telling Harriet:

> "But I don't want just power. I only see that somebody must have power, so those should have it who don't want it selfishly, and who have some natural gift

> for it, and some reverence for the sacredness of it." (98)

Later in the novel Somers concludes: "'I am a fool. I neither want love nor power. I like the world. And I like to be alone in it, by myself'" (206). Somers finds Kangaroo's posturing as a Jehovah irritating after a while and desires "my own mere manliness" (214). Even the possibility of a powerful leader becomes repugnant to him if power becomes an end in itself. Rather, he maintains the significance of "the innate majesty of the purest *individual*, not the strongest instrument, like Napoleon" (309). Here Somers intimates in "purest" a sense of altruism, disinterestedness and responsibility. Any attempt on a leader's part to assume god-like attributes by denying the power of individuality becomes destructive. Somers recoils from Kangaroo, who "wants to be God Himself, and save everybody, which is just irritating, at last" (310).

Jack, then, rather than the Lawrencian protagonist Somers, incorporates the traits of the authoritarian personality. In addition to Jack's desire for power, he exhibits a manipulating manner in his relations with other individuals. This manner is calculated to charm, but his inability to care genuinely for those around him severely limits his friendships. Lawrence presents him as exerting the "same breezy intimacy with all of them, and the moment they had passed by, they didn't exist for him" (54). Other human beings are instruments to accomplish the ends that he seeks. Somers, playing chess with Jack, notes:

> [Jack's] bearing was soft as it were submissive, and Somers was put quite off guard. He began to play with his usual freedom. And then Jack wiped the floor with him, and left him gasping.... (35)

Somers feels this manipulation "by a certain guilt, almost sly intention in Jack's voice, and a certain false deference in his bearing" (35). Later, when Jack tries to recruit Somers' support for Kangaroo's Digger movement, Somers is reluctant, largely because he is aware of being used and manipulated:

> The only thing he mistrusted was the dryness in Jack's voice: a sort of that's-how-it's-got-to-be dryness, sharp and authoritative.... Jack was trying to put something over him – in some way, to get a hold over him. He felt like an animal that is being lassoed. (91-92)

William James notes the similarly manipulative charisma in Kangaroo's approach to people when he says, "it's wonderful what a spell he can cast over you" (128). It is this element in Kangaroo that Jack especially admires, as if it signifies power and superiority above ordinary human standards. The ability of the propagandist is evident in Kangaroo when Jack notes that "...he can talk straight enough – and crooked enough as well, if it comes to that" (101). Any means, honest or otherwise, are apparently justified to attain power over other individuals. After meeting Kangaroo, Somers is somewhat dazed by the eloquence of the man; Jack laughingly clarifies such "eloquence" as instrumental and consciously manipulative when he says, "that's how he leaves you when he makes a set at you" (114). *What* Kangaroo says is not as important to Jack as the persuasive style he uses to manipulate and psychologically overpower his subject.

Further manipulation is evident in Jack's use and treatment of women as instruments and stereotypes. Somers is initially shocked at Jack's "liberal," unconcerned attitude regarding his wife's flirtation, and concludes that the Australian perception of the marriage bond may be looser than is his own. But one statement Lawrence makes about Jack's feelings towards his wife indicates her instrumentality to Jack:

> If his wife was good to him and satisfied him in so far as *he* went, then he was pledged to trust her to do as she liked outside his ken, outside his range. (29)

This attitude is not really indicative of an open, "no-strings-attached" marriage; rather, it resembles Robert's indifference to Julia's affairs with other men in *Aaron's Rod*. Victoria, like Julia, is neither valued nor cared for deeply enough by her husband for him to become possessive about her. The apparent "liberal" attitude is not liberal at all: it is Jack's inability to care about another human being, to love. Jack and Victoria's rather vulgar love-making offends the more reserved European couple, but Jack is unaware that he is insensitive: "He looked at the Somers pair with eyes gone dusky, as if unseeing..." (44). Victoria's behavior in this scene is stereotyped – coy and dishonest – as if this is the only female response such a "consciously manly man" will understand. Indeed, Jack treats his wife like a child and toy, much as Minette, with her babyish lisp, is treated by Gerald in *Women in Love*. At one point Jack comments:

> "And the ladies can punish the piano again meanwhile, if they feel like it. I bought something to sweeten the melodies with..."
>
> "That means a pound of chocolates," said Victoria, like a greedy child. "And Mrs. Somers will come and help me to eat them. Good!" And she ran in home. Somers thought of a picture advertisement in

the *Bulletin*:

> "*Madge:* I can't think of what you see in Jack. He is so unintellectual."
>
> "*Gladys:* Oh, but he always brings a pound of Billyer's chocolates."
>
> Or else: "Sweets to the Sweet. Give her Billyer's chocolates." or else:
>
> "Billyer's chocolates sweeten the home." (49)

Somers' ironic attitude toward the gift of chocolates and Victoria's childish reaction emphasize the parody of conventional sexual stereotypes. Similarly, Jack jokingly threatens to discipline his wife:

> "You'd be shut up in the coal-shed for the night before you got half-way through with it if ever you started trying it on." (140)

This is a form of black humor, since in another mood Jack could easily carry out this mock threat.

Harriet and Richard Somers simply do not interact like this. Jack's chauvinism is evident in his patronizing attitude towards the women's singing and piano playing. They "can punish the piano"; earlier, he called their singing "throat stretching" (40). Females, in Jack's view, are objects to be patronized and not considered seriously.

Jack's concept of sexuality on the whole is stereotyped and vulgar. He is the only individual in the novel who consistently finds "dirty" connotations in any discussion of love and sex. Adorno finds that in the typical authoritarian personality type, the "isolation of sex experience … is connected with an ambivalent *underlying disrespect for, and resentment against the opposite sex* often hidden behind an externalized and excessive *pseudoadmiration*" (399). Jack expresses his disrespect for and resentment against women in his remark about William James:

> "I always feel as if Jaz had got a bit of Chinese blood in him. That's what makes the women like him, I suppose.... I believe he'd make any woman like him, if he laid himself out to do it. Got that quiet way with him, you know, and a sly sort of touch-the-harp-gently, that's what they like on the quiet." (60)

Harriet's friendly visit with William James is reduced by Jack to a cheaply flirtatious encounter when he tells her, "You must have given him a glad eye" (71). Jack seems unable to conceive of warmly congenial relationships between men and women. He views Harriet, too, in terms of her "usefulness":

> "She's a fine woman, she is. I suppose I ought to say lady, but I prefer woman, myself, to a lady, any day.... A woman like that ought to stop in a new country like this and breed sons for us. That's what we want." (346)

Jack's emphasis on the term "woman" in contrast to "lady" carefully distinguishes Harriet's worth: women breed sons for men; that is their function. "Lady" implies character, innate superiority, maturity or goodness, none of which Jack would admit to in a woman. Somers' reply is a snub to Jack's coarse definition of femininity because, when he says, "I suppose if she wanted to stop and breed sons she would," he is pointing out to Jack that it is her choice, that she has a mind.

Finally, Jack's exasperation with his fellow country-men's apathy toward Australia is contemptuously couched in sexual terms, using the stereotyped, authoritarian's division of "pure" and "bad" women: "'They treat the country more like a woman they pick up on the streets than a bride, to my thinking'" (74). Jack's inability to conceive of women as equal human beings parallels his lack of understanding of human sexuality in terms of sensitive relationships. He protects his own hyper-masculine image, which makes it impossible for him to relate fully to Victoria, who in turn senses in Somers a fuller human response than her own husband is capable of. Victoria herself is conventional and immature in her approach to heterosexual ties, and thus is confused as to why her husband, who "was a man, and everything a man should be, in her eyes" (72), does not fulfill all of her needs. He seems in his isolated masculinity to be separate from her, "like a piece of driftwood drifting on the strange unknown currents in an unexplored nowhere, without any place to arrive at" (72). Jack's lack of introspection and self-analysis leave him with an "inner emptiness," again very similar to the emptiness that Gerald Crich feels.

What Victoria does see in Jack, and what probably only reinforces her set image of the masculine man, is his underlying violence, which at times is directed against her. This exists alongside of his coddling: the two set patterns of behavior merely represent two extremes in "handling" other human beings. Jack's surface will and self-control are in place at all times when he visits with the Somers, yet Richard Somers senses that Victoria:

> seemed a little afraid of him – physically afraid – though he was always perfectly good humoured with her. And this evening she sounded like that – as if she feared his coming home, and wanted the Somers to shelter her. (48)

The combination of fear and sensuality which Victoria experiences with Jack is reminiscent of Gerald and Gudrun's violent and sensual attraction for each other. Jack's manner as a husband is authoritarian; this can and does erupt suddenly into extremely violent anger. It is evident in the following passage that Victoria has experienced this anger in Jack before:

> "Don't you move," thundered Jack, and she relapsed into silence. She knew, when he had one of his hell-moods on him, it was best to leave him absolutely alone. (325-6)

Jack's surface control is governed by an iron will of repression. Underlying such control, however, is the violence that erupts aggressively when Jack finds a conventionally justified situation. Somers' early description of Jack is that he "had a sort of passion, and a passionate identity. But not what Somers called human. And threaded on this ironical stoicism" (55).

Lawrence's portrait of Jack Callcott parallels that of Gerald Crich in many ways. The qualities that Adorno has shown as defining an authoritarian, including a lust for power, the iron will hiding a repressed inner violence, a manipulative approach to the world around him, and an inability to understand oneself, or to care genuinely for others, are all very much present in both Gerald and Jack Calcott. The following description indicates Jack's psychological vacuum or "inner emptiness," as well as the aggressive violence that his conventionally willed exterior usually manages to cover up:

> The great indifference, the darkness of the fern-world, upon his mind. Then spurts of energy, spurts of sudden violent desire, spurts of gambling excitement. But the mind is a kind of twilight sleep.... Yet there was a queer light in his eyes, as if he might do something dangerous. (181)

Gerald's confused and hostile response to the external world was overlaid with a callow idealism that was not examined rationally. Similarly, Jack Callcott dwells in a "twilight sleep"; his usual response to the world around him is a confused, empty indifference. Such indifference is alleviated only by outbursts of irrational aggression or extreme emotion. Thus, he exhibits:

> an indifference based on real recklessness, an indifference with a deep flow of loose energy beneath it, ready to break out like a geyser. Ready to break into a kind of frenzy, a berserk frenzy, running amok in wild generosity, or still more wild smashing up. The wild joy in letting loose, in a smash-up. (182-83)

After the release of repressed violence, the authoritarian personality reverts back to the only means at his disposal – his willed control of self – since he cannot understand his behavior and is afraid to admit its existence. Jack's underlying violence rarely disrupts the surface of his daily existence. He maintains a strict self-control that is intellectually indifferent to the world, while emotionally it is hostile and confused:

> he was nearly all check. He sat there apathetic, nothing but body and solid, steady, physical indifference … he was like some creature that has lost its soul, and simply stares. (184)

Somers senses that Jack is representative of the men attracted to Kangaroo's movement. They have tacitly agreed that they will act, but that Kangaroo will think for them. Their pent-up hostility will be released in a "smash-up," which reduces really to an ugly, vicious aggressiveness. The theoretical part of Kangaroo's program – supposedly based on "love" – is uninteresting and perhaps incomprehensible to the majority of the diggers:

> And Somers felt again so distinctly they were doing it all just in order to have something to do, to put a spoke in the wheel of the present bosses, to make a change.... There was all the time the excitement. Damn the consequences. (189)

This statement recalls both Noltë's comment that "ideology [is] of a secondary and instrumental nature in fascism," since the movement is largely for emotional and psychological release, as well as Stern's "distinct cultural type ... [whose] nationalism was an idealistic abstraction ...[and who] cast their discontent into political visions which were as divorced from reality as their creators were from their society" (326-27). Like Jack Callcott, "[t]hey were conservative out of nostalgia and revolutionary out of despair" (Stern 327).

Jack's most revealing action, indicative of his authoritarianism, is his joy in killing violently three socialists at the meeting. Neither Lawrence nor Somers condones this extreme behavior. Lawrence again portrays the perverse mixture of violence and sensuality that characterized Gerald and Gudrun's relationship:

> He turned round to Somers, and the strangest grin in the world was on his face, all the lines curved upwards.
>
> "Tell you what, boy," he said in a hoarse whisper, "I settled *three* of 'em – three!" There was an indescribable gloating joy in his tones, like a man telling of the good time he has had with a strange mistress – "Gawr, but I was lucky. I got one of them iron bars from the windows, and I stirred the brains of a couple of them with it, and I broke the neck of a third. Why it was as good as a sword to defend yourself with, see –."
>
> He reached his face towards Somers with weird,

> gruesome exultation, and continued in a hoarse, secret voice: "Cripes, there's *nothing* bucks you up sometimes like killing a man – *nothing*. You feel a perfect *angel* after it."
>
> Richard felt the same torn feeling in his abdomen, and his eyes watched the other man.
>
> "When it comes over you, you know, there's nothing else like it. I never knew, till the war. And I wouldn't believe it then, not for many a while. But it's *there*. Cripes, it's there right enough. Having a woman's something, isn't it? But it's a flea-bite, nothing, compared to killing your man when your blood comes up."
>
> And his eyes glowed with exultant satisfaction.
>
> "And the best of it is," he said, "you feel a perfect *angel* after it. You don't feel you've done any harm. Feel as gentle as a lamb all round. I can go to Victoria, now, and be as gentle–" He jerked his head in the direction of Victoria's room. "And you bet she'll like me."
>
> His eyes glowed with a sort of exaltation.
>
> "Killing's natural to a man, you know," he said. "It is just as natural as lying with a woman. Don't you think?"
>
> And still Richard did not answer. (326-27)

Jack's comparison of heterosexuality as a "flea-bite" of a thrill compared to murdering another human being illustrates his use of love-making as a means to vent pent-up aggression, as well as the utter emptiness of his psychological make-up that must regress to the primal state before it experiences a joyful relief. It is difficult and embarrassing to hear Jack saying so innocently "what a perfect angel" he feels afterwards, "as gentle as a lamb." The enormous demands of repression are finally released, and he feels "reborn," albeit through acts causing death.

This is the destructive cost of over-repression, of authoritarianism.

If we recall Freud's sombre warning at the end of *Civilization and its Discontents* (1930), then Lawrence's acute perception of the same phenomenon seven years earlier is astounding. Freud ascertains that:

> ...the problem before us is how to get rid of the greatest hindrance to civilization – namely, the constitutional inclination of human beings to be aggressive towards one another; and for that very reason we are especially interested in what is probably the most recent of the cultural commands of the superego, the commandment to love one's neighbour as oneself.... In our research into, and therapy of, a neurosis, we are led to make two reproaches against the super-ego of the individual. In the severity of its commands and prohibitions it troubles itself too little about the happiness of the ego, in that it takes insufficient account of the resistances against obeying them – of the instinctual strength of the id [in the first place], and of the difficulties presented by the real external environment [in the second].... The commandment, "Love thy neighbour as thyself," is the strongest defence against human aggressiveness and an excellent example of the unpsychological proceedings of the cultural super-ego. The commandment is impossible to fulfil; such an enormous inflation of love can only lower its value, not get rid of the difficulty. (89-90)

Somers understands the difficulty of modern repression thoroughly. He observes Jack's elation, and recognizes the destructive aggression for what it is, the Freudian "id" breaking through the surface repression of moral "love." Somers calls this cultural repression "a vast white strangling octopus." It is the white or innocent, Christian-cultural love ideal[1] that "strangles human nature's basic vitality." Human vitality will, at times, break through the layers of self-control, willed inhibition and repression, but in a distorted and perverse manner, so that it becomes aggressive and destructive:

> He thought of Jack, and the strange, unforgettable up-tilted grin on Jack's face as he spoke of the satisfaction of killing. This was true, too. As true as love and loving. Nay, Jack was a killer in the name of Love. That also has come to pass again.
>
> "It is the collapse of the love-ideal," said Richard to himself. "I suppose it means chaos and anarchy. Then there will have to be chaos and anarchy, in the name of love and equality.... Love is perhaps an eternal part of life. But it is only a part. And when it is treated as if it were a whole, it becomes a disease, a vast white strangling octopus." (335)

Neither Lawrence nor Reich would have accepted Freud's final conclusion, however, that rational repression is the only solution to avoid the destruction of civilization. Like Wilhelm Reich, Lawrence hoped for more. No amount of repression, which leaves the condition of men in the present world unchanged, could avert disaster. Lawrence and Reich instead pursue the utopian desire for a transformation of human nature. Freud recognizes the need

---

[1] Note how Somers argues with the Christian Beatitudes:
"*Blessed are the poor in spirit*. It depends. If it means *listening*. Not if it means taking up a permanent attitude.
Blessed are the peace-makers. It depends. If it means *answering*. Not if it means enforcing the peace, like policemen.
Blessed are the meek. It depends on the occasion." (273)
Lawrence recognizes that such rules make impossible and absolute demands on human nature.

for transformation, but views the practical enactment as a socialist ideal that cannot possibly be fulfilled:

> I too think it quite certain that a real change in the relations of human beings to possessions would be of more help in this direction than any ethical commands; but the recognition of this fact among socialists has been obscured and made useless for practical purposes by a fresh idealistic misconception of human nature. (90)

Lawrence, on the contrary, hopes, like Somers in *Kangaroo*, that:

> Afterwards – afterwards – in the far-off, far-off afterwards, a different sort of men might arise to a different sort of care. (342)[2]

Jack rationalizes his underlying violence as an inevitable part of his life. Because he is not capable of self-examination, he interprets what happens to him and around him through projecting his own hostilities onto the outside environment. Like other authoritarians in Lawrence's work, Jack believes man's ability is not limited by his human condition; a supernatural force above human understanding must exist that has the power to decide and control events. We are all, Jack feels, guided by fate, some higher power of understanding than we can com-

[2] Adorno's findings show that the authoritarian personality feels that "there is no utopia and, one may add, there should be no utopia. One has to be 'realistic.' This notion of realism, however, does not refer to the necessity of judging and accounting on the basis of objective, factual insight, but rather to the postulate that one recognizes from the very beginning the overwhelming superiority of the existent over the individual and his intentions, that one advocates an adjustment implying resignation with regard to any kind of basic improvements, that one gives up anything that may be called a daydream, and reshapes oneself into an appendage of the social machinery. This is reflected by political opinion in so far as any kind of utopian idea in politics is excluded altogether" (695).

prehend. The propensity to shift the responsibility for problem-solving in one's life to an external power is, Adorno says, a definite tendency of the authoritarian personality:

> religion tends to assume the function of an external authority deciding what is good and what is bad, thus relieving the individual from making his own decisions and assuring him at the same time of membership in a privileged group. (310)

Jack reiterates over and over his belief in a supernatural absolutist fate which decides how his life will be lived. Somers, in contrast, appears skeptical of this belief:

> "Your instinct brought you here – and brought you straight up against me. Now that I call fate."
>
> He looked at Somers with dark, burning questioning eyes.
>
> "I suppose following one's deepest instinct is one's fate," said Somers, rather flatly. (51)

Somers prefers the individual's volition to be his "fate," thus making fate dependent upon man's judgment. Somers cannot identify with an external force because to do so would be to deny individual worth. But Jack repeats again that "I'm a believer in fate, absolute.... And when I feel my fate, I absolutely give myself up to it" (51-52). Through identification with a superior force, he feels more powerful and confident himself. The belief in fate implies power without responsibility; Jack's belief relieves him of the responsibility to analyze his own actions and feelings objectively. This superstitious approach to life makes Somers uncomfortable; here is another Lawrencian protagonist who exhibits a good deal of rational skepticism. Somers distrusts superstition, fate and irrational idealism. He mistrusts, as he says, "seventh heavens and all heavens in general.... In some strange way Somers felt he had come to the end of transports: they had no more mystery for him; at least this kind: or perhaps no more charm" (131-32). At another point in the novel, Somers succinctly derides "blind fate":

> So, it was just Thomas Hardy's Blind Fate? No, said Lovatt to himself, no. *Fata valentem ducunt, nolentem trahunt*. The Fates lead on the willing man, the unwilling man they drag.
>
> The Fates? What Fates? It takes a willing man to answer. Man is not a creature of circumstance, neither is he the result of cause-and-effect throughout the ages, neither is he a product of evolution, neither is he a living mind, part of the Universal Mind. Neither is he a complicated make-up of forces and chemicals and organs. Neither is he a term of love. Neither is he the mere instrument of God's will. None of these things.
>
> Man lives according to his own idea of himself. (268)

Similarly, Somers rejects any formal ideal of institutionalized religion, which has become the "strangling white octopus" of our civilization. The absolute demands of the "ideal God [who] is a proposition of the mental consciousness, all-too-limitedly human" (271). Rather, like Reich, Somers believes in man himself, in "the profound unconscious of man" (271); this exists within the individual's latent potential to save himself.

Altogether, Richard Somers exhibits a skepticism and rational clarity that elude Jack Callcott completely. Jack's repressive lack of rational thought underlies his superstitious belief in fate and his irrational outbursts of violence. Nowhere has he examined Kangaroo's theoretical program; he is attracted simply to the spirit of revolt and aggression.

Given the time and circumstances of Lawrence's writing in 1923, one can hardly say that he predicted a fascist movement like National Socialism; however, his presentation of Kangaroo as a military leader under the slogan of love certainly brings the identification to mind. If Gerald Crich sentimentalizes the "organization" of industry into "harmony," Kangaroo desires, above all, "order" and somehow translates order into the ideal of love:

> "... the greatest danger to the world to-day is anarchy, not bolshevism. It is anarchy and unrule that are coming on us and that is what I, as an order-loving Jew ... do not want. I want one central principle in the world: the principle of love." (211)

This lack of clear thought on Kangaroo's part may well be intentional; indeed, the authoritarian disposition welcomes Kangaroo's intention: "to take away the strain, the nervous tension out of life, and let folks be happy again unconsciously, instead of being unhappy consciously" (118). In this sentence, Lawrence has, in essence, summarized Fromm's *Escape from Freedom*.

Whereas Jack Callcott barely listens to the ideological cant of Kangaroo's platform, Somers is repelled by the absolutist demands it makes on individual freedom. He argues that he is "tired of one central principle in the world" (211), since this is too absolute a demand on the individual's unique personality. Somers recognizes Jack's lack of clear thinking and irresponsible gullibility, and this criticism by Somers is at centre the real criticism of fascism and any totalitarian system that effects a loss of individual volition: "'What I feel, is that the bulk of you just don't care what the chief does, so long as he does something'" (189). Jack's reply confirms Somers' suspicion that they are unthinking and blind in their support:

"Oh, we don't lose our sleep at nights. If he likes to be the boss, let him do the thinking. We know he's our man, and so we'll follow him. We can't all be Peter and Paul and know all about it." (189)

This wilful suspension of human reason lies at the bottom of fascism's appeal and recalls once again Noltë's dictum that ideology is of secondary importance in fascism (24); it is submerged under the emotional fervour and charisma that allow the authoritarian psychological make-up a release from repression. Jack is presented as the authoritarian personality imminently susceptible to such a government, but, in contrast, Somers questions him rationally and analyzes the basis of the movement. If Somers remains open to rational speculation, he is aligned towards the end of the novel with the equally common-sensical Jaz; both are portrayed as opposites to Jack. Jack's character is indicative at times of a blank, empty stupidity, as when Somers observes him watching a football game:

> Occasionally the tail-end of a smile would cross his face, occasionally he would take his pipe-stem from his mouth and give a bright look into vacancy and say, "See that!" Heaven knows what it was that he saw. The game, the skill? Yes. But more, the motion, the wild combative motion. And most of all, fate. Fate had a fascination for him. It was the only real point of curiosity left in him: how would chance work things out. Chance! Now then, how would chance settle it? Even the football field, with its wildly scurrying blues and bits of red, was only a frenzied shuffling of fate, with men for the instruments. The living instruments of fate! (182)

Jaz, in contrast, appears at times the most rational character in the novel. He maintains, like Somers, a strongly individual stance: "I'm not one of anybody" (69), he states early in the novel. It is he who restrains Somers' instinctive reaction to "let go" at the uprising during the labour meeting: "Jaz, quiet, persistent, drew him gradually out into the street.... Jaz was leading him by the arm – leading him away–" (331-2). Jaz has enough rational control and awareness to rise above the physical violence around him. His rational, commonsensical character contrasts sharply to that of Jack Callcott's immediately following the clash:

> "What time is it?" asked Richard.
>
> "Blowed if I know," answered Jack, like a drunken man.
>
> "Half-past eleven," said Jaz quietly.... Jaz's plump, pale face was still impassive, inscrutable and his clothing was in order. (324-5)

Later, when Jack brags about having killed some of the socialists, Jaz cautions him to restrain his elation and thereby avoid arrest by the police:

> "And I *did* do one or two of 'em in. See the brains sputter out of that chap that shot 'Roo?"
>
> "And suppose they arrest you to-night and shove you in gaol for manslaughter?" said Jaz.
>
> "I wouldn't advise anybody to lay as much as a leaf of maiden hair fern on me tonight, much less a finger."
>
> "They might to-morrow. You be still, and go home" (325).

The contrast is stark: the ecstatic Bacchanite figure of Jack beside the quiet, reasoned caution of Jaz presents the central polarities presented in the characters of *Kangaroo*. Jaz is the responsible, thinking individual, who, like Somers, can never quite bring himself to identify with the larger group. Jack, in contrast, has little essence as a solitary individual and functions only as an appendage of the larger group. Somers, in defining the authoritarian denial of the self, or the individual's freedom, simultaneously summarizes Jack's character:

> The mass does not act by reason. A mass is not even formed by reason. The more intense or extended the collective consciousness, the more does the truly reasonable, individual consciousness sink into abeyance. (304)

The mass includes the ordinary, everyday people that we intermingle with throughout our life, yet many of these people are at the least susceptible to, or at the most have a propensity toward authoritarianism. The western world educates its populace *just* enough, as Somers says, to "get by," but the over-riding concerns of this society are not with individual sensitivities or awareness. Gerald Crich, Jim Bricknell and Jack Callcott all carry a sense of inner emptiness and confusion that at times is relieved only by a violent emotional outburst to give them some sense of identity and meaning in an alienated, hostile world. None of these three examples of the authoritarian make-up is capable of self-examination, and along with it, the ability to express affection, love or any pleasure in beauty or art. The world as they see it is a "jungle"; the stakes are survival and the accumulation of power. But their natures lack the introspective ability to analyze their motives or the hostilities that exist within them. Somers observes Jack's lack of introspection:

> Over a great field he was quite indifferent to thought and hostile to consciousness. It seemed to him more manly to be unconscious, even blank, to most of the great questions. (36)

Jack's indifference is really a psychological vacuum that has nothing to offer other human beings. The price of maintaining the set masculine "tough" image is really a limited consciousness, and relationships that can only remain unfulfilled. Harriet ridicules Jack's superficial mask as non-human and unreal:

> "If they *were* real men I wouldn't mind. But look at your Jack Callcott.... 'Clip in, old man!'" She imitated Jack's voice and manner. (65)

Harriet is more mature, and certainly more sensitive to human relationships than Jack is, and readily discerns Jack's inability to care for others:

> What was the consecutive thread in the man's feelings? Not his feeling for any particular human beings, that was evident. His friends, even his loves, were just a series of disconnected, isolated moments in his life....
>
> The only consecutive thing was that facetious attitude. (54)

Jack's treatment of Victoria has been examined; his coddling of the pet-woman-child can as easily turn into the brutish temper of the stronger towards the weaker. If his tone towards her is usually affectionate, it is a conventionally assumed masculine stance, since Victoria remains *distrustful* of his approach. To interact with her husband at all, she assumes a helpless, coy mien as a polarization of femininity, since this is presumably the only kind of female Jack understands. Such a relationship does not mirror mature loving and understanding; think how different, in contrast, is Richard Somers' realization of his wife Harriet's individuality and, consequently, how beautiful it is to him. This is a perception that Jack Callcott could never feel:

> his eyes opened once more to the delicacy of Harriet's real beauty, which he knew as none else knew it, after twelve years of marriage. And once more he realized her gay, undying courage, her wonderful fresh zest in front of life. (62)

Somers is not reflecting on her physical beauty as much as realizing another human being's identity, or "essence" outside of his own, and he feels joy in his perception. Jack, on the other hand, is described mechanistically, much like Gerald; he functions, primarily physically, like a mechanical automaton. He is predominantly physical, leaving little impression on the other person's mind or spirit. This is why Somers resents Jack's "hand on his shoulder," or being called "old man" (104). These are superficial expressions of friendship that do not really penetrate the surface. Somers feels these gestures are cold, merely "part of the colonial bluff" (104).

Gerald Crich's identification with mechanical automatism became readily evident once the authoritarian patterns began to emerge in his character. This identification is perhaps more straightforward than in Jack Calcott's case, because Gerald runs industry, prides himself on the "organization" of men as instruments and seems to function as a machine himself (he is often described through the use of metallic imagery). Jack Callcott appears as the ordınary working man with a breezy disposition and easy-going nature. The far-off world of industrialization seems left behind in England. Yet the portrait that Lawrence draws of Jack is finally as definitively authoritarian as Gerald Crich's character. Gerald's surface confidence and charm disarmed most people, yet, like Jack, the inner man, the part of the human being that reaches out to understand and connect, is blank. The "personality" of each is a façade to hide the empty confusion and hostility within. This description of Jack again exemplifies his inner nullity:

> He just leaned back and stretched himself in that intense physical way which Somers thought just a trifle less than human. The man was all body: a strong body full of energy like a machine that has got steam up, but is inactive. He had no mind, no spirit, no soul. (183)

The stereotyped, romantic male hero of fiction – the "tall, dark, silent stranger" – often turns out to be silent because he is stupid; this is an equally wry analysis of Jack Callcott, since the masculine mode he assumes is unsupported by what he is capable of feeling. He assumes the strong, silent image because, firstly, it is most conventionally acceptable, and secondly, because he really has nothing much to say. Jack, like Gerald Crich before him, has just "to keep enough grip to run the machinery of the day: and beyond that, to let yourself drift, not to think or strain or make any effort to consciousness whatsoever. That was Jack" (185).

In contrast to Jack Callcott, Somers moves throughout the novel to a better understanding of what the political programs around him will actually demand in practice. He is attracted to each one in turn, but recoils when the attraction demands too absolute a response. Over and over again, Somers is tempted by the idealism each political stand embodies, but when he tries to envision the enactment of this absolute ideal, he falters. When Jack states "'You'd like to see the power of money, the power of capital, *broke*,'" Somers replies: "'Theoretically, yes. Actually, I really don't know'" (41). His response remains skeptically rational; he is sensible and cautious about the actual enforcement of utopian ideals. Jack's endeavor to claim Somers' complete loyalty similarly receives a cautious and noncommital response. Jack wants, as he tells Somers, to "*trust you with everything*" (52), but Somers replies that he doesn't understand him: "*Everything*! It means so much, that it means nothing" (52). Time after time, Richard Somers feels the urge to pledge himself to "the cause," but ends by realizing that "he couldn't. Not quite. Something stopped him" (102). "He had come to the decision, or to the knowledge that mating or comradeship were contrary to his destiny. He would never pledge himself to Jack, nor to this venture in which Jack was concerned" (105).

Somers is never completely entranced by any absolute demand made by either political program in the novel. At the height of his attraction to Kangaroo, he is still able to view him objectively as "so absolute" (112). Kangaroo's view of people as "my children" implies not the love that he claims he feels for them, but the manipulation that he will exert on their irresponsible natures. Somers senses this manipulative note in Kangaroo's claim of love, and defines precisely what his followers lack and why they – like the authoritarian personality – are susceptible to political manipulation: "'They haven't got the last everlasting central bit of soul, solitary soul, that makes a man himself'" (131). And he rationally and skeptically persists in a demand for fact. Kangaroo's charismatic promises of ideal love are not enough to convince him: "Where is one carried to when one is carried away?" (131). Somers demands that the mature individual must be independent, self-reliant and rationally alert. This demand denies Kangaroo's central dictum of salvation – one shared by all absolutist political regimes – that "folks be happy again unconsciously, instead of unhappy consciously" (118). Such an "escape from freedom" is perhaps portrayed best fictionally in Dostoyevsky's "Grand Inquisitor" chapter in *The Brothers Karamazov*. It is the central irony of utopia: to enact the ideal requires a loss of selfhood and individual freedom. Kangaroo's demand is that "Either you are with me … or you cease to exist for me" (212-13), but Somers recoils from "this all-in- all thing" (334), realizing that it would imprison rather than liberate him. Instead, Somers recognizes a central liberal tenet that secures individual freedom at all costs: "Life makes no absolute statement: the true life makes no absolute statement. Life is so wonderful and complex, and *always* relative" (272-3).

Kangaroo, then, is a novel that demonstrates a basic sympathy for the working class. It is also a novel in which Lawrence works out his own ambivalence towards socialism and the authoritarian political structure represented by Kangaroo's party. Though both systems express a utopian ideal, Somers finally decides that he cannot support either of them. The authoritarian nature of Jack Callcott becomes representative, in this novel, of the authoritarian-fascistic nature of the party he belongs to. Lawrence's conception of utopia is more personal than either of the options indicated in this novel. *Kangaroo* is therefore an intermediate novel, leading to the political utopia of *The Plumed Serpent*.

Chapter 7

Fascism and Authoritarianism in *The Plumed Serpent*

If Lawrence views the working classes as portrayed in *Aaron's Rod* (1922) in a primarily positive and sympathetic manner, he has become more ambivalent toward them by the time he writes *Kangaroo* (1923). In *Aaron's Rod* he praises the Italian peasants' *"looseness"; in Kangaroo* he still shows the working men of Australia as friendly and open on the one hand, but also as overly assertive and bullying on the other. By the time Lawrence wrote *The Plumed Serpent* (1926), however, a more pervasive change of view had occurred: Kate shows contempt and fear for the Mexican peasant who sits on her feet at the bull fight, and her perception would also appear to be Lawrence's at this point.

This reversal in attitude towards the working classes parallels Lawrence's changing perception of himself – a changing self-image – throughout the three novels. Lawrence's two main characters in *Aaron's Rod*, Aaron and Lilly, *are* from the working class, echoing Diana Trilling's earlier observation that Lawrence chose protagonists who resembled himself. As such, they are patronized and treated in a condescending manner by the upper classes throughout that novel. But *The Plumed Serpent* has Kate, born of an aristocratic family, as the protagonist. The social structure that Lawrence encounters in Mexico is also very different from that of England, and even that of the earlier novels, *Aaron's Rod* and *Kangaroo*. The "working class" that Lawrence emerged from in England is defined differently in Mexico. Lawrence uses Kate as the mouthpiece for some of his own experiences, showing the contempt and hatred of the Mexican working classes toward her as one of the "rich":

> The rich class was a freak class, like dogs with two heads or calves with five legs. To be looked upon, not with envy, but with the slow, undying antagonism and curiosity which "normals" have toward "freaks." (*Plumed Serpent* 233)

Kate is astounded to find herself viewed this way, since she is poor by European standards: "To her, who had nothing, *could* never have anything, Kate was one of that weird class, the rich" (233). Thus, there is a reversal of class roles in this novel: bullying by the upper classes through patronage and condescension has given way to bullying by the Mexican peasant.

This reversal in some part points to a shift in Lawrence's social and political view. In 1921 he saw socialism as the most feasible political platform, if it could only be implemented properly (*Movements* 316-17). Equality of man is the ideal. But by 1926, having experienced socialist uprisings and revolutions, Lawrence is critical of a political program that appears inevitably to result in bloodshed and chaos. He also points out in *The Plumed Serpent* what he sees as the central flaw in socialism, once it has been implemented: that it results in an empty, mechanical society, a lack of vitality and spirit. The imagination does not blossom under socialist regimes. *The Plumed Serpent* depicts disillusionment with socialism in practice, but it is worth noting that the utopian vision Lawrence offers by the end of the novel does not include the abolishment of socialism in Mexico. Rather, Lawrence's utopia is a combination of socialism politically and the Quetzalcoatlian movement religiously. Both movements are aligned in their opposition to the reactionary, fascist Knights of Cortes.

Lawrence's disillusionment with socialism is not difficult to understand within the context of the novel. Mexican socialism is a nationalistic socialism – a contradiction in terms – and Lawrence's utopian ideal extends beyond national borders at the very least:

> "When they forget all about the Patria and Mexico and all that stuff, they're as nice a people as you'd find. But as soon as they get national, they're just monkeys." (36)

Mexican nationalism hardly resembles "the brotherhood of man," as the Major's experience in the National Museum illustrates:

> "I walked into the National Museum the other day," said the Major quietly.... "I'd been there about ten minutes when somebody suddenly poked me on the shoulder. I turned round, and it was a lout in tight boots. *You spik English*? I said yes! Then he motioned me to take my hat off: I'd got to take my hat off. *What for*? said I, and I turned away and went on looking at their idols and things: ugliest set of stuff in the world, I believe. Then up came the fellow with the attendant – the attendant of course wearing his cap. They began gabbling that this was the National Museum, and I must take off my hat to their national monuments. Imagine it: those dirty

> stones! I laughed at them and jammed my hat on tighter and walked out. They are really only monkeys, when it comes to nationalism." (36)

The absolutist bullying of such nationalism is repugnant to Kate, who wonders, "What does nationalism and all that rubbish matter, really!" (182). The criticisms found throughout the novel are aimed directly at the nationalism that masquerades as socialism, while implicitly denying the idealism of the program.

Lawrence also establishes the atmosphere of constant insecurity and chaos that accompanies the inauguration of the new Socialist regime. Montes, the Laborite leader, attempts to gain support, while General Angulo tries to gain control of the army (35). That such a political situation is fearsome and threatening is clear, but Lawrence especially underlines the violent nature of such regimes. A labour victory is "just freedom to commit crime" (30), since the absolute nature of national socialism will not tolerate dissenting views: "The Labourites … marched to the Hotel Francia to shoot all the gringoes and the Gachupines. The hotel manager had pluck enough to harangue them, and they went off to the next hotel. When the man came out there to talk to them, they shot him before he got a word out" (35-36). Bolshevism is clearly tied to chaotic violence throughout the novel, recalling the fearful "male slashing sound" of the socialist mob in *Aaron's Rod* (220). It "smashes your house or your business or your skull" (*Plumed Serpent* 44).

The high-flown slogans of equality and brotherhood are not achieved in practice. Instead, such a regime manipulates the masses of people with "pious catchwords, to catch the poor" (*PS* 111). The socialist agitators "all talk so nobly beforehand. If only their deeds followed their words" (34). But Lawrence especially criticizes the spiritual emptiness created by this regime. The artist in Lawrence finds the propagandistic art of the Mexican socialists repugnant, since the common people are used as symbols for "these maniacal ideas of socialism, politics, and La Patria" (55). The young didactic artist "was as mechanical as a mousetrap. Very tedious" (55). He has adopted the abstract idealism of socialism but no longer recognizes the intrinsic value in either the human being or in art itself. Thus, his work portrays "flat Indians" as:

> symbols in the great script of modern socialism, they were figures of the pathos of the victims of modern industry and capitalism. That was all they were used for: symbols in the weary script of socialism and anarchy (54).

The central dilemma presented in the novel is voiced by Kate: "'How can you make a people free, if they *aren't* free'" (183). Socialism, nationalism, western democracy all attempt to improve the lot of mankind externally – socialism especially promises freedom from poverty and an equal distribution of goods. But Kate's point – and Lawrence's – is once again that an external reconstruction of life styles will not and cannot work unless there is a corresponding *internal* change in the human consciousness. Lawrence's underlying utopian tenet is that freedom cannot be imposed on masses of people if the individuals who comprise the mass are not intrinsically free. Don Ramón states this concept clearly, and in doing so dissociates his attempt to form a utopian society from the world of politics:

> "Politics, and all this *social* religion that Montes has got is like washing the outside of the egg, to make it look clean. But I, myself, I want to get inside the

> egg, right to the middle, to start it growing into a new bird." (210)

Such a transformation of human nature is utopian in origin: it relies on the belief that man's potential for a full, creative existence has been limited and repressed by external forces throughout the ages. Reich parallels Lawrence's belief that the potential for this kind of transformation is latent within the human consciousness, and that it must be reborn for man to survive. Kate rediscovers this latent creativity when she looks at Don Ramón, partly undressed, and extends her perception beyond the external appearance to his inner being, "forever still and clothe-less, and with another light about it, of a richer day than our paltry, prying, sneak-thieving day" (201). Don Ramón embodies the utopian goal that succeeds, at least in part, within this novel. Thus, Lawrence describes "a new world ... unfolding ... we turn to life; and from the clock to the sun and the stars, and from metal to membrane" (393-95). The new world as Lawrence describes it is an unreal, idealized pastoral, but no sooner does he envision this world positively, than he undercuts it with Kate's sometimes cynical and always independent view. Cipriano's instructions to his men also illustrate the basic contradiction inherent in utopian enactment: "Each company of a hundred must learn to act in perfect unison, freely and flexibly" (402). Human individuals acting in "perfect unison" are neither free nor flexible as individuals; rather, the individual resembles the bull let out into the ring at the beginning of the novel. He rushes out "blindly, as if from the dark," into the free space of the arena. But like the individual who has surrendered self responsibility to a totalitarian regime, he suddenly finds that he is "not free, but surrounded in an unknown way" (11). Lawrence tries, within the novel, to justify the loss of individuality by having Cipriano and Don Ramón admonish Kate for her strong ego and self-will: "'The individual, like the perfect being, does not and cannot exist, in the vivid world'" (426). But this rationale breaks down when it leads to Kate's amoral assumption of individual irresponsibility. Finally, if the individual does not have to make decisions and bear the burden of responsibility for his actions in life, all becomes relative, and consequently meaningless. Thus, Kate wonders: "What do I care if he kills people?… What do I care, what Cipriano Viedma does, or doesn't do? Or even what Kate Leslie does or doesn't do?" (431). Had Lawrence ended the novel at this point, with this denial of individual human worth, the utopianism embodied within the work would have remained absolute, irresponsible and finally immoral. But he did not end there, and in the remaining fifty-six pages, Kate constantly criticizes the utopia.

Kate senses the underside of the hero-worship amongst the Mexican people toward Ramón:

> Kate somehow felt their latent grudging. Perhaps they took more satisfaction in ultimately destroying their heroes, than in temporarily raising them high. The real perfect moment was when the hero was downed. (442)

Further, the Quetzalcoatlian utopia seems to work, but it takes constant preoccupation and will power to keep it working. Once again, Kate wonders at the:

> steady, urgent, efficient *will* which had to be exerted all the time. Everything was kept going by a heavy exertion of will. If once the will of the master broke, everything would break, and ruin would overtake

> the place almost at once. No real relaxation, ever.
> Always the sombre, insistent will. (444-45)

In an ironical reversal of authoritarian personality traits, Lawrence here portrays the utopian concept in the same terminology he earlier used to describe the repressed personalities of Gerald Crich and Jack Callcott. The utopia is held together entirely by the force of the will, or the superego; if the underlying violence of the repressed society should burst out, it would do so in a perverse and utterly destructive form. The individual microcosm has, in a sense, become the macrocosm in this novel.

Toward the end of the novel, Kate feels pressured to choose between her individual existence and a communal life with Cipriano and Ramón. She concludes that "I must have both" (484), which is, of course, the underlying contradiction in utopian practice, as she finds out. She *cannot* have both without counterfeiting something in herself: "'*What a fraud I am! I know all the time it is I who don't altogether want them. I want myself to myself. But I can fool them so they shan't find out*'" (486). Ramón recognizes her duplicity, and she reverts to the irresponsible plea with which the novel ends: "You won't let me go!" (487). But Kate is an individual, and therefore not a good follower; consequently, her submission to the communal utopia of Quetzalcoatl is unconvincing. Much like her early reaction of disgust for the "macho" all male atmosphere of the bull-fight at the beginning of the novel, Kate rebels against the authoritarian demands of Ramón's new order. While unthinking followers inevitably incorporate the qualities that have been defined as authoritarian, Kate utterly fails to do this. Rather than approaching life with stealth and hostility, she views it with "disinterested amusement" (42). She experiences three of the most vibrant, spontaneous exhibitions of emotion in the novel. She suffers over and identifies with the hurt, tortured bird, not, as others, "Blind to the creature as a soft, struggling thing finding its own fluttering way through life" (241). She feels the spirit and enjoyment of the horse dancing in the lake (357), and takes great pleasure at discovering the newly born baby donkey (477). Such spontaneity suggests a full, creative individual capable of both affection and love. Kate's natural vivacity constantly struggles to emerge, and she feels especially claustrophobic around "these mechanical connections. Every one of them, like Villiers, was like a cog-wheel in contact with which all one's workings were reversed" (113). Kate's central tenet becomes:

> *"Let me still believe in some human contact. Let it not be all cut off for me!*
>
> *...Give me the mystery and let the world live again for me!... And deliver me from man's automatism."* (113-14)

Kate does not desire the "mystical" as much as the joyful recognition of genuine "human contact." Such a "mystery" is identified with vitality and creativity.

Kate's spontaneous response to the life around her is gradually restricted more and more by the wilfulness of Ramón's utopia. She protests that there is, "at the centre of all things, a dark, momentous Will sending out its terrific rays and vibrations, like some vast octopus" (423). Lawrence has previously used the image of the octopus in *Kangaroo* to describe the too-demanding absolutist idealism of western democracy, "the *almost* automatic white octopus of the human ideal" (272). In both that novel and in *The Plumed Serpent*, the octopus is a negative image that indicates the grasping, possessive nature of repressive, conventional idealism, and its deadening effect on the individual, cancelling any expression of spontaneity. Kate cannot reconcile her refreshing desire for the "mystery" of renewed human contact with the restrictiveness of "the Godhead as a sheer and awful Will" (*PS* 424).

Kate is also characterized – repeatedly – as a nonconformist strong enough to stand apart from conventional standards. Lawrence describes her variously as having "her own unconventional way.... She was never *in* any society" (42); "She was never 'smart'" (63). During the Rain Dance, she is the one individual who, however much intrigued, does "not lift her arms" (217). The whole communal role urged upon her is distasteful to her because of her strongly individualistic stance: "'I dislike the masses of people – anywhere.... So how could I pretend to join any – any – any sort of Salvation Army?'" (274). She exhibits a healthy rational skepticism and sensitivity throughout the book, being suspicious of supernatural beliefs: "I never understood mystical things. They make me uneasy" (406). She is not readily gullible, finding that "people – yes, they are all monkeys to me" (275). Most of all, she quickly perceives manipulation by others, especially by the men in her life. She rebelliously states at one point: "I am sick of these men putting names over me" (407). Obviously, she is angered by such names that serve only to identify her as a possession or property of the male. The Quetzalcoatlian utopia similarly demands the submission of the female, a demand that Kate finds hard to swallow: "Where was the woman, in this terrible interchange of will? Truly only a subservient, instrumental thing" (424). Kate's reaction to the absolute demands of the Quetzalcoatlian utopia is one of indignation; she views it as coercive and deceptive and decides that she "would not have this thing put over her! She would break free, and show them!" (472). Although she appears to adore Don Ramón, she decides finally that he is "too abstract and overbearing for me.... Ramón needs far too much submission from a woman, to please me" (475).

Two incidents in the novel do portray Kate as exhibiting authoritarian traits. At one point the narrator points out Kate's élitist pride in her aristocratic birth:

> Kate was of a proud old family. She had been brought up with the English-Germanic idea of the *intrinsic* superiority of the hereditary aristocrat. Her blood was different from the common blood, another, finer fluid. (456)

Yet this élitist pride – needing to belong to "the right sort" – is directly contradicted by the narrator earlier in the novel when he asserts that "Kate was no snob. Man or woman, she cared nothing about the social class" (87). When she encounters an inebriated group of natives, she is "a bit afraid" (48) of them, but feels more sympathy with them than with the Burlaps, that "bloodless, acidulous couple from the Middle-West, with their nasty whiteness" (48), whom she has just left. The pride she takes in her aristocratic birth does not prevent her from relating to the human beings around her, irrespective of class.

The second authoritarian trait she exhibits, at least at one point, is an underlying desire for violence. She is simultaneously attracted and repelled by Don Ramón, as she stares at the "soft, cream-brown skin of his back!" (201). Attracted by the sensual nudity, she finds herself repelled by his remote arrogance:

> In spite of herself, she could not help imagining a knife stuck between those pure, male shoulders. If

> only to break the arrogance of their remoteness. (200-201)

While the underlying, repressed violence breaks through Kate's consciousness, this in itself is not necessarily authoritarian. The importance of self-understanding, of questioning and examining the source of the eruption of crude violence differentiates the "liberal" from the authoritarian personality. Jim Bricknell, in *Aaron's Rod*, immediately covers up the violence of his punch at Lilly by protestations of affection for Lilly, thus projecting the violent act onto the victim ("it's all his fault"). Kate does not react in this projective way; she is suffused with guilt and shame and accepts fully the enormity of her aggression:

> The moment Kate had imagined a knife between his shoulders, her heart shrank with grief and shame, and a great stillness came over her. Better to take the hush into one's heart, and the sharp, preying beams out of one's eyes. Better to lapse away from one's own prying, assertive self, into the soft, untrespassing self, to whom nakedness is neither shame nor excitement, but clothed like a flower in its own deep, soft consciousness, beyond cheap awareness. (201)

Kate experiences the moment of aggression as a cheapening of the self, of the human soul's sensitivity and awareness of a fellow human. She exhibits complete awareness of her aggression and consciously feels shame. This ability to self-question and self-admonish is, in fact, indicative of the liberal rather than the authoritarian personality: "the extremely unprejudiced individual tends to manifest a greater readiness to become aware of unacceptable tendencies and impulses in himself" (Adorno 474). Kate's momentary aggression at this point must also be placed against another incident in the novel. Her agony over the Mexican boy's torture of a crippled bird shows her fine sensitivity to all living creatures outside of herself. Here she offers a damning criticism of human insensitivity:

> The curious void.
>
> He could not see that the bird was a real living creature with a life of its own.... Blind to the creature as a soft, struggling thing finding its own fluttering way through life. (241)

Kate's sensitivity is supported by a good deal of common sense. Upon seeing the Mexican peasants throwing stones at cattle to make them move, she retorts: "Drive it sensibly" (241). Above all, her clear thinking reiterates a basic Lawrencian tenet found throughout his works, namely that "One must keep a certain balance" (55), which asserts the necessity of individual responsibility and rational sense. She preserves a healthy skepticism, a sense of balance and fear of extremism amidst the absolute demands of Ramón's regime:

> At the same time, as is so often the case with any spell, it did not bind her completely. She was spell-bound, but not utterly acquiescent. In one corner of her soul was revulsion and a touch of nausea. (423)

Her intrinsic self remains questioning, non-conforming and never totally subservient. She "would always be a good deal alone" (460). These characteristics certainly place Kate in the "liberal" category rather than defining her as an authoritarian.

There are, however, authoritarian characters in *The Plumed Serpent*, and Kate, through her commonsensical astuteness, discerns who they are:

> Kate sat by the window, and laughed a little. The primeval woman inside her laughed to herself, for

> she had known all the time about the two thieves on the cross with Jesus; the bullying, marauding thief of the male in his own rights, and the much more subtle, cold, sly, charitable thief of the woman in *her* own rights, forever chanting her beggar's whine about the love of God and the God of pity. (381)

Kate here pinpoints Dona Carlota and Don Cipriano as the "bullies" of the novel.

Dona Carlota is, on the surface, the conventional wife and mother, submissive, timid and eager to please. She is a "good" woman, a devoted Christian and intimidated by Ramón's attempt to begin a new, strange, religious movement. She is not a full character in the sense that Kate is; Lawrence does not develop her as fully or with the same complexity; more to the point, there is not much substance to develop in a character like Carlota's. Her strong adherence to conventions indicates the inner dearth of creative life in this woman. The established, institutionalized religion *must* be right; she refuses to entertain more flexible theories of rebirth, and instead condemns her husband's eccentricity as "such *nonsense*. How dare he!" (180). Her sense of conventionality is outraged as well by her husband's new peasant attire. The Carrascos are landowners, and Carlota's need to be differentiated as "the right sort" is foiled by her husband's humble costume:

> "You didn't know my husband had become one of the people – a real peon – a Senor Peon, like Count Tolstoy became a Senor Moujik?" said Dona Carlota, with an attempt at raillery. (184)

Later she asks Kate whether "Ramón is wise, to wear the peasants' clothes, and the huaraches?" (189). The word "wise" has two connotations here: on the surface, Dona Carlota seems fearful that her husband's attire may incite the surrounding peasantry to revolt. Her real outrage, however, is the pseudo-righteous indignation of the smug upper class, the outrage against her husband identifying himself, and by association her, with the peasantry.

While Carlota is extremely "moral," her religiosity is not accompanied by true compassion or flexibility; she exhibits, instead, a fanatical, absolutist tone: "'Could *you* give up the Blessed Virgin? – I could sooner die!'" (207). Kate's earliest impression of Carlota was of "an intense, almost exalted Catholic. She exalted herself in the Church, and in her work for the Cuna" (172). The word "exalted" implies Carlota's hunger for power rather than religious ecstasy. Indeed, Carlota's emphasis on the need for charity becomes a disguise for her desire for power. There is little spontaneous compassion in her. Instead, "she loved now with her *will*: as the white world now tends to do. She became filled with charity: that cruel kindness" (228). Cipriano sees through the charitable image when he later taunts her as "you impeccable wife, you just woman" (381). Similarly, he equates charity with a *lack* of compassion, as if the two go together naturally: "'You have been charitable and compassionless to the man you called your own'" (380). Charity maintains the *status quo*; by helping only a little, the lower classes are kept in their place and the real problems of poverty are ignored. Kate is initially impressed with Carlota's orphanage work, but she senses the futility of it:

> Kate listened with uneasy interest. She felt there was so much real human feeling in this Mexican charity: she was almost rebuked. Perhaps what Dona Carlota was doing was the best that could be done, in this

> half-wild, helpless country. At the same time, it was such a forlorn hope, it made one's heart sink. (172-73)

Dona Carlota is further characterized as willful; even her love "was now nearly all will" (171). She is described as totally lacking in spontaneity, substituting instead her willfulness: "Even as the spontaneous mystery died in her, the will hardened, till she was nothing but a will: a lost will" (228). And again:

> Life had done its work on one more human being, quenched the spontaneous life and left only the will. Killed the god in the woman, or the goddess, and left only charity, with a will. (229)

Even Carlota's love for Don Ramón is presented as willful and manipulative. He is her property, her possession. When she visits him in his room, "she sat down on the unmade bed, as if asserting her natural right. And in the same way she glanced at his naked breast – as if asserting her natural right" (229). Ramón feels her manipulative treatment of him, as if he were an object that she owned; there is no genuine interaction or equality in their meetings:

> She claimed him and he restrained himself in resistance. Even his very naked breast, when Carlota was there, was self-conscious and assertively naked. But then that was because she claimed it as her property. (278)

Carlota's perception of Ramón as her property is further borne out in her disillusionment with him: "He was not what I would have him be" (380), she states, and reveals simultaneously her inability to recognize him as an individual human being in his own right.

That such a moralistic, conventional and seemingly timid character should conform to the pattern of the authoritarian personality is further supported by the surprising element of repressed violence and hatred present in Carlota. Ramón bears the primary brunt of her manipulation, and he best senses the deadly anger in her toward him. If she cannot have an obedient, conformist, Christian Ramón, she would rather negate him. Ramón senses this death- wish in her: "'Carlota … how happy you would be if you could wear deep, deep mourning for me. – I shall not give you this happiness'" (229).

When Carlota breaks down into insanity, she betrays her violent hatred of Ramón by asking God to kill him:

> Her voice had gathered strength till it rang out metallic and terrible.
>
> "Almighty God, take his life from him, and save his soul." (376-77)

Carlota is self-righteous even in her hatred, believing that she alone understands what goodness and love are; Ramón is better off dead so he can no longer upset the established and conventional order of her life. Ramón sees through Carlota's hypocrisies and realizes the aggression underlying her surface charity:

> "the white Anti-Christ of Charity, and socialism, and politics, and reform, will only succeed in finally destroying [Mexico]… – You, Carlota, with your charity works and your *pity* … surcharged with pity for living men … but really with hate." (230)

While Carlota is a stereotyped pattern of fanaticism, rather than a complex human being, Lawrence creates a more subtle and complex character in Don Cipriano. Cipriano is a foil to Don Ramón, and assures a Lawrencian balance of opposites in the novel. Ramón resembles a meek and gentle Jesus too much to achieve this balance by himself; he shows very little human ambivalence and primality, and would simply become another strangling "white octopus of the human ideal" (*Kangaroo* 272), another form of moralistic aggression were it not for Cipriano's countering force. Cipriano ostensibly represents or provides the power/strength leadership polarity to counterpoise Ramón's altruism and love, though Ramón remains Cipriano's superior and always has the final word. If these two characters create the balance of love and power for the utopian society that is formed in *The Plumed Serpent*, they also embody very different, though still opposite, psychological characteristics.

Lawrence introduces Don Cipriano in a way that is reminiscent of his initial portrayal of Gerald Crich in *Women in Love*. Gerald's stealth and instinctive hostility to the world around him were symbolized in the image of the northern wolf. Cipriano, portrayed throughout the novel with the same qualities of stealth, is symbolically identified with the image of the southern snake. Both characters exhibit the underlying hostility and violence of the wild animal carefully repressed under a strong will and conventional exterior. Cipriano, says Lawrence:

> spoke in a peculiar quiet voice, rather suppressed, and his quick eyes glanced at her, and at his surroundings, like those of a man perpetually suspecting an ambush. But his face had a certain silent hostility, under his kindness. (20)

Lawrence describes him, at different times, as having "watchful, calculating eyes ... opposing her in an animal way" (40), and a pleasant conventional expression which does not really reflect any inner warmth: "An amused little smile quickly lit his face, though his eyes did not smile. They looked at her with a black, sharp look" (41). Like Gerald's conventional sense of decorum, Cipriano observes social etiquette, but observes only the form without being truly involved in the essential human interaction:

> Cipriano, on the other hand, remained mute and disciplined, perfectly familiar with the tea-table routine, superficially quite at ease, but underneath remote and unconnected. (42)

His eyes are especially indicative of the way in which he views his outside environment, alternately described as "wary" (87), "insolent black eyes" (88), "a curious, lurking sort of insolence" (205), or "the black eyes of Cipriano glanced at her in hostility" (280). At times Kate is repelled and frightened by his presence, which "seemed sinister to her, almost repellent" (260). The inner fear with which he approaches life lies just beneath his wilfully composed exterior. Kate feels that "he seemed to be watching, watching for something" (338). Even in the midst of a group of people, Cipriano, although conventional and proper in his behavior, "stayed outside the conversation altogether, in a dusky world of his own, apart and secretly hostile" (344). The atmosphere of human interchange does not touch his essence; his projected image is, like Gerald's, solely concerned with form. His conventional self-image functions mechanically, repressing the emotional turbulence within him:

> Curious he was! With a sort of glaze of the ordinary world on top, and underneath a black volcano with hell knows what depths of lava. And talking half-abstractedly from his glazed, top self, the words came out small and quick, and he was always hesitating, was saying: No? It wasn't himself at all talking. (339)

Adorno emphasized conventionality as an authoritarian attribute because authoritarians "need external support – whether this be offered by authorities or by public opinion – in order to find some assurance concerning what is right and what is wrong" (476). Conventionality in this context includes "Good manners, attainment of success and status, self- control, and poise" (478). Cipriano clearly exhibits these conventional attributes, yet Kate senses the inner psychological vacuum underlying the correct exterior. It is equally important for Cipriano to be identified on the "right" or winning side. He is the élitist out of a necessity for survival, or so he thinks. He projects himself as a leader of the masses, but at the same time, his contempt for the people is noticeable in his comment that "These people are nothing if not perverse, nowadays" (272).

This comment is made in response to Don Ramón's concern that the Quetzalcoatlian hymns will not be read by the people because the priests are forbidding them. Cipriano's response shows a contempt for the perversity of the people who will read the hymns, rather than a positive belief in their courage to disobey the priests. Kate recognizes the negativism and cynicism of Cipriano's view of the peasants. It is, in fact, an ironic inconsistency of this novel to find Kate, a life-affirming individual, aligning herself with a man who is so much her opposite, especially since she so often and consistently exposes his psychological deficiencies. Some of her remarks and thought patterns regarding Cipriano are framed in the weary, cynical tone that in itself connotes a negative character. Kate thinks to herself with some wryness that "Here at last he was not a *will*" (430), but this comment merely points out that willfulness is his usual mode. Similarly, she notes that "Cipriano, for once, was faithful" (442), which does not denote loyalty as his usual behavior.

In fact, at this particular point, he is faithful only to himself as the semi-divine Huitzilopochtli.

Cipriano initially appears to support rational sense and scientific knowledge in his explanation of why he rejected Roman Catholicism:

> "I used to think it was the images of Jesus, and the Virgin, and the Saints, that were doing everything in the world.... Only in England I learned about the laws of life, and some science. And then when I knew why the sun rose and set, and how the world really was, I felt quite different." (73)

Here Cipriano offers a valid argument against his former religious belief in a supernatural agency. In the same passage, he tells Kate about his god-father, Bishop Severn, Bishop of Oaxaca, who looked after Cipriano's education. Cipriano describes the bishop in highly positive language, as "a very well-known man … very rich, too" (72). Again, "The Bishop was a very good man, very kind" whom he liked "very much" (73). Cipriano is clearly glorifying the bishop's character, as well as exhibiting a superstitious belief in the bishop's supernatural power; at the same time Cipriano explains how he has rejected religion in preference for "the laws of life, and some science":

> "When I was a little boy I came running to my father, when the Bishop was there, with something in my hands – so!" – and he made a cup of his hand. "I don't remember. This is what they tell me. I was a small child – three or four years of age – somewhere there. What I had in my hands was a yellow scorpion, one of the small ones, very poisonous, no?… Well, the Bishop was talking to my father, and he saw what I had got before my father did. So he told me at once, to put the scorpion in his hat – the Bishop's hat, no? Of course I did what he

> told me, and I put the scorpion in his hat, and it did not bite me. If it had stung me I should have died, of course" (72-73).

Cipriano's life is, thus, saved by the Bishop's magical power. There is a ready submissiveness to the bishop's command to put the scorpion into his hat. While the incident itself happened to a three or four-year-old child, and thus would not necessarily carry any external significance, it attains an importance and carries emotional connotations through Cipriano's memory, which embues the occurrence with the magical elements that he has since come to identify with Catholicism and with the bishop. Throughout his later life, he tells Kate, "I felt I must do what my god-father wished" (73), and "I couldn't marry, because I always felt my god-father was there, and I felt I had promised him to be a priest – all those things, you know" (74). Cipriano has submitted fully to the bishop until the latter's death, which makes it all the more astonishing later on in the novel to witness the vituperative hatred Cipriano exhibits towards Roman Catholicism:

> "The old Jesuit, he only wants to keep his job and his power, and prevent the heart's beating. I know them. All they treasure, even more than their money, is their centipede power over the frightened people, especially over the women."
>
> "I didn't know you hated them," laughed Ramón.
>
> "Waste no more breath on them, my dear one," said Cipriano. (292)

Cipriano's glorification of the Bishop and his willing submission to his wishes during his life seem inconsistent with this later outburst. Under the auspices of the church, the bishop *has* helped Cipriano, saving him from a life of peasant drudgery. But Cipriano exhibits only the extremes of stereotyped glorification/obedient submission on the one hand, and violent hatred on the other. Similarly, the authoritarian may exhibit a:

> stereotyped, rigid glorification of the parents, with strong resentment and feelings of victimization occasionally breaking through on the overt level.... Usually, however, only admiration for the parent is accepted by the subject. The underlying hostility has to be kept ego-alien for several reasons: it is too strong to be fully admitted; and it interferes with the desire to be taken care of by the parents. This conflict leads to a submission to parental authority on the surface and a resentment underneath which, although not admitted, is the more active under the guise of mechanisms of displacement. (Adorno 357)

Cipriano's intense ambivalence towards his god-father is an area of his psychological make-up that he seems unable to question or understand. The extremes in his personality point out his inability to examine his own psychological make-up, or to even think rationally and clearly. Combined with this inability is Cipriano's need for a strong leader or authority. Kate goads Cipriano into admitting that his submission to Ramón is not based on love or on the belief in Ramón's mission; Cipriano's submission is based on one factor only, and that is power:

> " ... you don't believe in him. You think it is like everything else, a sort of game.... You don't *really* believe, in anything."
>
> "How not believe? I not believe in Ramón? – Well, perhaps not, in that way of kneeling before him and spreading out my arms and shedding tears on his feet. But I – I believe in him, too. Not in your way, but in mine. I tell you why. Because he has the

> power to compel me. If he hadn't the power to *compel* me, how should I believe?"
>
> "It is a queer sort of belief that is compelled," she said.
>
> "How else should one believe, except by being compelled? I like Ramón for that, that he can compel me. When I grew up, and my godfather could not compel me to believe, I was very unhappy. It made me very unhappy. – But Ramón *compels* me, and that is very good. It makes me very happy, when I know I can't escape." (224)

The need for submission to power figures is exclusively characteristic of the authoritarian personality. The insecurity of such a personality "leads to the acceptance of absolute authority and to a value for authoritarian forms of social interaction." Further, what authoritarians "admire most in others is power, strength, authority, rugged masculinity. While the aggressive-assertive needs of authoritarian individuals are the most conspicuous ... the dependent-submissive needs are equally if not more important" (599-600). Cipriano's real preoccupation in the novel is not so much with Kate; it is with his glorification of Ramón as his leader.

Ramón himself is not emphatically authoritarian with his own sons, nor is the Ramón-Carlota marriage exclusively patriarchal. The emphasis on patriarchal authority is, therefore, most evident in Don Cipriano's intense need to "be compelled," to submit to a power figure above him. Cipriano has, in essence, projected his need for an authority figure, which was previously fulfilled by the bishop, onto Ramón. Wilhelm Reich points to this same pattern:

> In the figure of the father the authoritarian state has its representation in every family, so that the family

> becomes its most important instrument of power.... And he reproduces his subservient attitude toward authority in his children, particularly in his sons. (53)

The true authoritarian patriarchal pattern of submission to a dominating power figure is very evident in Don Cipriano. Don Ramón *as* a leader is not harshly strict, nor aggressively masculine. In fact, Ramón as a natural father is gentle, teasing and patiently resigned in face of his sons' condemnation, hardly the typical authoritarian disciplinarian.

Cipriano, on the other hand, exhibits an intense and slavish desire to be dominated by a higher, more powerful figure, one that *compels* his loyalty and behavior which, in turn, relieves him of the burden of responsibility and decision-making. Also, such compulsion *must* be controlled by a *more* powerful authority than his own – this coincides exactly with his enormous respect *for* power and authority. The bishop's authority is shaken for him by an English education, and he ends by vehemently rejecting his fallen idol. Similarly, Don Ramón is astute enough to realize how, as Cipriano's superior, he had better guard against revealing any human vulnerability, since this would disillusion Cipriano, who would reject him just as decisively as he did the bishop; Ramón admits to himself that "Cipriano would betray him. Given one little vulnerable chink" (212). Ramón simultaneously reveals his own introspective quality by acknowledging to himself, "what man can be invulnerable?" (212).

Don Cipriano's respect for power and authority are in direct relation to his own desire for power; it is difficult, in fact, to understand what other benefits the

Quetzalcoatlian movement have for him. Like Jack Callcott before him, he enjoys being boss:

> "he wants to be in command of the soldiers.... He has great power with his regiments.... He has that power ... to make many others want to follow them and fight for them." (173-74)

Lawrence emphasizes Cipriano's military characteristics throughout the novel, but the military image is not of a patriot so much as of a mercenary. Personal ambition and willfulness are the primary motives driving this soldier:

> Cipriano ... slipped back into the inevitable Mexican General, fascinated by the opportunity for furthering his own personal ambition and imposing his own personal will. (278)

Even in his treatment of the Roman Catholic bishop of the West, he asserts his power through the thinly veiled threat of physical violence: "'Adios, Senor!' said Cipriano, clicking his spurs, and putting his hand on his sword as he turned to the door" (292).

Cipriano's total presence as a military general "exude[d] pride and arrogant authority" which "were not to be laughed at" (293). The underlying stealth with which Cipriano moves within his environment is supported by a willfulness that controls his reactions in all situations. As it is for Gerald Crich before him, the universe is a hostile place for Cipriano; his "self" is an unknown reservoir of confusing emotions, which threaten to break out in aggressive ways. His conventional image and surface control are enforced by the constant strength of his will. The power that he achieves is felt by Kate to be a product of this unrelenting and watchful will: "he had a curious power. Almost she could *see* the black fume of power which he emitted ... the heavy power of the *will* that lay unemerged in his blood" (340). His relationship with Kate bears out his willfulness; he must be the undisputed boss, the dominant partner at all times. She views him at various times as "the old dominant male" (341) or "the master" (343). In their relationship, she soon realizes that his attitude to her as the female is totally unbending, demanding complete submission: "[h]e would never woo; she saw this" (342). Their heterosexual relationship demands "submission absolute ... the supreme passivity" (342) on Kate's part. Such submission is really unquestioning obedience, and recalls again Reich's emphasis on fascism beginning in and constantly being reinforced by the patriarchal family unit. The blind obedience of the woman to the man is a microcosmic version of Cipriano's own need to submit to an absolute system of leadership. With Kate, however, he "could not bear even to be the least bit thwarted" (365). At other times Lawrence describes him as "very sharp and imperious in his orders" (352). Altogether, Cipriano is very often described negatively – as a thoroughly unlikable person:

> Kate looked at him, and mistrusted him. In the long run he was nobody's man. He was that old, masterless Pan male, that could not even conceive of service; particularly the service of mankind. He saw only glory; the black mystery of glory consummated. And himself like a wind of glory. (344)

This description pinpoints Cipriano's utter selfishness and self-absorption. He is not truly interested in the idealism of the utopia; unlike Ramón, his concern is not with improving man's nature and creative life; rather, it is with the amount of power and glory he can accumulate. Such a megalomaniacal personality exhibits surprising pettiness in asserting his power. The smallest occurrences *have* to be under his control; he virtually *cannot* recognize another human being's feelings. Kate's agonizing decision to escape from Mexico for awhile angers him so – since she is acting independently of him – that he thinks of using police force to stop her:

> He was thinking, superficially, that if he liked, he could use the law and have her prevented from leaving the country – or even from leaving Sayula – since she was legally married to him. (479)

The fact that such physical force would not really change or control her feelings and thoughts is immaterial to Cipriano. He views Kate solely as an instrument for his own use. Throughout the novel, Kate feels treated as an object, manipulated and coerced by Cipriano: "Kate could not help feeling that it was a sort of intense, blind *ambition*, of which she was partly an object" (258). Their interpersonal connection is solely physical – Cipriano is incapable of recognizing another human individual's nature outside of himself. Kate perceives that his "desire seemed curiously impersonal, physical, and yet not personal at all" (259). She is at times mesmerized by his dominant attitude towards her, but because of her strong sense of self, she can recognize the manipulation: "Yet surely, surely he was only putting his will over her?" (260).

Ramón likewise discerns Cipriano's manipulative use of other human beings. His analysis of Cipriano's "attraction" to Kate is acute, and it illustrates neither love nor affection on Cipriano part: "'He will let you go when you've had enough; and he's had enough. He is a *general* and a very great *jefe*'" (280). When Kate admits to Don Ramón that Cipriano "'just wants something of me ... he would never meet me. He would never come forward himself, to meet me. He would come to take something from me and I should have to let him'" (297), Ramón immediately understands what she means. The area where Cipriano would not "meet" her is the psychological-spiritual realm of human interconnectedness, and Cipriano has nothing in this realm with which to connect. Ramón here sums up his staunch disciple as the person he really is: "a man who wants just to take, without giving, ... a creature of prey" (298). He exposes Cipriano's inability to love and simultaneously admits his own cynicism toward Cipriano.

By implication, then, if Ramón recognizes Cipriano's inability to care for Kate in a strong, mature way, he is certainly aware of the superficial level of Cipriano's devotion towards himself. Kate's disillusionment with the absolute demands of the utopia is precisely reflected in her discomfort under Cipriano's domination. At one point, she says: "You treat me as if I had no life of my own" (406-7). At another point in the novel, the narrator tells us that "Cipriano could not see Kate as a being by herself" (425). Her instrumentality to Cipriano is underlined and emphasized in passages such as the following:

> The tiny star of her very self he would never see. To him she was but the answer to his call.... Alone, she was nothing.... As an isolated individual, she had little or no significance. (425)
>
> The little general, the strutting little soldier, he wanted Kate: just for moments. He did not really want to marry her. He wanted the moments, no more. She was to give him his moments, and then he was off again, to his army, to his men. (437)

This description of Cipriano is especially derogatory.

While Cipriano's manipulative use of Kate is underlined throughout *The Plumed Serpent*, Lawrence also presents Kate herself as manipulative, using the male as instrumentally as he uses her. This female quality is similarly perceived in Lottie and Fanny in *Aaron's Rod*. But in *The Plumed Serpent*, Lawrence distinguishes between two kinds of manipulation. While Kate acutely recognizes and resents the way Cipriano coldly uses her, Cipriano only *partially* acknowledges his use of Kate. Lawrence indicates here that Cipriano's egotism and self-centeredness prevent him from perceiving someone else's manipulation. Thus, Cipriano "knew this too: though perhaps not well enough" (425).

There are other gaps in Cipriano's thinking. While he praises the British education that helped to de-mystify religion for him, his thought processes are never clearly rational or questioning. He is described as "indifferent and fatalistic" (75). In a discussion with Kate about the desirability of peace, Cipriano questions its value. Kate replies:

> "... there is another peace: the peace that passes all understanding. Don't you know that?"
>
> "I don't think I do," he said.
>
> "What a pity!" she cried.
>
> "Ah!" he said. "You want to teach me! But to me it is different. Each man has two spirits in him. The one is like the early morning in the time of rain, very quiet, and sweet, moist, no? – with the mocking bird singing, and birds flying about, very fresh. And the other is like the dry season, the steady, strong

> hot light of the day, which seems as if it will never change."
>
> "But you like the first better," she cried.
>
> "I don't know!" he replied. "The other lasts longer."
>
> "I am sure you like the fresh morning better," she said.
>
> "I don't know! I don't know!"
>
> He smiled a crumpled sort of smile, and she could tell he really did *not* know. (204)

Cipriano has very limited ability to examine and understand himself; he has no desire to probe his inner nature, and categorizes the time spent with a female as the "time of rain"; conversely, the "dry season" in his dichotomy is illustrative of power, of when he "wants to be a very big man, and master of all the people" (205). What is interesting about Cipriano's "rainy" and "dry" seasons is that the personality here is so strictly dichotomized into extremes of tenderness and succour versus a harsh self-control and disciplined abstinence exercised to attain power. A more balanced psychological make-up would at least include overlapping areas and boundaries. A creative, fulfilled personality would certainly have the two extremes permeating each other throughout, so that there is discipline with tenderness. Cipriano's confusion finally resolves into a greater trust in the "dry season," where no respite exists, nor succour, but where the intensity of his primal unconscious – carefully and constantly repressed – is the ever-present reality. Because he lacks self-understanding, his primal urge for power is the over-riding reality and value in his life. As with Gerald Crich before him, the female is a relief from such internal psychological pressure, but the recognition of her as a distinct individual is beyond both Gerald and Cipriano. Lawrence describes Cipriano as totally impervious to human contact: "Nothing came forth from him to meet with one outside. All oblivious of the outside, all for himself" (222).

Cipriano's lack of introspection and affection is again obvious in the blunt statement, "There was no kindness in Cipriano" (343). The lack of human compassion is evident throughout Cipriano's relationship with Kate. He feels no desire or need to communicate with her; she is an object at his disposal. In this inability to love, he again resembles Gerald, although Lawrence seems to be even more definite and damning in his presentation of Cipriano's character. We may sympathize with Gerald at the end of *Women in Love*; Gudrun's viciousness helps to ensure such sympathy. But nowhere do we feel sorrow or sympathy for Cipriano. Lawrence has not made him attractive as a character, either physically or psychologically. One wonders how Kate *can* like him, because Lawrence – perhaps only unconsciously – does not like him and consistently portrays him as lacking or limited. It is possible that Lawrence attempts to punish the domineering independence of the modern woman in Kate by coupling her with this very rigid and limited male. Kate actually respects Ramón far more than she does Cipriano, admitting to herself that "Ramón [was] a greater man than Cipriano" (449). Cipriano blatantly uses Kate for his own satisfaction, never troubling about her feelings or responses: "His words said nothing; would never say anything ... impersonal.... Cipriano hardly talked to her at all" (352-3). At another point, Cipriano "did not look very definitely at Kate, or even take much definite notice of her. He did not like talking to her, in any serious way" (462). In fact, right near the end of the novel, she is still lamenting the fact that Cipriano "is such a stranger to me" (452). Kate ends by pleading with him to compel her to stay and to believe, but the reader feels extremely uneasy with her behavior. It does not correspond to her perceptions of Cipriano throughout the novel. The following ironic thought sums up her estimate of him as a human being: "'Ah!' said Kate to herself. 'I'm glad Cipriano is a soldier, and doesn't get wounds in his *soul*'" (446). The implication is clear: he *has* no soul.

Lack of a soul is simply another way of stating the quality of inner emptiness and confusion which the authoritarian personality embodies. Cipriano is characterized throughout as psychologically repressed, conventionally controlled on the surface, but hiding a confused turmoil of aggressive emotion underneath:

> He relapsed into blank silence. Peculiar how his feelings flushed over him, anger, diffidence, wistfulness, assurance, and an anger again, all in little flushes, and somewhat naive. (21)

The emptiness in Cipriano seeks reassurance and succour in Kate. Much like Gudrun's recoil from Gerald's incessant need of her ("Had she asked for a child, whom she must nurse through the nights" [*WL* 524]), Kate also senses that it was "the incompleteness in Cipriano that sought her out, and seemed to trespass on her" (207).

Such inner emptiness characterizes the authoritarian personality's hunger for identity and meaning through identification with power and authority figures. Cipriano turns to Ramón to satisfy this need, much as he turns to Kate; there is no strong individualistic self in him that can think independently. Because of the hyper-masculine aggressive stance a personality of this kind assumes, one tends to overlook the underlying childish desire for submission. Submission to a leader is virtually the only sense of safety possible for him. Thus, Cipriano turns to Ramón in order to relieve the psychological void within himself:

> Cipriano, still gazing into the other man's face with black, wondering, childlike, searching eyes, as if he, Cipriano, were searching for *himself*, in Ramón's face. (200)

Like Jack Callcott, Cipriano's demeanor is often blank and "so still, so unnoticing" (349). The following description could serve to describe Jack Callcott as well: "The range of him was very limited, really. The great part of his nature was just inert and heavy, unresponsive, limited" (340). Cipriano's superficial conventionality ensures that his behavior and social responses will be correct and appropriate, yet Kate senses their falsity. Cipriano never truly feels what his social actions portray; he is devoid of the compassion that would help him to empathize:

> How curious Cipriano was! He stated things as if they were mere bare facts with no emotional content at all. As for its being painful to Kate to go to Jamiltepec, that meant nothing to him....
>
> "They might have killed me too," she said.
>
> "Yes! Yes! They might!" he acquiesced. (339)

Cipriano exhibits so many authoritarian qualities that he can be classified as a well-delineated authoritarian personality – perhaps the fullest portrait of the authoritarian that Lawrence offers. But no quality indicative of authoritarianism shines through in his character as completely and emphatically as his underlying violence and aggression. His superficial gentility is constantly belied by the threat of repressive aggression. He is by far the most violent character in *The Plumed Serpent*, probably because he is totally unaware of his aggression. Lawrence describes him as having "quietness, and his peculiar assurance, almost aggressive" (22). At his most charming, however, Kate is still not fully relaxed and trustful around him, and what seems to frighten her the most are his eyes, signalling that the gaiety and charm are only on the surface. Even when he impresses her, "speaking Oxford English in a rapid, low, musical voice, with extraordinarily gentle intonation" (28), she is not fooled, but notes "those black, inhuman eyes" (28). Her perception of him is almost like that of an animal, acting instinctively rather than rationally:

> the movement of his hand was so odd, quick, light as he ate, so easily a movement of shooting, or of flashing a knife into the body of some adversary, and his dark-coloured lips were so helplessly savage, as he ate or briefly spoke, that her heart stood still. There was something undeveloped and intense in him, the intensity and the crudity of the semi-savage....
>
> So that unconsciously she shrank when his black, big, glittering eyes turned on her for a moment.... They were black, as black as jewels into which one could not look without a sensation of fear.... She felt somewhat as the bird feels when the snake is watching it. (71)

At another point, Kate admits to herself that "Cipriano made her a little uneasy, sitting beside him" (340). Fear plays a definite role in her attraction to Cipriano, and the fear is due to her recognition of his latent aggression, so the relationship takes on a perverse slant. Like Victoria Callcott, Kate "was a bit afraid of him too" (487). Cipriano, as the typical authoritarian, wants to inspire fear in the people he deals with; his primary goal is not to connect but to control. Thus, it is not surprising to find him saying:

> "Get used to it that there must be a bit of fear, and a bit of horror in your life.... The bit of horror is like the sesame seed in the nougat, it gives the sharp wild flavour. It is good to have it there." (259)

Once again the association of fear with a sensual image – food – gives Cipriano's interpretation a perverse implication. Jack Callcott's thrill over killing would be the extreme of such perversity, one which Cipriano seems to share.

Cipriano is the only character in the novel who glorifies aggressive violence and force. He is consistently the first to propose coercion as a means to an end. Ramón notes this quality in his disciple: "Already he saw in Cipriano's eye the gleam of the Holy War" (272). At another point, he notes Cipriano's love of violence when he explains that he is "'[c]hasing rebels in the State of Colima.... Anyhow, Cipriano will enjoy chasing them" (319). Cipriano "was for meeting metal with metal" (394), and the purpose of such aggression would be, ironically, to enforce the Quetzalcoatlian religion. His absolute devotion to Ramón causes him to erupt in blind fury at the suggestion that Ramón could be assassinated. Cipriano seems to take leave of all rational sense at moments like these:

> The volcano was rousing.... His eyes took on that fixed glare of ferocity, staring her down.... the ferocity melting in a strange blind, confiding glare, that seemed sightless, either looking inward or out at the whole vast void of the cosmos, where no vision is left. (340)

Such violent anger resembles ecstasy; Cipriano at such moments is lost in blind primal rage. Kate senses that underneath the conventional character armour lies "a black volcano with hell knows what depths of lava" (339).

Because of his primal nature, Cipriano is unaware of and uninterested in the human beings around him. It is as if some part of his self – as a child, autistically or retardedly – has not matured, but remains in a world of the child. Just as earlier he entertains, quite coldly and dispassionately, the possibility that Kate might have been killed, so he views the act of killing itself. When questioned about how many lives he has taken after chasing the rebels, he shows little interest or concern: "'Some! Not many, no? Perhaps a hundred.... Maybe two hundred?' He waved his hand vaguely" (338). This kind of attitude is also examined by Hannah Arendt, who analyzes Eichmann as the "type" of the "totalitarian murderer." Stephen Whitfield summarizes the results of her research, and the resulting personality portrait bears an uncanny resemblance to Cipriano:

> Eichmann could not be regarded as a psychopathic killer writ large: he was not simply an ordinary criminal who had been given an S.S. colonel's uniform and some railroad schedules and allowed to gratify his lust for blood.... Eichmann was peculiarly scary because of his diligence and devotion, which safeguarded him against the realization of his own wickedness.... "the Nazi destruction of Jewry could be so thorough and so effective in part because its instruments were not rampaging Cossacks but clerks scrupulous in their obedience to the law.... It was preponderantly a credulous normality ... that stamped the features of this horror. It has shattered the image of man more lastingly than ever the collective outbreak

> of base passions could have done." ... Had Eichmann *not* obeyed his Fuehrer, his conscience would have troubled him. (Whitfield 224-6)

Whitfield also notes that "While it would be preposterous to suggest that anyone would be capable of doing what Eichmann did, a willingness to commit abhorrent acts under cover of authority can hardly be said to be confined to the small minority who may be psychopaths" (226). Whitfield then describes the Milgram experiment, in which, under the auspices of a learning test, and upon the authority of presumably accredited scientists, ordinary citizens – participants in the experiment – were instructed to administer electric shocks to other people. Milgram's results showed that "two-thirds of the subjects showed an "extreme willingness ... to go to almost any lengths on the command of an authority," even when the maximum voltage was supposed to be highly painful and very dangerous.... The ordinary person who shocked the victim did so out of a sense of obligation – a conception of his duties as a subject – and not from any peculiarly aggressive tendencies" (Whitfield 227). It is not surprising, while assessing how well Cipriano fits this type of "totalitarian killer," to find him the official executioner in the Quetzalcoatlian movement. The executions are of traitors and, in themselves, not as shocking as they may seem at first. Few democracies – especially during war time – could be exempted from executing traitors. But the personality of the executioner in this case is well suited to his line of work.

Finally, Cipriano's underlying violence shows up the utter futility and pessimism that he feels. Supposedly an integral figure in a new utopia bent on the rebirth of man, Cipriano exhibits little hope or belief in such idealism.

Like Jack Callcott, he is involved in the movement for the excitement, the personal gain, and because it offers a socially acceptable means of venting all the accumulated violence that he must repress on a daily basis. Ideologically he remains uninvolved and uninterested. In fact, his truest ideology reduces to the opposite of a rebirth of the human spirit. It is the annihilation of the human world that he truly desires, as his comment to Ramón clearly indicates: "wouldn't it be good to be a serpent, and be big enough to wrap one's folds round the globe of the world, and crush it like that egg?" (211). This attitude makes up the base of authoritarian psychology, in which, in addition to "an element of overt antipacifist opinion, there is contempt for men and acceptance of the 'survival of the fittest' idea as a rationalization for aggressiveness" (Adorno 246). Such contempt precludes any utopian goal; an authoritarian like Don Cipriano desires only the destruction and eventual annihilation of man.

Don Ramón stands in sharp contrast to the authoritarian nature of Cipriano. As the leader of the utopian Quetzalcoatlian religion, his altruistic desire for the rebirth of mankind is intrinsic to his character. Lawrence portrays him so positively, in fact, that he becomes a little boring. However, he exhibits none of the qualities of the authoritarian personality. There is no lack of an inner life in Ramón; the blank emptiness which Cipriano embodies contrasts to Ramón's ability for creative thought. His stance as the new utopia's leader is definitely anti-conformist; Carlota is bothered as much by Ramón's lack of conventional clothes as by his lack of conventional beliefs.

The power that Cipriano desires so absolutely is not reflected in Ramón's definition of leadership. He states firmly, instead:

> "We will be masters among men, and lords among men. But lords of men, and masters of men we will not be.... I will not command you, nor serve you.... Yet I will be with you, so you depart not from yourselves." (196)

This definition of leadership sounds more democratic than authoritarian. His statement that "I will be with you" implies his presence "in spirit" or "in essence," rather than in terms of harsh discipline. Similarly, Ramón does not manipulate the individuals around him. Instead he declares: "'The men and women of the earth are not manufactured goods, to be interchangeable'" (273). Ramón admits to an earlier manipulative use of women, but introspectively indicates that he has outgrown such a superficial approach to mere sensuality: "'Wine, woman, and song – all that – all that game is up. Our insides won't really have it any more'" (300). There is a self-realization here that questions and admits to error; Cipriano is incapable of such insight.

Ramón is characterized by clear, rational thought. He praises the socialist leader as "sensible" (210), indicating his predisposition for rational, objective knowledge. When Cipriano indicates his desire to "crush ... [the world] like that egg" (211), Ramón for a moment is humourously in agreement, but the primal emotive impulse does not win out. Instead,

> he checked himself, and gathered himself together.
>
> "What would be the good!" he said heavily. "If the egg was crushed, and we remained, what could we do but go howling down the empty passages of darkness. What's the good, Cipriano?" (211)

Ramón quickly recognizes the death-headedness in Cipriano's suggestion. Similarly, when Kate passes off Carlota's death with the conventional superstition that "her hour had come!" (469), Ramón immediately questions her lack of rational objectivity. He replies: "Can you set one's hour as one sets an alarm clock?" (469). He is not given to either superstition or, ironically, to a belief in the supernatural.

This is one of the most interesting qualities that Ramón possesses. He is the leader of a new religious utopia and yet he does not himself believe in the religion. He uses religion as the only possible means to change men's hearts and minds, to effect the most complete rebirth. He states that "Only religion will serve; not socialism, nor education, nor anything" (289). Religion is for him the tool to bring about the transformation of human nature, but unlike an authoritarian, he does not really believe in a higher supernatural power that has infinitely greater understanding than his own. It is somewhat shocking to realize that Ramón does not really believe in Quetzalcoatl, that he is deliberately and rationally mythologizing to achieve the rebirth of the masses:

> "Quetzalcoatl is to me only the symbol of the best a man may be, in the next days. The universe is a nest of dragons, with a perfectly unfathomable life-mystery at the centre of it. If I call the mystery the Morning Star, surely it doesn't matter! A man's blood can't beat in the abstract. And man is a creature who wins his own creation inch by inch from the nest of the cosmic dragons." (299)

Clearly, Ramón has invented a new religion in order that, as Reich and Lawrence would both agree, the latent human potential for creative life may be achieved. He states firmly to Kate that "I am a man who has no belief" (299). And in a similar vein, he admits his pretense – a necessary life-giving pretense – very honestly to his son. The elder boy says:

> "They say, also, that you pretend to be the Aztec god Quetzalcoatl."
>
> "Not at all. I only pretend that the Aztec god Quetzalcoatl is coming back to the Mexicans." (295)

Ramón's desire to create a new religion is in good part based on his disgust with and skepticism of the established conventional religions in Mexico. Don Ramón is critical of the Mexicans' superstitiousness and fatalism; he desires that each man develop greater responsibility and realistic awareness:

> "when the child dies, the parents say: *Ah, he will be an angel*! So they cheer up and feel as if they had been given a present. Sometimes I think they enjoy it when their children die. Sometimes I think they would like to transfer Mexico *en bloc* into Paradise." (66)

The emphasis that the Christian religion places on heaven as the only happiness to be achieved has led the peasantry to a hopeless fatalism that Ramón would willingly erase. Thus, his new utopia has "no Before and After, there is only Now" (193). True reactionary and authoritarian stances never condemn established conventional religion. In fact, the strong pressure to conventionality and obedience within the church coincides with the same pressures in a fascist program. In *The Plumed Serpent*, the reactionary forces, the Knights of Cortes, join the church in a fight against Ramón, who hopes to be aligned with the socialists. Ramón distinguishes his program from Montes' socialism, but it would seem that they can work side-by-side without interference or rancour, although Ramón remains suspicious. The Quetzalcoatlian movement is explicitly defined by Ramón as non-political, *outside* the extremes of the right-wing Roman Catholic Church, the Knights of Cortes, or even Montes' left-wing socialism (271). Throughout the novel, in fact, Lawrence makes it very clear that Ramón is, in the first place, *not* political, secondly, that his movement is religious in name only, and finally, that he is attacked and hated far more by the reactionary right than by Montes on the left. The one portrait of a fascist in the novel is little more than a caricature; Lawrence ridicules his pretentious, overly-ceremonious behavior – which may, in part, be based on the strutting arrogance of Mussolini. Kate sees:

> the stout figure of her landlord on the walk outside the window, taking off his cloth cap and bowing low to her. A cloth cap! – She knew he was a great Fascista, the reactionary Knights of Cortes held him in great esteem.
>
> Kate bowed coldly.
>
> He bowed low again, with the cloth cap.
>
> Kate said not a word.
>
> He stood on one foot, then on the other, and then marched forward up the gravel walk, towards the kitchen quarters, as if he had not seen either Kate or General Viedma. In a few moments, he marched back, as if he could not see either Kate or the General. (338-39)

Ramón bears no resemblance whatsoever to such a character. Ramón has little sense of his own self-importance and superiority as he interacts with those around him.

Above all, Ramón possesses the ability to analyze himself and question his own motives. At one point – in despair – he admits that he is mistaken and feels a fool for having begun the new religion:

> "I don't know who is prince. But in the kingdom of fools, I believe it is I." ... "I am a prince of fools!" Why have I started this Quetzalcoatl business? Why? Pray tell me why?" (296-97)

Similarly, though he fears appearing vulnerable in front of a blind follower like Cipriano, he knows readily enough that he *is* vulnerable, and sometimes wrong: "'Who am I, even to talk about Quetzalcoatl, when my heart is hollow with anger against the woman I have married and the children she bore me?'" (299). Such self-reproach not only illustrates introspection; there is considerable humility in forcing oneself to look this closely at the discrepancy between self-image and actuality. The sensitivity with which Ramón approaches his sons also illustrates a more humble mien than Cipriano would ever use. Far from being the authoritarian disciplinarian, Ramón is a gentle, affectionate father whose "heart yearned over them" (391).

Ramón, lastly, is the greatest of contrasts to Cipriano in his consistent avoidance of violence. Unlike Cipriano's readiness to fight – for whatever cause – Ramón tries to avoid aggression:

> Mexico is not Mexico for nothing, however, and already blood had been shed on both sides. This Ramón particularly wanted to avoid, as he felt that violent death was not so easily wiped out of the air and out of the souls of men, as spilt blood was washed off the pavements. (287)

Where Cipriano's impulse is to destroy – "My hand is to hold a gun" (396) – Ramón recognizes that aggressive power is nullifying, that the only real value in life is to awaken the human spirit, rather than to batter it into submission: "'It's never half so brave, to carry something off, and destroy it, as to set a new pulse beating'" (319). Ramón, unlike Cipriano, will use diplomacy and kindliness; he is willing to negotiate rationally rather than use force: "All the time, Ramón tried as far as possible to avoid arousing resistance and hate" (394). His dictum to his people is sensible, being neither so meek as to elicit inhuman repression – which the "turn the other cheek" demand finally does in Christianity – nor at all aggressive: "'Lay forcible hands on nothing, only be ready to resist if forcible hands should be laid on you'" (396). This is a psychologically healthy attitude that contains reverence for creative life, while retaining a rational sense of "individualistic" self-respect. The greatest difference between Cipriano and Ramón is drawn by Teresa: "a man like [Ramón] is more gentle than a woman. He is not like Cipriano. Cipriano is a soldier" (476).

What Lawrence finally illustrates in *The Plumed Serpent* is that the leader of the utopian religion *is* a genuinely altruistic, disinterested and compassionate human being. There are no grounds at all for labelling Ramón as an authoritarian leader. However, Lawrence also shows – perhaps inadvertently – that such a leader would only be supported truly and absolutely *by* an authoritarian, in the character of Cipriano. Kate, as a questioner and individualist, would be a poor follower. Further, Lawrence's portrait of Cipriano is a negative one; while the goals of Ramón's utopia remain praiseworthy and desirable, the type of personality that would follow is proven to be undesirable and destructive. Utopia in itself is not reprehensible, but the kinds of absolutist followers that it attracts are destructive.

Given Ramón's life-affirming personality, however, the novel also illustrates the need, even within a utopian framework, for the authoritarian, enforcement role that Cipriano occupies. Lawrence could not envision a utopia without an enforcement arm, and enforcement inevitably carries with it an authoritarian element. Whitfield points out the authoritarian quality of average Americans in the way they knowingly applied electric shocks to others when asked to do so by an authority figure. The leader/follower concept is integral to any social system, and with this concept there must necessarily exist a measure of authoritarianism. In *The Plumed Serpent*, Lawrence envisions a balance between the life-affirming leadership of Don Ramón and the authoritarianism of Cipriano. Should this balance shift, however, putting the Ciprianos in control, then the spectre of fascism or totalitarianism quickly becomes a realizable possibility.

Conclusion

The analysis of the novels within the terms of this study has indicated that Lawrence was certainly very aware of authoritarianism as a negative element within the human personality. Gerald Crich dies when, feeling the need for love, for a reciprocal relationship, he is unable to achieve it because of his inner emptiness, his inability to share any part of his life with others. Characters like Jim Bricknell, Jack Callcott and Cipriano simply do not understand themselves; neither do they feel any need to examine the motives behind any of their actions. Their lack of introspection, and their unthinking adherence to specific programs, make them destructive individuals. These are the strong adherents of the *status quo*, the unthinking followers of convention, of religion, or of any reactionary movement such as Kangaroo's. These are also the individuals who will make up the body of any totalitarian or fascist force, because they live their lives in accordance with authoritarian principles. On the other hand, the Lawrencian heroes who think and feel, characters like Rupert Birkin, Lilly, Richard Somers and Kate Leslie, are intense and passionate in their denial of an empty life. These are the people who, though often stumbling, at times making ridiculous statements and proclamations, nevertheless lead society toward regeneration.

If Rupert Birkin, Lilly and Somers are regenerative forces, how should Lawrence himself be viewed? From a negative perspective, he has been variously characterized as reactionary, authoritarian, and even fascistic – note Russell's view that Lawrence's theory of "blood-consciousness" led "straight to Auschwitz." But he is undoubtedly also, in Fritz Stern's definition of the term, a "cultural critic." How closely, then, does he resemble the personalities that Stern defines, and where would this place him with regard to the political spectrum of "Left" and "Right?"

Stern, in *The Politics of Cultural Despair*, formulates "a particular type of cultural despair," which indicates that not all cultural criticism is identical. Stern's study isolates the specific type of personality that exhibits a "mixture of cultural despair and mystical nationalism" (3), which he finds particularly personified in the three figures he examines: Lagarde, Langbehn, and Moeller van den Bruck. These men are credited as being at times incisive and just in their criticism of German culture (1). Their thought, however, finally resembles the authoritarian attitudes of some of the Lawrencian characters examined in this study; Langbehn, Lagarde and Moeller share a world with Gerald Crich, Jim Bricknell, Jack Callcott and Cipriano, insofar as "their reforms as well as their criticisms reflected the strong subjective element of their thought" (Stern 3). Like the authoritarian characters in Lawrence's novels, the men studied by Stern made a "leap from despair to utopia across all existing reality" (1). Gerald Crich's translation of mechanical order into "harmony" represents this kind of warped thinking, irrational in its subjectivity and the need to obtain self-approval, while ignoring the reality of the miners who suffer because of his actions. The way Stern describes Lagarde, Langbehn and Moeller resembles Lawrence's descriptions of Gerald, Cipriano, Jim Bricknell and Jack Callcott much more closely than it does a description of Lawrence himself. Stern identifies Lagarde as "a lonely, embittered man" (2), who was characterized by "his crabbed manner and his extravagant presumption" (113).

Stern pinpoints the flaw in Lagarde's thinking:

> The form of Lagarde's attack, as always, consisted of three parts: the statement of extravagant expectations and ideals, a distorted and hypercritical view of actual conditions, and a prescription of concrete reforms. (104)

His first two steps are the crux of his irrational thought; the utopian ideal he holds is blatantly unrealistic and is further undercut by any practical view of the existing reality.

Lawrence's emphasis on "blood intimacy" in his writing has led many critics to assume that he forsakes a rational approach to reality, yet this study has demonstrated that Lawrence recognizes very clearly the distinction between the rational and irrational in thought processes. Lawrence does not resemble Lagarde, except perhaps for the superficial label that characterizes each of them as "cultural critics."

Stern introduces Langbehn in a similar manner to Lagarde, as "a failure and a psychopath" (2). Langbehn's personality, although remembered by many as charming and intelligent, is dominated by an ego-centered perception of reality that is very similar to that of Gerald Crich or Jack Callcott. At one point in his life, Langbehn "went to absurd lengths to conceal his obscure identity, to disguise what no one was particularly anxious to discover. He alternately cherished and resented his self-centered isolation" (138). There is little resemblance to Lawrence here, whose own isolation from his fellows and country was the result of being ostracized, rather than a romanticized self-imposition. Neither is there any similarity between the two men's thought. Langbehn's writing, states Stern:

> leapt from laments to prophecies, from wild charges against the present to sublime visions of the future. But no argument, no bridge of reason that could be challenged or discussed – nothing, except an occasional foe or scapegoat that accounts for the presence of evil. (154)

Stern's study illustrates a central irrational element in the personalities of both Lagarde and Langbehn. Moeller van den Bruck is, however, more complex and, in Stern's words, "the most admirable" (231) of the three men:

> an outsider who made a Nietzschean virtue of having drifted into isolation. How many youths of his time dignified their retreat from life by invoking Zarathustra, as if that superb self-conqueror had preached resignation and passivity in the face of an uncongenial culture! The abstract and fanciful quality of Moeller's thought was undoubtedly conditioned by his prolonged loneliness, as was his passionate desire to lead his people to a new community. (232-33)

Moeller stands solidly, however, as "a talented *litterateur*" (2), whose "critical survey of German literature after Nietzsche is an impressive achievement" (235), and who translated a twenty-three volume collection of Dostoyevsky's works (260). These are laudable achievements for any intellectual and give Moeller van den Bruck a certain credibility. The flaw in his thought, however, occurs when he applies his aesthetics to external reality:

> Actually, Moeller intended to be more than a critic of literature; he sought to discover the spirit of his age in its esthetic creations. Accordingly he wrote a kind of didactic, subjectivist history – a willfully self-created past as a guide to an imaginary, ideal future. (236)

Moeller subjectively reinterprets historical fact and political reality as a myth of aristocratic, heroic greatness that never actually existed. Lawrence's Ramón does this as well, but he does so consciously, in order to promote the rebirth of the spirit in his people. He does not really believe in his own myth-making. Most importantly, Ramón's rewriting of history is done within a fictional context, while Moeller rewrites history in actuality, offering it as truth. Lawrence's own history book, *Movements in European History*, certainly carries his own imaginative interpretation of history, but does not use the presentation of historical fact to promote a rigid platform for utopian reform. Stern criticizes van den Bruck's hazy irrationality:

> His politics were never the result of an analysis of existing historical conditions or of actual need, but always a projection of an esthetic judgment and a criticism of culture. (251)

Stern asserts that Moeller "was no armchair strategist, but a kind of metaphysician of crisis, a searcher after the deeper causes and prospects of the great trial" (266). While both Lawrence and Nietzsche could also be considered "metaphysicians of crisis," their theories remain grounded in reality and rational fact. As Moeller aged, he "preserved an exasperating indifference to fact or historical complexities" (302). One example of this tendency in his thought was his adoration of Dostoyevsky, who simply came to symbolize Russia in van den Bruck's mind; this unrealistic and unquestioning view of Russia as a positive force therefore became part of his thought. Such a subjective, irrational flaw in thinking – "because he mistook his abstract ideal of Russia for the live concrete society" (302) – is very similar to Gerald's translation of concrete, mechanized order into an abstract, mystical harmony.

While Lawrence's characters, Gerald Crich, Jim Bricknell, Jack Callcott, and Cipriano, all parallel Stern's three figures because of their irrational subjectivity, Lawrence himself cannot be accused of thinking irrationally, as his portrayal of the authoritarian personality in his novels shows. Some confusion regarding Lawrence may exist because he *can* be grouped with Lagarde, Langbehn and Moeller van den Bruck as being *anti*-rational in his role as a cultural critic, but that does not mean his thought is *ir*rational. Lawrence's life simply does not resemble the romanticized, tortured, self-imposed isolation of Stern's three theorists. Lawrence's vivid mimicry of propriety, his love of nature and spontaneity, his humble pleasure in simple work and living an ordinary, unostentatious life are all part of a more concrete and realistic approach to reality. There is a commonsense tone in Lawrence's memoirs, as in all his writing, that precludes the dominance of a subjectively mystified self-image.

Another stereotype that is often applied to Lawrence is that of the "right-wing" artist. George Watson places Lawrence on the "Right" side of the political spectrum. Watson's over-riding criterion for this placement seems to be that Lawrence was a writer of the 1920s decade, rather than the 1930s, the era that Watson believes ushered in the proponents of the "Left." Watson's chart reads as follows:

RIGHT	LEFT
W.B. Yeats, 1865-1939	Bloomsbury, etc.: Leonard and Virginia Woolf, Maynard Keynes, Lytton Strachey, E.M. Forster, Bertrand Russell ...
P. Wyndham Lewis, 1882-1957	Cecil Day Lewis, 1904-72
T.E. Hulme, 1883-1917	Christopher Isherwood, b. 1904
D.H. Lawrence, 1885-1930	William Empson, B. 1906
Ezra Pound, 1885-1972	W.H. Auden, 1907-73
T.S. Eliot, 1888-1965	Louis MacNeice, 1907-63
T.E. Lawrence, 1888-1935	Stephen Spender, b. 1909
Roy Campbell, 1901-57	
Evelyn Waugh, 1903-66	

(Watson 88)

Watson's categorizations allow him to isolate some characteristics that are common to the members of each group, for example, the youthfulness of the literary Marxists in the '30s in contrast to the members of the Right in the '20s. He also points out that the people on the "Left" are "more upper- class in origin than the Right" (90). The artists belonging to the Right were "of barely middle-class parentages" (90). Finally, he notes that the Left comprises more native Britons than does the Right:

> The Left, then, was not only socially superior to the Right, and younger, and more of a kind; it was also more British. If you were fairly well-bred and expensively educated, born in the first decade of the twentieth century and of a literary bent, then your chances of not being a Marxist by the mid-Thirties were low. (91)

This is a fairly superficial categorization that does not really represent the complexity of many of the artists Watson discusses.

Lawrence was not preoccupied with right-wing politics; rather, his recognition of the authoritarian personality enabled him to portray it as a destructive force, and to prophesy the totalitarian-fascistic society that it could lead to. Lawrence cannot, therefore, justly be labelled as right-wing or authoritarian. Instead, he possesses the characteristics of the "genuine liberal" in Adorno's sense of the term:

> The subject in whom [liberalism] is pronounced has a strong sense of personal autonomy and independence. He cannot stand any outside interference with his personal convictions and beliefs, and he does not want to interfere with those of others either. His ego is quite developed but not libidinized – he is rarely "narcissistic." At the same time, he is willing to admit id tendencies, and to take the consequence – as is the case with Freud's "erotic type." One of his conspicuous features is moral courage, often far beyond his rational evaluation of a situation. He cannot "keep silent" if something wrong is being done, even if he seriously endangers himself. Just as he is strongly "individualized" himself, he sees the others, above all, as individuals, not as specimens of a general concept. He shares some features with other syndromes found among low scorers [liberals]. Like the "Impulsive," he is little repressed and even has certain difficulties in keeping himself under "control." However, his emotionality is not blind, but directed towards the other person as a *subject*. His love is not only desire but also compassion – as a matter of fact, one might think of defining this

> syndrome as the "compassionate" low scorer. He shares with the "Protesting" low scorer the vigor of identification with the underdog, but without compulsion, and without traces of overcompensation: he is no "Jew lover." Like the "Easy-Going" low scorer [liberal] he is antitotalitarian, but … consciously so, without the element of hesitation and indecision. It is this configuration rather than any single trait which characterizes the "Genuine Liberal." Aesthetic interests seem to occur frequently. (781)

Certainly there are some very close similarities between Adorno's description of the liberal and Lawrence (as well as some of his "liberal" protagonists like Rupert Birkin and Richard Somers). As the English cultural critic and prophet of the 1920s, Lawrence's outspoken chastisement of his countrymen is well-known. His independent sojourn throughout Europe and America, and his willingness to stand apart from conventional society are also well documented facts.

Whereas a theorist like Langbehn is easily recognized as being narcissistic, the writer of poetry such as Lawrence's "New Heaven and Earth" is hardly so. Here, he shows a hatred of solipsism, where "everything was tainted with myself" (*Complete Poems* 256). The rebirth of the spirit is achieved only when "I put my hand out further, a little further / and felt that which was not I …" (*Poems* 259).[1] Lawrence's belief in the redemptive power of human sexuality asserts his "willingness to admit id tendencies, and to take the consequences" (Adorno 781). The compassionate expressions of love in his writing are always directed toward another human being as a "subject," rather than an object. This is perhaps the very basis of

[1] See also Pritchard, *D.H. Lawrence: Body of Darkness* 19.

Lawrence's message. Most of all, Lawrence embodies the "moral courage" that also characterizes the genuine liberal; he could never "keep silent" where he saw social wrongs committed, regardless of the cost to himself, and the cost was, many times, considerable. His lifetime was spent decrying the wrongs he saw. Lawrence is not always a *nice* author to read; no doubt he was also not always easy to live with. In describing the "genuine liberal," Adorno also draws a portrait of a personality that would not always be "nice," or "easy-going." This individual demonstrates a healthy anger toward injustice, and a strong sense of his own personal rights.

The results of this study, then, would indicate that Lawrence is, indeed, a deeply "committed" artist. He sees clearly the wrongs, the injustices that exist, and points the way toward the rebirth of society through the regeneration of the self. Perhaps the most remarkable feature of this artist is the clarity with which he views the threat of authoritarianism, totalitarianism and fascism within his time, and the precision with which he documents these perceptions within many of his characters.

Works Cited

Adorno, T.W. et al. *The Authoritarian Personality*. New York: Harper and Row, 1950.

Ackroyd, Peter. *T.S. Eliot: A Life*. New York: Simon and Schuster, 1984.

Arendt, Hannah. *The Origins of Totalitarianism*. New York: Harcourt, Brace and World, 1968 [1951].

Barr, Barbara Weekley. "Memoir of D.H. Lawrence." *D.H. Lawrence: Novelist, Poet, Prophet*. Ed. Stephen Spender. New York: Harper and Row, 1973.

Boadella, David. *The Spiral Flame: A Study in the Meaning of D.H. Lawrence*. [Reprinted as Nos. 50-51 (December 1977) of *Paunch*. Buffalo, New York: 1978].

Brontë, Emily. *Wuthering Heights*. Oxford: Oxford University Press, 1981.

Burgess, Anthony. *Flame Into Being*. London: Heinemann, 1985.

Cameron, Elspeth. "The Inner Wars of Timothy Findley." *Saturday Night*. Vol. 100, No. 1 (Jan. 1985).

Carswell, Catherine. "The Café Royal Episode." *D.H. Lawrence: Interviews and Recollections*. Ed. Norman Page. London: Macmillan, 1981.

Carey, John. "D.H. Lawrence's Doctrine." *D.H. Lawrence: Novelist, Poet, Prophet*. Ed. Stephen Spender. New York: Harper and Row, 1973.

Caudwell, Christopher (Christopher St. John Sprigg). *Studies in a Dying Culture*. Intro. by John Strachey. London: J. Lane the Bodley Head, 1938.

Cohn, Norman. *The Pursuit of the Millenium: Revolutionary Millenarians and Mystical Anarchists of the Middle Ages*. New York: Oxford University Press, 1970.

Cox, C.B. and A.E. Dyson, eds. *The Twentieth-Century Mind*. Vol. III: 1945-1965. London: Oxford University Press, 1972.

Delany, Paul. *D.H. Lawrence's Nightmare: The Writer and His Circle in the Years of the Great War*. New York: Basic Books, Inc., 1978.

Didion, Joan. *Slouching Towards Bethlehem*. New York: Washington Square Press, 1968.

Douglas, Norman. *Looking Back: An Autobiographical Excursion*. New York: Harcourt, Brace and Co., 1933.

Eagleton, Mary and David Pierce. *Attitudes to Class in the English Novel: From Walter Scott to David Storey*. London: Thames and Hudson, 1979.

Eagleton, Terry. *Criticism and Ideology: A Study in Marxist Literary Theory*. London: NLB, 1976.

Eliot, T.S. *After Strange Gods: A Primer of Modern Heresy*. The Page- Barbour Lectures at the University of Virginia. London: Faber and Faber, 1933.

Eysenck, Hans J. and Glenn D. Wilson. *The Psychological Basis of Ideology*. Lancaster: MTP Press, 1978.

Fielding, Daphne. *Emerald and Nancy: Lady Cunard and Her Daughter*. London: Eyre and Spottiswoode, 1968.

Ford, Ford Madox. "An Editor's Impressions." *D.H. Lawrence: Interviews and Recollections.* Vol. I. Ed. Norman Page. London: Macmillan, 1981.

Freeman, Mary. *D.H. Lawrence: A Basic Study of His Ideas.* Gainesville, Florida: Univ. of Florida Press, 1955.

Freud, Sigmund. *Civilization and Its Discontents.* Ed. James Strachey. New York: W.W. Norton, 1961.

Fromm, Erich. *Escape From Freedom.* New York: Avon Books, 1969 [1941].

Garnett, David. "In Germany and Italy." *D.H. Lawrence: Interviews and Recollections.* Ed. Norman Page. London: Macmillan, 1981.

Goodheart, Eugene. Review of Yudishtar's *Conflict in the Novels of D.H. Lawrence,* Colin Clarke's *River of Dissolution,* and David Cavitch's *D.H. Lawrence and the New World. Modern Fiction Studies,* 16 (Summer 1970), pp. 230-34.

Goodheart, Eugene. *The Utopian Vision of D.H. Lawrence.* Chicago: Univ. of Chicago Press, 1963.

Hardy, Barbara. "Women in D.H. Lawrence's Works." *D.H. Lawrence: Novelist, Poet, Prophet.* Ed. Stephen Spender. New York: Harper and Row, 1973.

Harrison, John R. *The Reactionaries.* London: Victor Gollancz Ltd., 1966.

Heschel, Abraham J. *The Prophets.* 2 Vols. New York: Harper and Row, 1962.

Hochman, Baruch. *Another Ego: The Changing View of Self and Society in the Work of D.H. Lawrence.* Columbia: Univ. of South Carolina Press, 1970.

Hough, Graham. *The Dark Sun: A Study of D.H. Lawrence.* New York: Octagon Books, 1956.

Huxley, Aldous. *Two or Three Graces and Other Stories.* London: Chatto and Windus, 1926.

Jenkins, Roy. *Asquith*. London: St. James Place, 1964.

Kermode, Frank. *The Sense of an Ending: Studies in the Theory of Fiction*. New York: Oxford Univ. Press, 1967.

Kreml, William P. *The Anti-Authoritarian Personality*. Oxford: Pergamon Press, 1977.

Lawrence, D.H. *Aaron's Rod*. Middlesex: Penguin Books, 1950.

Lawrence, D.H. *The Complete Poems of D.H. Lawrence*. Eds. Vivian de Sola Pinto and Warren Roberts. New York: Viking Press, 1964.

Lawrence, D.H. *Fantasia of the Unconscious*. New York: Viking, 1960 [1921].

Lawrence, D.H. *Kangaroo*. New York: Viking, 1923.

Lawrence, D.H. *Movements in European History*. Oxford: Oxford University Press, 1981 [1921].

Lawrence, D.H. *Phoenix: The Posthumous Papers of D.H. Lawrence*. Ed. Edward D. McDonald. New York: Viking Press, 1964.

Lawrence, D.H. *Phoenix II: Uncollected, Unpublished, and Other Prose Works by D.H. Lawrence*. New York: Viking Press, 1970.

Lawrence, D.H. *The Plumed Serpent*. New York: Vintage Books, 1959 [1926].

Lawrence, D.H. *The Quest for Rananim: D.H. Lawrence's Letters to S.S. Koteliansky, 1914 to 1930*. Ed. George J. Zytaruk. Montreal and London: McGill-Queen's University Press, 1970.

Lawrence, D.H. "The Reality of Peace." *Phoenix: The Posthumous Papers of D.H. Lawrence*. Ed. Edward D. McDonald. New York: Viking Press, 1964.

Lawrence, D.H. "Return to Eastwood." *Phoenix II*. New York: Viking Press, 1968.

Lawrence, D.H. "Study of Thomas Hardy." *Phoenix. New York: Viking Press, 1964.*

Lawrence, D.H. *Women in Love*. Middlesex: Penguin Books, 1983.

Leavis, F.R. *D.H. Lawrence: Novelist*. Middlesex: Penguin, 1955.

Lerner, Laurence. *The Truthtellers: Jane Austen, George Eliot, D.H. Lawrence*. New York: Schocken, 1967.

Lipset, Seymour Martin. *Political Man: The Social Bases of Politics.* Garden City, N.Y.: Doubleday & Co., 1960.

MacLeod, Sheila. *Lawrence's Men and Women*. London: Heinemann, 1985.

Mailer, Norman. *The Prisoner of Sex*. Boston: Little, Brown and Company, 1971.

Marx, Karl and Friedrich Engels. *The Russian Menace to Europe*. Glencoe, Illinois: Free Press, 1952.

Millett, Kate. *Sexual Politics*. Garden City, N.Y.: Doubleday & Co. Inc., 1970.

Moore, Brian. *Conversations With Canadian Novelists*. Toronto: Macmillan, 1973.

Moynahan, Julian. *The Deed of Life: The Novels and Tales of D.H.* Lawrence. Princeton, N.J.: Princeton Univ. Press, 1963.

Noltë, Ernst. *The Three Faces of Fascism: Action Française, Italian Fascism, National Socialism*. London: Weidenfeld and Nicolson, 1963.

Ortega y Gasset, José. *The Revolt of the Masses*. New York: Norton, 1932.

Orwell, George. *Coming Up For Air*. New York: Harcourt, Brace and Company, 1950.

Orwell, George. "Politics and the English Language." *Norton Anthology of English Literature*. Fifth ed. Vol.2. New York: W.W. Norton, 1986.

Page, Norman, ed. *D.H. Lawrence: Interviews and Recollections*. 2 vols. London: Macmillan Press Ltd., 1981.

Parmenter, Ross. *Lawrence in Oaxaca: A Quest for the Novelist in Mexico*. Salt Lake City: Peregrine Smith Books, 1984.

Patmore, Brigit. "'Searching Not Flattering.'" *D.H. Lawrence: Interviews and Recollections*. Ed. Norman Page. London: Macmillan Press Ltd., 1981.

Pritchard, R.E. *D.H. Lawrence: Body of Darkness*. London: Hutchinson Univ. Library, 1971.

Reich, Wilhelm. *The Mass Psychology of Fascism*. New York: Farrar, Straus and Giroux, 1970.

Ruderman, Judith. *D.H. Lawrence and the Devouring Mother: The Search for a Patriarchal Ideal of Leadership*. Durham, N.C.: Duke Univ. Press, 1984.

Russell, Bertrand. "A 'Brief and Hectic' Friendship." *D.H. Lawrence: Interviews and Recollections*. Vol. I. Ed. Norman Page. London: Macmillan, 1981.

Ruthven, K.K. "On the So-Called Fascism of Some Modernist Writers." *Southern Review* (Adelaide), 5:3 (September 1972), 225-30.

Sagar, Keith. *D.H. Lawrence: Life Into Art*. Middlesex, England: Viking, Penguin Books Ltd., 1985.

Sanders, Scott. *D.H. Lawrence: The World of the Five Major Novels*. New York: The Viking Press, 1973.

Scheckner, Peter. *Class, Politics, and the Individual: A Study of the Major Works of D.H. Lawrence*. London and Toronto: Associated Univ. Presses, 1985.

Schneider, Daniel J. *D.H. Lawrence: The Artist as Psychologist*. Lawrence, Kansas: Univ. Press of Kansas, 1984.

Schneider, Daniel J. "D.H. Lawrence and the Early Greek Philosophers." *D.H. Lawrence Review*.

Schoenbaum, David. *Hitler's Social Revolution: Class and Status in Nazi Germany 1933-1939*. New York: Doubleday and Co., 1966.

Sharaf, Myron. *Fury on Earth: A Biography of Wilhelm Reich*. New York: St. Martin's Press, 1983.

Spender, Stephen, ed. *D.H. Lawrence: Novelist, Poet, Prophet*. London: Weidenfeld and Nicolson, 1973.

Stern, Fritz. *The Politics of Cultural Despair: A Study in the Rise of the Germanic Ideology*. New York: Doubleday, 1961.

Tindall, William York. *D.H. Lawrence & Susan His Cow*. New York: Cooper Square Publishers, 1972 [1939].

Trilling, Diana. *We Must March My Darlings: A Critical Decade*. New York: Harcourt, Brace, Jovanovich, 1977.

Trilling, Lionel. *The Liberal Imagination: Essays on Literature and Society*. New York: Viking Press, 1950.

Updike, John. *Rabbit Run*. New York: Knopf, 1960.

Watson, George. *Politics and Literature in Modern Britain*. London: Macmillan, 1977.

Whitfield, Stephen J. "Banality on Trial." *Into the Dark: Hannah Arendt and Totalitarianism*. Philadelphia: Temple University Press, 1980

Woolf, Virginia. *The Letters of Virginia Woolf*. Vol. II. London: Harcourt, Brace, Jovanovich, 1976.

Woolf, Virginia. *Orlando: A Biography*. Middlesex: Penguin Books, 1970.

Yudhishtar. "The Changing Scene: *Aaron's Rod*. *D.H. Lawrence: A Collection of Criticism*. Ed. Leo Hamalian. New York: McGraw-Hill, 1973.

Zaslove, Jerald. Review of Baruch Hochman's *Another Ego: The Changing View of Self and Society in the Work of D.H. Lawrence*, and Tom Marshall's *The Psychic*

Mariner: A Reading of the Poems of D.H. Lawrence. West Coast Review. October 1971.

Zytaruk, George J., ed. *The Quest for Rananim: D.H. Lawrence's Letters to S.S. Koteliansky, 1914-1930*. Montreal: McGill-Queen's Univ. Press, 1970.

Index